UNITED STATES

v.

MEMBERS OF THE ARMED FORCES

UNITED STATES

v.

MEMBERS OF THE ARMED FORCES

The Truth Behind the Department of Defense's Anthrax Vaccine Immunization Program

Dale F. Saran
Major, USMCR, Judge Advocate

United States vs. Members of the Armed Forces

Major, USMCR, Judge Advocate
dalesaran@gmail.com

ISBN: 978-1-7346293-0-9 (paperback)
ISBN: 978-1-7346293-1-6 (ebook)

Editing, cover, ebook formatting, and print design by
Elizabeth Beeton, b10mediaworx.com.

Note: All emphases in cited works belong to the author.

CONTENTS

Prologue 1

Chapter 1: History 9

Chapter 2: The Nuremberg Code 19

Chapter 3: "The General Did What?" 30

Chapter 4: Judicial Remedies? 39

Chapter 5: The FDA, DHHS, & Vaccines: Anthrax Slides By 51

Chapter 6: The Gulf War Drugs 63

Chapter 7: Congress Acts: 10 U.S.C. §1107 81

Chapter 8: It's Illegal! 98

Chapter 9: History of the Ava 107

Chapter 10: The Vaccine Fails 117

Chapter 11: United States versus Stonewall 132

Chapter 12: The Dod "Evolves" on the AVA 147

Chapter 13: Defense Delay 169

Chapter 14: Cohen's "Four Points" 176

Chapter 15: The Stay 192

Chapter 16: Guard Pilots Quit 195

Chapter 17: Science Intervenes & Project Badger 208

Chapter 18: The Walking Wounded 220

Chapter 19: Fighting Behind the Scenes 230

Chapter 20: Why? 239
Chapter 21: Back to Okinawa 257
Chapter 22: Why, Indeed 263
Chapter 23: Conviction 272
Chapter 24: After Action 279
Present Day 282
About the Author 291

PROLOGUE

"This court will come to order in the case of United States versus Petty Officer David M. Ponder, United States Navy, at Marine Corps Base Camp Foster, Okinawa, Japan."

I'm nervous, like I am at the beginning of every trial, but I don't show it. It's just an arraignment anyway. We're mostly here to arrange dates for trial and I've already talked to the prosecutor, known as the "trial counsel" in the military, a professional Marine officer by the name of Captain Chris Kolomjec; we've agreed to push the dates out a bit on this case. Like me, he had another specialty in the Marine Corps before becoming an attorney, so we have a fairly collegial relationship. Chris is going on temporary duty to an exercise in Thailand called "Cobra Gold" and I'm in the beginning stages of a plan to plead this case out under very favorable terms if I can get in to see the Convening Authority—my client's Commanding Officer—while Kolomjec is out of town. In courts-martial, the prosecution has 120 days to be ready to go to trial and the arraignment stops that clock from running. In David Ponder's case, stopping the clock is mutually agreeable, but we have to coordinate our plans with the judge's trial schedule.

I put on the required lawyerly mask of indifference, but inside, my guts are twisting a little. A trial is like the start of a "big" game in sports, except the stakes are a lot higher. I am, as you might expect, extremely competitive, particularly in sports, but I've played enough to have perspective: At the end of a game, even after a loss, nobody goes to jail, gets busted, kicked out of the service, or loses their pay. On the other hand, as a defense counsel, I have a standard line to my clients: "At the end of the day, I'm not the one going to jail. I'm going home to my wife and four daughters." Notwithstanding this act, I have always keenly felt the possible punishment awaiting my clients, the mythical sword of Damocles hanging there waiting to fall. On the defense side of the table, it is your intellect, initiative, imagination—along with a ball point pen and legal pad—against "The United States of America." While that is a unique challenge I relish, it is also daunting. Anyone who feels otherwise is either another class of lawyer than I am or a fool.

I edge a little closer to Petty Officer Third Class Ponder, a sailor who refused the controversial anthrax vaccine. My move closer might appear to outsiders as a sign of my solidarity with my client and in Ponder's case, it's got some truth. We've only just met, but I like him. In most cases, however, being proximate to my client makes me feel less alone. I am six months removed from Naval Justice School, nine months from passing the Bar, 11 months from law-school graduation, and a lifetime away from my former occupation in the Marine Corps as a Cobra attack helicopter pilot.

Captain Kolomjec finishes reciting his bona fides and how the court came to be created by the Commanding Officer of Naval Mobile Constriction Battalion Seventy-Four, Petty Officer Ponder's C.O. This part really was boring, scripted, and I waited for my turn to speak.

"Captain Saran?" The military judge, Lieutenant Colonel Tim Miller, looks up from his Military Judges' Benchbook in my direction, my cue to do my part.

"Sir, I have been detailed to this court-martial by Major J.R. Woodworth, Senior Defense Counsel, Legal Services Support Section, Third Force Service Support Group, Camp Foster, Okinawa, Japan. I am qualified and certified under Article 27(b) and sworn under article 42(a) of the Uniform Code of Military Justice." I don't need to look down at my trial guide for this, which is a script for Navy and Marine Corps trial proceedings for the repetitive parts in the process. It keeps everyone tracking where the trial is, but the real reason for it is to make for better records of trial. Anyone who receives a punitive discharge in the military gets an automatic appeal up to their service specific appellate court. Given the number of courts-martial in the military, this helps the appellate courts do their jobs. Arguably, it also helps the accused get a better, cleaner trial. The familiar recitation helps my nerves dissipate; I suspect it has something to do with being raised Catholic.

"I have not acted in any manner which might tend to disqualify me in this court-martial and no other defense counsel, either military or civilian, has either been detailed to or are on this case." I start to sit down but decide to stay on my feet in anticipation of my client standing up when the judge speaks to him for the first time—just as I instructed him to do.

"Are you Petty Officer Ponder, the accused in this case?"

Ponder stands to the position of attention. "Yes, sir." Firm, not too loud, perfect. He looks good in his uniform, as well. I know because I inspected him myself before we came into court.

The defense shop keeps an extra set of uniforms, spare ribbons and devices, and whatever else we can scavenge for our clients when they're brought in by the chasers—military escorts—from the brig. They come over in those ubiquitous orange jumpsuits in shackles. While their units are supposed to provide the uniforms for them, we always wind up with clients missing ribbons and sundry uniform items, so we have a small stock available.

"Okay, Petty Officer Ponder, you may take a seat and you may remain seated unless I otherwise direct you to stand." Lieutenant Colonel Miller nods gently from behind his glasses. I notice he's still rubbing his hand as he continues, a habit since the pins were removed. The judge had flipped over the handlebars of his bike and busted his wrist up pretty badly and I knew the scar must itch where the pins had come out. Reconstructive shoulder surgery at 15 left me with an intimate understanding of that feeling.

We finish with the preliminaries. I rattle off all the awards Ponder had earned during his three years as a Navy Seabee. The judge goes through my client's rights to counsel, military and civilian, and then his own qualifications. He then gives us a chance to challenge him or ask any questions if we think he might be partial for any reason, a formality at this point because I'm pretty sure that Lieutenant Colonel Miller isn't even going to hear this case if we go to trial. He's likely to pass it to Major Eric Stone, the other military judge on Okinawa, because of some scheduling conflicts with other cases in the Pacific region, which includes mainland Japan and Korea. We all do a good bit of traveling because of the odd and disbursed units that have occasional courts-martial, but the bulk of the work is on Okinawa.

I look over at my client. Ponder looks young to me and I just turned thirty. He has the beginnings of a moustache, but it's just that, the beginnings. The good thing is that he likes to keep his hair short by Navy standards, which helps in a Marine court. He's also a genuinely squared-away sailor. I liked him, which is supposed to be irrelevant to attorneys, but it's not. Everyone gets the same level of representation; it's just a question of whether you like defending them or not and whether or not you'll feel badly if they're convicted. It also helps in generating the emotional energy to work late nights and long hours cheerfully as opposed to drearily.

"Petty Officer Ponder," the judge says, breaking into my thoughts, "I now ask you: How do you plead? But before accepting your pleas, I advise you that any motion to dismiss or grant any other relief should be made at this time. Captain Saran?"

I stand up, my stomach now fully settled, which is great because we're just about done. We have our dates for trial, but I'm thinking this gets pled to a summary court-martial, where my client can get no more than 30 days in the brig and no punitive discharge. He's probably going to have to waive his right to an Administrative Discharge Board, though, and they'll kick him out with "bad paper"—an "Other Than Honorable" discharge—which is like being fired from the military.

"Sir, at this time Petty Officer Ponder requests to defer entry of pleas and motions in accordance with the schedule the court has already set forth."

The judge goes through the dates Kolomjec and I have already picked for motions, responses, witness requests, and discovery. All parties are agreed.

"Anything else from either party before we adjourn?"

"No, sir," both Kolomjec and I answer after glancing at each other.

"Then this court is in recess."

"All rise!" Kolomjec intones.

I'm already on my feet and Ponder joins me as the judge passingly says, "Carry on" before departing.

As my client and I walk out, we almost bump into David Allen, a reporter from the *Stars and Stripes*. I've only been here a short while, but my reaction is immediate—I step in and tell Allen we'll give a statement at some point and he'll be the first to know.

The first thing any decent defense attorney wants regarding his client's talking—to *anyone*, but particularly law enforcement and the press—is for him to STFU and let the lawyer do the talking. The cop shows and movies are dead-on in one respect: Anything you say *can* and *will* be used against you. Plus, offhand I can't remember either the Code of Professional Responsibility or the more stringent Navy Instruction for all Judge Advocates on speaking to the press. I know generally it's frowned upon if not outright verboten to speak to the press. Add to that my natural aversion to the media as a military officer and I'm curt, but polite.

Oddly enough, this is one of the few times it likely won't matter. It's not as if Ponder could say anything damning—he had refused a direct order to take the anthrax vaccine and even talked about it in interviews with local media in his homeport of Biloxi, Mississippi. There isn't a whole lot of dispute factually. I don't want to give the government any additional ammunition for sentencing, however, should we ever get there. A jury or military judge would probably not look kindly on someone who was bashing the military in the local paper. So, we pass on the "exclusive."

Back in my office, I drop into my chair.

"Sir," Petty Officer Ponder begins, "what happens now?"

"Well, you heard the dates for motions. That's the next big milestone. It's likely that the prosecutor will file a motion asking the judge to find the order to take the vaccine lawful. That's been the standard in the few other anthrax cases that have gone to trial. The good thing is that Captain Kolomjec leaves for Thailand the day that our response is due. Likelihood is he won't be around in the afternoon when I drop the response off on the prosecution. He also won't be back until right before the motions session and I'm betting no one else is going to pick up our response and run with the ball. So, it may not win the day, but it will certainly limit his time to be ready to answer our motion."

Ponder nods, but I can tell he's nervous. I would be, too, if I were in his shoes.

"Sir, did you get in touch with Major Bates's attorney, Mister Smith, at that number I gave you?"

"Yeah. I talked to him. Interesting conversation."

Ponder had put me in touch with an attorney in the States named Bruce Smith, an administrative judge in North Carolina and Major in the Air Force Reserve. He defended Air Force Major Sonnie Bates, who was the highest-ranking officer to refuse the anthrax vaccine and had been discharged with "good paper" as a result of a plea negotiation. When I spoke to Mister Smith, he calmly asked me if I could consider that the order to take the anthrax vaccine was unlawful. Not quite expecting the question, I had hesitantly said, "Sure." In my own mind, I figured he was a loon, a conspiracy theorist, but he had gotten a good result for Major

Bates, so what did I have to lose by listening to the guy? He told me to look up a particular federal statute and then said he would send me some other materials and asked if I would please keep them "close hold." His manner was so cordial, I casually agreed, thinking nothing of it.

My boss, Major John Woodworth, figured he had done me a favor by assigning me—a brand new judge advocate—three of the four anthrax refusal cases on the island of Okinawa. The assumption was that these were guys looking for an excuse to get out of the military and the units would likely agree to Summary Court deals with an Admin Board waiver and that these would be over in short order. Like Tom Cruise in *A Few Good Men*, I came to Ponder's case with the goal to get him the best deal possible, and do it quickly and quietly. I also had several major cases pending, including a rape defense involving an Okinawan national woman that had garnered its own share of attention from the local media.

I got the first three of my anthrax shots just before coming to Okinawa. I took them somewhat reluctantly, as I had read an article in a major news magazine about the possibility of some experimental substance called squalene being in the anthrax vaccine given to soldiers during Desert Storm. I had sat in the medical clinic at Naval Justice School in Newport, Rhode Island, discussing the matter with another Marine attorney. Both of us had served previously as officers in the Fleet Marine Force and while we tended to think that squalene had been used in the anthrax vaccine, our leaders wouldn't allow it to be used now. Quite simply, we trusted our chain of command, our senior officers.

Ponder breaks into my thoughts.

"Do you think my C.O. might consider not court-martialing me or something if you explained this to him?" The question is laden with ethical implications that I'm glad I had explained to him. While the anthrax vaccine is getting a lot of attention in the press back in the States, and the issue is very interesting legally, I can't let that interfere with my duty to my client: to advocate for his interests. If he wants to deal, to plead guilty, no matter how much I might like to litigate the issue, it's his ass on the line and I explained as much to him from the start. Ponder doesn't have a Juris Doctor, but he's sharp and understood the bottom line.

"Well, I'm going to set up a meeting while Kolomjec's away and see if the C.O. won't listen to what we've got to say. I'll get back to you as soon as I get out of that meeting, okay?" I smiled at him.

"Okay, sir. I'm going to change up. Where can I go to have a smoke?"

"Out on the stairs at the end of the building."

I nod toward the general direction and once he leaves, I go back to work. I'm concerned with the 15 other clients who are counting on me to keep them out of jail.

At the time, I had no idea that Ponder's case would take me from Okinawa to the highest military court of appeals, the doorstep of the Supreme Court, and eventually in front of Congress. It would eventually cost me my active-duty career, but that was a long way off.

CHAPTER 1
HISTORY

> "I think it speaks to the undercurrent of distrust of the government and the military," said Lt. Gen. Ronald R. Blanck, the Surgeon General of the Army, the service that oversees the [anthrax] vaccination program. "Agent Orange. Nuclear tests in the '50s. People say, 'How can you say this is safe?' Clearly, we have a credibility problem."[1]

The United States Armed Forces have a long and not-so-illustrious history of testing nuclear, biological, and chemical weapons … on its own citizens. From at least the 1940s on (and if you want to include Native Americans, we can go back a lot further!), the Department of Defense (DoD) has conducted experiments on U.S. service members using "unconventional" weapons.[2] A report prepared by the staff of the Senate Committee on Veterans' Affairs in 1994 concluded that "[f]or at least 50 years, [the] DoD has intentionally exposed military personnel to

---

[1] Myers, Steven Lee. "Armed Services Opt to Discharge Those Who Refuse Vaccine." First appeared in *The New York Times*, 11 March 1999. Archived at https://gulfwarvets.com/anthrax3.htm, last accessed 30 April 2020.

[2] An Institute of Medicine report looking at the history of mustard and lewisite gas found the Armed Forces researching chemical warfare after World War I and up through World War II. The report even traces some research back before the Civil War.

potentially dangerous substances, often in secret[.]"[3] That report followed a Government Accounting Office (GAO) inquiry into experiments conducted on service members by the DoD.[4] The GAO report detailed many different programs, some of which the DoD still lists as classified, in which service members were given experimental drugs and other treatments without their knowledge or consent. A few of the more stunning examples of experimentation are worth discussing in detail, not simply to attack the DoD or the military establishment, but rather as context because it is against this history that the DoD's anthrax program was launched. And it is against this background of secret experimentation and tests conducted on coerced subjects that the DoD asks members of the Armed Services to "trust us" with regards to vaccines and inoculations claimed to be safe and effective.

In the 1940s, the Department of the Navy began soliciting volunteers to participate in a program to test protective clothing. In reality, the program was designed to test mustard and lewisite gases, chemical agents that the United States thought might be used by the desperate Axis powers at the end of World War II. There are some who claim that the tests were done simply to see what effect mustard gas had on soldiers in order to determine the offensive potential of chemical weapons. The truth is likely that these are not exclusive propositions. Either way, the program solicited potential "volunteers" with the promise of two weeks

---

3 United States. Congress. Senate. Committee on Veterans' Affairs. *Is Military Research Hazardous to Veterans' Health?: Lessons Spanning Half a Century: A Staff Report.* Washington: U.S. G.P.O., 1994.

4 The Government Accounting Office (GAO) is the watchdog arm of Congress that investigates government agencies. Conahan, Frank C, United States. Congress. House. Committee on Government Operations. Legislation and National Security Subcommittee, and United States. General Accounting Office. *Human Experimentation: An Overview on Cold War Era Programs: Statement of Frank C. Conahan, Assistant Comptroller General, National Security and International Affairs Division, Before the Legislation and National Security Subcommittee, Committee on Government Operations, House of Representatives.* Washington, D.C.: The Office, 1994.

of extra leave or some other similar incentive.[5] "Due to the strategic importance of these experiments [however], the Navy deemed it inappropriate to inform potential volunteers as to the precise nature of the tests. Instead, the "volunteers" were led to believe that they would be testing uniforms for use in tropical climates."[6] These "volunteers" were sworn to secrecy and threatened with court-martial if they told anyone about the program for which they had just "volunteered." Of course, at this point, because no one had told them exactly what they volunteered for, it was relatively easy to extract such a promise. It is rather doubtful that most members would have agreed had they known that they were about to be experimented upon with chemical weapons.

Nathan Schnurman was a young sailor who figured he could use the extra few days off. He had just finished boot camp and was stationed at Bainbridge, Maryland, awaiting further orders when he volunteered for the program. He was put on a bus for Anacostia, Maryland, where the experiments actually took place. Young Nathan Schnurman, along with the other volunteers, was given a bunk in a Quonset hut and some blankets for that evening. All of the volunteers were issued protective clothing, including a gas mask, given a physical, and the next morning the experiments began. The protective clothing and masks were fitted and checked and then the 10 volunteers were led to the testing building. At this point, the volunteers had still only been told that they were testing clothing for tropical weather.

> The building itself was a simple structure with an entrance platform and test chamber. A single door separated the platform from the chamber and an intercom allowed for communication between the subjects inside the chamber

5 Few things have amazed me more in my time in service than what members of the Armed Forces—even more so Marines—will do for just a few extra days of leave or liberty. I am still not sure what that says about the military, but leave and liberty are the promised land to most service members.

6 *Schnurman v. United States*, 490 F. Sup. 429, 430 (E. D. Va. 1980).

> and the corpsmen on the platform. The subjects were told that, once inside, a vapor was to be introduced into the chamber and that they were to remain in the chamber for one hour. The subjects were not told what the vapor was, but were told that it might produce a slight irritation on the subjects' skin, similar to a sunburn. The subjects were admonished not to discuss the experiment with anyone.[7]

The volunteers were exposed to the vapor for the one hour, as advertised. After that, they were instructed to continue to wear the protective clothing for another four hours, to eat meals and pass the time in their Quonset hut. They later disrobed and were given physical exams to check primarily for burns on the skin. This routine repeated itself the next day. The second day's physical was the last one that any volunteer ever received as a part of the experiment.

> The hour-long gas exposures continued on a daily basis for the next four days without incident, save the departure of a few of the subjects due to painful burns. On one of those days, just prior to the morning's exposure, plaintiff [Schnurman] was informed by a corpsman that they would be testing mustard and lewisite gas that day.

On the sixth test day, while inside the chambers, plaintiff's gas mask malfunctioned and plaintiff breathed the noxious vapor being tested. The inhalation of the gas produced extreme nausea and a burning in his eyes, nose and throat. Before being helped out of the chamber, plaintiff regurgitated in his mask. Once outside the chambers and free of his mask, plaintiff continued to experience nausea and dizziness, plus an

[7] *Schnurman*, at 431.

intense pain in his chest. After further vomiting, plaintiff lost consciousness. No record was made of this incident.

Upon regaining consciousness, plaintiff was informed that he would no longer be needed for the experiment and that he could return to Bainbridge. He was not given any physical examination or treatment with the exception of local treatment for the minor burns on his skin. Plaintiff left the site of the experiment and traveled to his home in Roanoke, Virginia for a 10-day leave.[8]

Mr. Schnurman went on with his life, experiencing long-term health problems. Sworn to secrecy, Schnurman felt that he could not tell his personal physician about the source of his ailments because of his oath and the threat of punishment. Thus, he did not provide essential information to his doctors about his health because of his fears of what would happen to him if he told. This scenario was not uncommon. A Mr. John T. Harrison described to a senate committee how he was sworn to secrecy in 1943 when mustard gas tests were conducted on him.[9] Because of this, it was not until much later in life that Mr. Schnurman learned of what had been used on him and he filed a lawsuit against the government.

A very similar incident happened to a John William Allen in 1945, according to a statement before the Senate Committee on Veterans' Affairs. Mr. Allen testified that the real purpose of the testing was to determine how much sulfur mustard a man could take before being overcome: These were known as "man-break tests." "He was exposed several times to sulfur mustard and was removed from further exposure on 5 May 1945, when he passed out in the gas chamber. A physical

---

[8] *Id.*

[9] United States. Congress. Senate. Committee on Veterans' Affairs. *Is Military Research Hazardous to Veterans' Health?: Lessons from World War II, the Persian Gulf, and Today: Hearing Before the Committee on Veterans' Affairs, United States Senate, One Hundred Third Congress, Second Session, May 6, 1994.* Washington: U.S. G.P.O., 1995.

examination on 14 May 1945, revealed many wounds as the result of exposure to mustard gas."[10]

It is important to understand that these are not isolated incidents. An Institute of Medicine report in 1993 estimated that some 60,000 military members were used as human subjects in the 1940s to test just for two chemical agents, mustard gas and lewisite, and the majority of these people were not informed about the nature of the experiments, nor were they given proper medical care or follow-up after the research.[11]

During the 1950s and 60s, the CIA and the Army engaged in experimentation on U.S. service members, both with and without their knowledge. In several different experiments, the DoD caused service members to unknowingly ingest hallucinogens. Most of the experiments centered around "mind control" and interrogation of persons under the effects of hallucinogens. This was prompted by the perception in U.S. intelligence that China and the Soviet Union had used, and were using, hallucinogens for "brainwashing" and interrogation of prisoners of war. This program was known by the code name MKULTRA. It involved giving LSD and another substance known as quinuclidinyl benzilate, a hallucinogen code-named BZ, to unsuspecting members of both the Armed Forces and civilian communities.

In 1958, Master Sergeant James Stanley responded to a posting on Fort Knox, Kentucky, that solicited volunteers to help the Army develop methods for testing and defending against chemical weapons. Ironically, the volunteers were told they would be testing protective clothing (just as in World War II). MSgt Stanley was transferred to Aberdeen, Maryland, for the

---

[10] United States. Congress. Senate. Committee on Veterans' Affairs. *Is Military Research Hazardous to Veterans' Health?: Lessons Spanning Half a Century: A Staff Report.* Washington: U.S. G.P.O., 1994, at 18.

[11] Institute of Medicine (U.S.). Committee to Survey the Health Effects of Mustard Gas and Lewisite, David P Rall, and Constance M Pechura. *Veterans at Risk: The Health Effects of Mustard Gas and Lewisite.* Washington, D.C.: National Academy Press, 1993, p. 3-4, 6-8, 50-52, 224-226.

testing. He did not learn until 17 years later that he had been given LSD during the program without his knowledge. He found this out accidentally in 1975 when contacted by Walter Reed Army Medical Center, which was conducting follow-up on those who had participated in the 1958 test. Walter Reed wanted to know of any long-term health consequences to MSgt Stanley from his ingestion of the hallucinogen. MSgt Stanley in the intervening years had suffered health problems and hallucinations that he had no explanation for that eventually led to a divorce.

In another instance, Lloyd Gamble, who enlisted in the U.S. Air Force in 1950, volunteered for a special program to (yet again!) test new military protective clothing in 1957.

> He was offered various incentives to participate in the program, including a liberal leave policy, family visitations, and superior living and recreational facilities. However, the greatest incentive to Mr. Gamble was the official recognition he would receive as a career-oriented noncommissioned officer, through letters of commendation and certification of participation in the program. During the 3 weeks of testing new clothing, he was given two or three water-size glasses of a liquid containing LSD to drink. Thereafter, Mr. Gamble developed erratic behavior and even attempted suicide. He did not learn that he had received LSD as a human subject until 18 years later, as a result of congressional hearings in 1975. Even then, the Department of the Army initially denied that he had participated in the experiments, although an official DoD publicity photograph showed him as one of the valiant servicemen volunteering for "a program that was in the highest national security interest."[12]

---

[12] *Id.*, notes omitted.

What is worth noting about these programs, beyond the experimentation on service members without their informed consent, are the arguments offered by the proponents and defenders of these programs. According to Sidney Gottlieb, a doctor and former CIA officer, MKULTRA was established to investigate whether and how an individual's behavior could be modified by covert means. Dr. Gottlieb testified before Congress that "it was felt to be mandatory and of the utmost urgency for our intelligence organization to establish what was possible in this field on a high priority basis."[13] Although many human subjects were not informed or protected, Dr. Gottlieb's defended these actions by stating, " … harsh as it may seem in retrospect, it was felt that in an issue where national survival might be concerned, such a procedure and such a risk was a reasonable one to take."[14]

These attitudes persist even today. Dr. Gottlieb's responses in the 1970s sound remarkably like the reasons offered to justify mandatory vaccination of troops today with unapproved, unlicensed, or investigational drugs. In a television appearance in 1997, Secretary of Defense Cohen held up a five-pound bag of sugar and stated that if the bag were filled with anthrax spores, it could wipe out half of the population of Washington, D.C.[15] In a later opinion editorial appearing in *Army Times*, Secretary Cohen wrote that

> At least 25 countries, including Iraq and North Korea, now have—or are in the process of acquiring and developing—weapons of mass destruction … This is not hyperbole. It is reality … The race is on between our

---

[13] United States. Congress. Senate. Committee on Human Resources. Subcommittee on Health and Scientific Research. *Human Drug Testing by the CIA, 1977: Hearings Before the Subcommittee on Health and Scientific Research of the Committee on Human Resources, United States Senate, Ninety-fifth Congress, First Session*, On S. 1893 ... 20-21 September 1977. Washington: U.S. Govt. Print. Off., 1977.

[14] *Id.*, p. 169-217.

[15] Richter, Paul. "Experts Assess Risk of 'New Terrorism' Threat." *Los Angeles Times*. 7 February 2000. https://www.latimes.com/archives/la-xpm-2000-feb-07-mn-61940-story.html, last accessed 30 April 2020.

> preparations and those of our adversaries. We are preparing for the possibility of a chemical or biological attack on American soil because we must. There is not a moment to lose.[16]

The truth of these matters will be examined in greater detail later. The point to be made here is that Secretary Cohen's defense of the anthrax program, and the justification for biological warfare programs generally, distilled to its essence, is nothing more than "the ends justifies the means." Where matters of national security (Gottlieb called it "national *survival*") are at stake, it does not matter how we go about defending ourselves, even if it means experimenting on unsuspecting troops, because it involves "National Security."

This is a particularly dangerous path for a number of reasons, some obvious and others not as obvious. While there are any number of moral points of view about using troops in this way, one's opinion about whether it is right or wrong to experiment on troops in this fashion depends largely on one's view of individual liberty for the citizen-soldier and the limits of a nation-state's ability to protect "itself." These arguments inevitably devolve into philosophical debates, punctuated by 12-letter words and citations of long-dead philosophers, spoken by people far removed from the gas chambers and vomiting victims on their hands and knees, much like Dr. Gottlieb's testimony in an air-conditioned chamber in front of politicians and cameras during the famous Church Committee hearings. More importantly, where "military" or "national security" matters are concerned, the academics inevitably defer to those wearing uniforms with stars on their collars.

It would appear on the surface that this issue was decisively concluded at the end of World War II in favor of the rights of the individual. In

---

[16] Cohen, William S. "Preparing for a Grave New World." *The Washington Post*, 26 July 1999. https://www.washingtonpost.com/archive/opinions/1999/07/26/preparing-for-a-grave-new-world/0e784cbe-e140-4af1-bb0cc9075c57f672, last accessed 30 April 2020.

August 1947, the Nuremberg Trials of the Nazi Doctors, including those such as Karl Brandt, came to a close, resulting in the death penalty for many of the doctors who conducted experiments on unwilling prisoners in concentration camps across Hitler's Reich. It is to this that we must turn briefly in order to understand the law of informed consent and how it applies to the military, if at all. But if it seems that his author is "laying it on a little thick," compare Secretary Cohen's above remark about the necessity of the mandatory anthrax vaccine program to this one: "We are not conducting these experiments, as a matter of fact, for the sake of some fixed scientific idea, but to be of practical help to the armed forces and beyond that to the … people in a possible emergency." This is from a letter written by Doctor Wolfram Sievers, Colonel in the German Army in November 1942, to Dr. Karl Brandt, both convicted Nazi War Criminals, excerpted from Prosecution Exhibit No. 263 at their trial.

CHAPTER 2
THE NUREMBERG CODE

> Members of the military are not shorn of their constitutional rights while they remain in the military service. Blackstone said: " … he puts not off the citizen when he enters the camp; but it is because he is a citizen, and would wish to continue so, that he makes himself for a while a soldier."[1]

After the Germans were defeated in World War II, it was not long before both an International War Crimes Tribunal was created and a separate Military Tribunal to try members of the German High Command and others for their "War Crimes, Crimes Against Peace and Against Humanity."[2] These military tribunals were held under the auspices of the four individual Zone Commanders, into which Germany had been divided at the end of the war. The Chief Prosecutor for the military tribunals in the American Zone was General Telford Taylor, U.S. Army. There were twelve separate trials held at Nuremberg by the American Military Governor, promulgated by Military Government Ordinance Number Seven, dated 25 October 1946. This ordinance was passed pursuant to the

---

[1] *U.S. v. Manuel*, 43 M.J. 282, 286 (C.A.A.F. 1995) (citations omitted).

[2] Germany (Territory under Allied occupation, 1945-1955: U.S. Zone). Military Tribunals. *Trials of War Criminals Before the Nuremberg Military Tribunals Under Control Council Law No. 10, Nuremberg*, October 1946-April 1949. Washington: U. S. Govt. Print. Off., 19491953.

authority granted by Control Council Law Number 10, which set forth exactly who and what could be prosecuted and how the process was to occur (including that someone sentenced to death would be executed no later than 30 days after the "decision has become final").[3] It was in the American occupation zone that the second "series" of trials occurred in 1947 against the doctors who performed medical experiments on Jews, Poles, and other persons who were being held prisoner. These trials came to be known as the "Doctors Trials" or the "Medical Trials." German scientists, some of them renowned in their fields, were tried as war criminals because of the experiments they had performed on behalf of the German High Command on unwilling citizen-victims.

Some of the experiments named in the indictment against the German doctors were startlingly similar to those detailed in Chapter 1. For example, Count II of the indictment, entitled War Crimes, [specification] Number 6 alleges that

> Between September 1939 and April 1945 all of the defendants herein unlawfully, willfully, and knowingly committed war crimes, as defined by Article II of Control Council Law No. 10, in that they were principals in, accessories to, ordered, abetted, took a consenting part in, and were connected with plans and enterprises involving medical experiments without the subjects' consent, upon civilians and members of the armed forces of nations then at war with the German Reich and who were in the custody of the German Reich in exercise of belligerent control.[4]

---

[3] *Id.*

[4] From the indictment, *U.S. v. Brandt, et al.* (The Medical Case), *2 Trials of War Criminals Before the Nuremberg Military Tribunals Under Control Council Law No. 10*, (1949).

The indictment goes on to list a number of different experiments, the most similar to American experiments of which were the *lost* (mustard) gas experiments. These were "[c]onducted at Sachsenhausen, Natzweiler, and other concentration camps for the benefit of the German Armed Forces to investigate the most effective treatment of wounds caused by *Lost* gas. *Lost* is a poison gas which is commonly known as mustard gas."[5] One of the most horrifying aspects of the experiments was *simultaneously* the *scientific precision* and *complete disregard for the subjects' humanity* with which the tests were carried out, as if they were being conducted on lab mice. Many of the experiments had obvious utility for all Armed Forces. The U.S. prosecutor at NUREMBERG acknowledged as much in his opening statement.

> A sort of rough pattern is apparent on the face of the indictment. Experiments concerning high altitude, the effect of cold, and the potability of processed sea water have an obvious relation to aeronautical and naval combat and rescue problems. The mustard gas and phosphorous burn experiments, as well as those relating to the healing value of sulfanilamide for wounds, can be related to air-raid and battlefield medical problems. It is well known that malaria, epidemic jaundice, and typhus were among the principal diseases which had to be combated by the German Armed Forces and by German authorities in occupied territories.
>
> To some degree, the therapeutic pattern outlined above is undoubtedly a valid one, and explains why the Wehrmacht, and especially the German Air Force, participated in these experiments. Fanatically bent upon conquest, utterly ruthless as to the means or instruments to be used in achieving victory, and callous to the

[5] *Id.*

> sufferings of people whom they regarded as inferior, the German militarists were willing to gather whatever scientific fruit these experiments might yield.[6]

There were high-altitude tests to determine how high pilots would be able to fly, as well as freezing tests on human subjects that examined how cold a person could get before dying, as well as what the best ways were to re-heat a freezing person. This had important implications for the Germans fighting on the brutally cold Russian front. Of more specific import for the anthrax vaccine herein discussed, the Germans conducted a number of tests involving chemical and biological warfare.

The experiments involving mustard gas involved gassing subjects and measuring its effect upon them. The Germans operated with the complete permission and authority of both their government and the society generally; given that the subjects weren't even German soldiers, but captured enemy civilians or belligerents, they went a step further and wounded some prisoners first to determine the effect the gas would have upon a wound under battlefield conditions. While it is important to state that none of the experiments involving the U.S. DoD (of which we are aware) involved this kind of treatment, the "baseline" experiments conducted by the German doctors were identical to the U.S. DoD's "man-break tests" conducted in the late 1940s and 1950s. In fact, the lawyers for several of the Nazi doctors argued at trial that the German experiments were identical to the experiments conducted by the U.S. and Britain using human subjects in the period between World Wars I and II. Of course, as has already been shown, the U.S. experiments were conducted, in most cases, *after* the Nuremberg Trials—and in secret—on U.S. soil and against U.S. citizens and soldiers.

---

6 *U.S. v. Brandt, et al.* (The Medical Case), *2 Trials of War Criminals Before the Nuremberg Military Tribunals Under Control Council Law No. 10* (1949), p. 37.

During their trial, the Nazi doctors offered several defenses to their actions, chief among these was that they, the doctors, had not known that anything they were doing was wrongful because the experiments (in some cases) were no different than ones which had been carried out by the Americans and Germans prior to the trial. In other words, the argument is essentially a combination of challenging the war crimes tribunal's charges as *ex post facto* laws, as well as a challenge to the notion of being on "notice" that one's actions are prohibited, i.e., the doctors argued that there existed no agreed-upon international common law on the use of human beings as subjects. While the world might say *now*, after victory, that the German doctors' actions were wrongful, there was no law in existence prior to their actions to let them know that what they were doing was criminal. This is a fundamental tenet of criminal law generally: the necessary existence of some law making the act criminal before it is committed, in order to provide notice to the actor that such acts are forbidden.[7]

Two doctors who worked with the prosecution at Nuremberg, Drs. Andrew Ivy and Leo Alexander, were concerned with the defense arguments about there being no previous international statement or standard regarding the treatment of human subjects and their consent in medical experimentation. In April 1947, Dr. Alexander submitted a memorandum to the American Counsel of six points regarding medical experimentation on human subjects. The verdict against the doctors was returned on 19 August 1947. In the verdict, each of the six points was covered and expanded into ten points under a section entitled "Permissible Medical Experiments." This came to be known as "The Nuremberg Code." The Nuremberg Code's first principle was that "the voluntary consent of the human subject is absolutely essential." The principles of the Nuremberg Code were adopted by the U.S. DoD in

---

[7] Four of the seven defendants charged with this crime (experiments involving lost or "mustard" gas) were acquitted.

1953 when the Secretaries of the Army, Navy, and Air Force all adopted a memorandum entitled "Use of Human Volunteers in Experimental Research." The first principle was verbatim from the Nuremberg Code. In 1964, the World Medical Association, in its "Helsinki Declaration," adopted the Nuremberg Code. Eventually, these principles were codified in U.S. law as Title 50, section 1520a, but this did not occur until 1977. One might well ask at what point the CIA and DoD doctors can be charged with conducting illegal experiments, but one may as well wonder when pigs will fly at this point.

There is a seminal case from the Supreme Court called *The Paquete Habana*, which international law professors will say stands for the proposition that international law, in the form of treaties, executive agreements, and international norms and customs, are an essential part of U.S. domestic law.[8] If that legal proposition is true, then the DoD's experiments on its own soldiers without their informed consent was patently illegal, and it is clear that in 1977, Congress thought something "wrongful" had happened with the CIA's MKULTRA program. At the opening of the hearings regarding the program, Senator Inouye, presiding, stated that "[i]t is also the purpose of this hearing to address the issues raised by any additional illegal or improper activities that have emerged from the files and to develop remedies to prevent such improper activities from occurring again."[9] Notice, however, what is conspicuously absent from that statement: any mention of holding people accountable for those putative violations of the law.

Admiral Stansfield Turner, director of the CIA, also believed that something illegal happened by noting that (a) he was cooperating with the Attorney General, and (b) reminding the committee that MKULTRA

---

[8] *The Paquete Habana*, 175 U.S. 677 (1900).

[9] United States. Congress. Senate. Select Committee on Intelligence, and United States. Congress. Senate. Committee on Human Resources. Subcommittee on Health and Scientific Research. *Project MKULTRA, the CIA's Program of Research in Behavioral Modification: Joint Hearing Before the Select Committee on Intelligence and the Subcommittee on Health and Scientific Research of the Committee on Human Resources, United States Senate, Ninety-fifth Congress, First Session, August 3, 1977.* Washington: U.S. Govt. Print. Off., 1977, p. 2.

did not occur on his watch, but was a program of another director and that the events were some 12 to 24 years past at the time of the hearings. MKULTRA lasted from 1953 to 1964 and was conducted in concert with the Department of the Army.[10]

Interestingly, no one ever stated exactly what law they believed had been broken and what the penalty was for this crime. There was not then, nor is there now, any federal *criminal* statute prohibiting a person or agency from conducting experiments on military members or ordinary citizens without their informed consent. Some members of the committees invoked a recently passed law in that year (1977) that was the product of a 1975 initial inquiry into these matters, but it wasn't a criminal statute—it simply mandated informed consent with no actual punishment or remedy listed for violations.[11]

This raises an uncomfortable moral/ethical/legal question: Which is worse, the German doctors who operated (they claimed) out of a genuine ignorance that their actions were wrong—and historically speaking they have a fair case for it—or the DoD and its doctors who clearly knew that their actions were wrongful in light of the German doctors' trials? Someone will undoubtedly want to take me to task for comparing the CIA's or DoD's doctors to the Nazi doctors of World War II; however, either the principles of the Nuremberg Code are the standards of the medical profession or they are not. They cannot be called principles if they can be bent to the will of the doctor performing the particular tests, or justified and waved away after the fact with vague references to "national survival" because the U.S. has never faced the kind of military pressure against the homeland as Germany did in World War II.[12]

---

[10] *Id.* at p. 9-14.

[11] Chapter 3 addresses at some length what legal recourse someone has against a government agent or agency conducting such experiments. Technically, an unconsented medical procedure would constitute a battery or an assault consummated by a battery, but there is no federal "battery" statute; criminal law is almost entirely a matter for the states.

[12] This is momentarily setting aside a doctor's Hippocratic oath to "do no harm."

The first principle enunciated in the Nuremberg Code is that "the informed consent of the subject is absolutely essential." There is nothing equivocal about that statement. It does not say, for example, that "the informed consent of the subject is *somewhat* or *mostly* essential." Nor does it manifest any limitation to only Nazi doctors or doctors of defeated Axis powers. As one author has noted, "[t]here is no exception for soldiers or for wartime."[13] Which all goes to this simple point: There is no "greater good" exception or argument against the principle, because that is exactly what the Nazi doctors said they were doing.

Sidney Gottlieb's statement that it was considered a matter of "national survival" has two dangerous flaws in it, one obvious, the other insidious. The first, obvious flaw is that it is exactly the same argument that the U.S. and other Allied powers forbade as a defense in Control Council Law Number 10. The Wehrmacht doctors certainly performed a number of experiments whose results had only one possible practical application and that was in the war effort in which they were engaged. In fact, the German doctors, involved as their country was in a losing battle against foreign powers with bombs dropping on them daily, probably had a much better claim to Gottlieb's "national survival" argument than the CIA or DoD had in the continental United States post World War II with the U.S. as one of the world's only two (nuclear) superpowers.

More insidious, and hidden in Gottlieb's argument, however, is a claim of moral superiority. Gottlieb's argument allows that either he, or someone else on behalf of the State, can take away the subject's right to decide the most fundamental question of humanity: the right to live. It is an objectification of the person—the person as tool of the State. As was pointed out by Supreme Court Justice William Brennan's dissent in the *Stanley* case, quoting a law review article,

---

13 Annas, George J. "Changing the Consent Rules for Desert Storm." *New England Journal of Medicine*, vol. 326, no. 11, December 1992, p. 770-773., doi:10.1056/nejm199203123261117.

> [Human experimentation authorized by the state] dramatizes the notion that the state is free to treat its nationals in the manner it chooses because it perceives itself as the source of all rights, and therefore as beyond the reach of law, rather than regarding rights as inalienable, that is, not subject to arbitrary cancellation by the State.[14]

This is more insidious because it sounds academic and benign, perhaps even agreeable, because, after all, doesn't each of us owe our way of life to the State? This simple yet bankrupt logic and consequent objectification of human beings can easily be turned on particular groups and yields exactly the kind of thinking that helped create the Holocaust in the first instance.

I do not want to oversimplify a tragedy on the scale of the Holocaust into one short sentence; it doesn't do it justice nor does it take into account the myriad other factors involving anti-Semitism in Europe that help account for what happened there in from 1933 to 1945. It is, however, critical to recognize arguments like Gottlieb's of "national survival" and follow them to their logical conclusion. Otherwise, tragedies like the Holocaust get put aside as historical anomalies, but when programs like MKULTRA, the Tuskegee experiments, and yes, even the current DoD anthrax vaccine are announced, apologists differentiate them because, *clearly*, *we* are not in any way morally comparable to the (gasp!) *Nazi* doctors ... even though we're violating the exact same principle in the same way.

It may be that they do not use the same specific means that the Nazi doctors did, which was brute force. Instead, like the CIA doctors in the MKULTRA program and the DoD doctors in the mustard and lewisite gas tests, or the AEC in its radiation tests on soldiers, it was deception or trickery via gunpoint, backed by the very credible threat of future

---

14 Bassiouni, M. Cheriff, et al. "An Appraisal of Human Experimentation in International Law and Practice: The Need for International Regulation of Human Experimentation." *The Journal of Criminal Law and Criminology (1973-)*, vol. 72, no. 4, 1981, p. 1597., doi:10.2307/1143248.

punishment (court-martial) in order to silence those who might bring the government's actions to light. In normal criminal trials, attempting to hide conduct is frequently admissible as "consciousness of guilt"—that is, evidence that the actor was aware of the wrongfulness of his actions.

Worse than Gottlieb's justification, however, is that in some cases, government actors consciously change history or the law: destroy documents, close test sites, classify evidence they don't want to become public, and then offer some higher moral calling as justification—the threat of an invisible enemy, international terrorism, the ticking time bomb. The end result is that these excuses either gain public acceptance or create a sense of public indifference to the rights of their fellow citizens.

Lest there be any question about whether this line of reasoning was ever explored by the Army or CIA doctors back then, some internal documents, which were accidentally discovered because they were misfiled and did not get destroyed like the rest of the source documents, became public and put a finer point on it:

In the 1977 hearings in front of the Senate, internal CIA documents revealed that the CIA believed that it must "conceal these activities from the American public in general," because public knowledge of the "unethical and illicit activities would have serious repercussions in political and diplomatic circles and would be detrimental to the accomplishment of its mission."[15]

In a 1959 Staff Study, the United States Army Intelligence Corps (USAINTC) even more candidly explained its justification for abandoning the principles of the Nuremberg Code:

> It was always a tenet of Army Intelligence that the basic American principle of dignity and welfare of the individual

---

[15] United States. Congress. Senate. Select Committee to Study Governmental Operations with Respect to Intelligence Activities. *Final Report of the Select Committee to Study Governmental Operations with Respect to Intelligence Activities, United States Senate: Together with Additional, Supplemental, and Separate Views.* Washington: U.S. Govt. Print. Off, 1976. S. Rep. No. 94-755, Book I, p. 385. Quoting CIA Inspector General's Survey of the Technical Services Division, 1957, p. 217.

> will not be violated. In intelligence, the stakes involved and the ***interests of national security may permit a more tolerant interpretation of moral-ethical values***, but not legal limits, through necessity ... Any claim against the US Government for alleged injury due to EA 1729 [LSD] must be legally shown to have been due to the material. Proper security and appropriate operational techniques can protect the fact of employment of EA 1729.[16]

That is to say, legal liability could be avoided by covering up the LSD experiments. If no one could prove they had been given the drug, no one on the administering side would ever have to pay the consequences for their actions.

Putting aside the moral reprehensibility of this position, the issue of the legality of the DoD's tests is beyond cavil: The experiments violated a slew of laws. They certainly violated the spirit and letter of the Nuremberg Code. They violated any number of state criminal battery or assault statutes, i.e., an unconsented drug in one's drink is a battery. In fact, the person administering such a treatment would be criminally liable for whatever happened to the person taking the drug.[17] These batteries would also be actionable in a tort suit for damages were the doctors in private practice. They violated the "common rule" and accepted standards of medical practice. They violated the civil rights of U.S. citizens. Interestingly enough, no one was ever prosecuted for these and other acts and no government agent or agency was ever forced to pay a servicemember a dime by any court for the harms done to them. The explanation as to why is a complicated bit of legal legerdemain.

---

[16] *Id.*, at 416-417. Emphasis added. Quoting USAINTC Staff Study, Material Testing Program EA 1729, 15 October 1959, p. 26.

[17] "During the Rockefeller Commission and Church Committee investigations in 1975, the cryptonym [MKULTRA] became publicly known when details of the drug-related death of Dr. Frank Olsen were publicized. In 1953, Dr. Olsen, a civilian employee of the Army at Fort Detrick, leapt to his death from a hotel room window in New York City about a week after having unwittingly consumed LSD administered to him as an experiment at a meeting of LSD researchers called by CIA." —prepared statement of Adm. Stansfield Turner, Director of the CIA, before a Senate Committee, 3 August 1977.

CHAPTER 3
"THE GENERAL DID WHAT?"

"Hey D, you got a minute?"

I looked up from behind my computer. I must have betrayed a look of impatience, because Justin looked back at me and said, "What?"

"I'm sorry, man. Sure, what's on your mind?" I pushed back from my desk and he leaned against the wall, all six-foot, two-hundred five pounds of him.

Justin Constantine and I had gone to Naval Justice School together back in Newport, Rhode Island. All of the sea services, the Navy, Marine Corps, *and* the Coast Guard, send their lawyers to NJS for 10 weeks of training in military Administrative law, Criminal law, and Civil law, with a heavy emphasis throughout on practical application and trial advocacy. I hadn't known Justin that well, as he was a new First Lieutenant and I was a relatively senior Captain, a year or two away from being on the selection/promotion board for Major. Despite that, when we found out that he and I, as well as another classmate of his, had orders for Okinawa straight out of Justice School, I made an effort to take them under my wing. As it turned out, Justin and I both got orders for the Defense shop and we found out we had rugby in common. After some long days as brand-new criminal defense attorneys, we also found our common love of drinking.

"Well, you know I got detailed to those three anthrax refusals from Up North, right?"

I nodded in reply. "Up North" referred to Camp Hansen, about an hour north of where we were at Camp Foster. While Camp Foster contained a lot of headquarters and support units, Hansen tended to have combat units like infantry battalions, an artillery regiment, and other front-line trigger-pullers. My assigned office was technically up there in the smaller Legal Services Support Team building, but I kept getting assigned cases in the south because of the fact that the Third Marine Air Wing was there and my boss always seemed to think my having been a pilot would somehow help the Marines who got into trouble in the Wing. It didn't seem that way to me.

I knew all about the anthrax cases Up North; in fact, I had lobbied our boss, Major John Woodworth, to give them to Justin.

"J.R.," I had said, "I know Justin is new, but he's solid, and I have the other anthrax cases. These are a great way for him to get his feet wet and we can work on them side by side."

I had been sitting in the only other chair in his small office in the Defense wing of the Legal Services building to discuss it, and I presumed to use his first name in private: We had known each other on a first-name basis for a couple of years, since we were both Captains and I was interning as a prosecutor at Camp Lejeune.

Although I had been commissioned the same year he had, the vagaries of our different career tracks made him senior to me now.

In order to recruit lawyers, the armed services must offer incentives; there is no way that the pay of an officer is comparable to what an attorney could get on the open market. One of the ways to make up that deficit is through a fiction known as "constructive service." An attorney who signs up at the beginning of law school actually gets a reversion back to the date they signed up once they've completed training, which means that upon completion of Basic School and Justice School, someone with only months in service gets promoted to First Lieutenant and then is in zone for Captain, something that usually takes four to five years for the "normally" accessed officer. This occasionally creates friction within the Marine Corps' rigid hierarchy because a Marine lawyer walking around with Captain's bars may have nine to 18 months of actual, real-life experience and time in the Corps, compared to a "regular" line officer Captain who has been through two promotion boards, several deployments, and could have as much as eight or nine or 10 years of service. After a few years it all irons itself out, but it's a difficult row to hoe for new attorneys, too. They're occasionally treated as *less than* officers by those who know the system.

"Well," J.R. had begun in his usual southern twang, "he's gotta mind his clients and you gotta mind yours, but these should all wind up as Summary Court Board waivers anyway. Help him out and let me know how it goes."

"Wilco, sir. Thank you." I had stood to attention in front of his desk briefly, spun smartly on my heel and toe as if we were doing an about face on the parade deck, and marched out of his office in an exaggerated high step, to his snickering.

Here, now, with Justin in front of my desk, I squinted, struggling to think of the case names.

"Stone-something, right? Not Stonehenge, but … ?" I tried to remember from our last defense meeting.

"Stonewall," Justin supplied, either missing or ignoring the joke. I knew something was on his mind. "I just got a call from one of my clients. You'll never believe what happened."

"Your guy confessed to the Kennedy shooting?" I didn't even smile. He looked frustrated in return. "Okay, okay. I'm sorry. What happened?"

"All three of my guys got called into a meeting with the Commanding General for Third MarDiv." I raised my eyebrows and sat forward. It wasn't often that our clients got called into the Division Commander's office for a chat. "So, of course, the Sergeant Major's in there, the Division SJA—"

"Colonel Favors was in there?" I asked, incredulous. I was curious as to why the Staff Judge Advocate, a lawyer for the entire Third Marine Division would need to be in there to talk to three anthrax refusers.

"—the regimental or battalion surgeon, and maybe one other C.O., either Battalion or Company C.O.," Justin finished and let that sink in.

"Okay, you got me, I give up, why the fuck was the C.G. Third MarDiv talking to one of your anthrax refusers?"

"Get this: They all were sitting out in the hall or waiting area and they get called in and have a talking to from the C.G. about why this vaccine is completely safe, and why won't they take this? and all this dis-information out there on the internet is just hype and conspiracy theorists and, now for the money ball, if they'll just take this shot, all will be forgiven. No court-martial, no NJP, nothing. The whole unfortunate incident will be put behind them." Justin had a deep, gravelly voice and everything he said tended to come out flat and monotone. A long time of hanging around him had taught me the subtle nuances of that monotone. I saw where he was heading.

"And no one ever called you, their lawyer?" He shook his head slowly from side to side. I whistled slowly and rocked back in my chair. "They've got charges preferred already, right?"

Justin nodded. "Yep."

There were several troubling things about that scenario from a defense counsel's perspective. First, commanders of units are the persons who actually create the courts in the military. They have incredible discretion to either prefer (bring) charges against a member of their unit or not, based on how they see the particular offense, after an appropriate investigation has been done. Convening authorities also grant search warrants, select the jury pool, can grant clemency after a court-martial and lessen the sentence a judge or jury awards, although they cannot increase the punishment. As a result, charges and dispositions can vary widely from unit to unit, depending upon how serious the particular commander views the offense. Prosecutors (known as "trial counsel" in the military) and staff judge advocates provide advice to commanders and tend to buff some of the differences out, but there can still be wide divergence on particular charges.

That all said, commanders generally stay out of the process once charges have preferred in order to avoid the appearance of impropriety and subject themselves to an unlawful command influence motion or make themselves into witnesses at a motions session. There are also, for all lawyers, some fairly strict rules of professional conduct for dealing with persons who are already represented. The general practice is to not talk to a criminal defendant who is already represented without consulting his attorney first. It just invites trouble.

So I was a bit shocked to hear that the SJA for the Division was present while the General talked to a criminal defendant about the charges he was currently pending, without even notifying his attorney. Furthermore, the charges in the anthrax refusal cases were not even convened by a General court-martial—that is, a court convened by a General officer—they were brought at a Special court-martial, a lower forum convened by the Battalion commander, where the accused could receive no more than 6 months' confinement, forfeiture of 2/3 pay per month for 6 months, reduction to the lowest enlisted paygrade, and a bad-conduct discharge. A General Court-Martial can award any punishment authorized for the particular offense, including death.

"And get this," Justin went on, "I heard from some of my sources that the C.G. was basically asking them 'Why don't you trust me?' and shit like that. One of my guys is a Sergeant and finally caved in, crying or very upset, after this long heart-to-heart and agreed to take the shot, so the surgeon took him right on the spot to medical." Now Justin's voice had a real edge to it. "Do you believe that?!"

"Curiouser and curiouser," I answered.

Justin looked at me and then caught on. "*Alice in Wonderland*?" he mouthed.

I nodded. My mind was trying to process what this meant, but more importantly, I was trying to find an angle that would help Justin's clients. I was stumped. I enjoyed these sessions we had in defense, frequently bouncing ideas off of one another to help focus our thinking. Justin's thought process, I had found, frequently mirrored my own.

"Let's ask Hites," I said finally. Although I had over eight years on active duty, I was as new as Justin as a lawyer, and I couldn't think of a rule or regulation that had technically been violated, so it was time to ask someone with more experience.

Major John Hitesman graduated from the Norwich Military Academy a year before I graduated from Boston University. Like me, Hitesman had a "life" before becoming a lawyer. He had been a "grunt," an infantry officer, stationed in Hawai'i before getting picked up for the Funded Law Program. Okinawa was his first tour as a lawyer, but he had been a defense attorney there for two years straight. He had a phlegmatic personality, utterly unflappable in my experience with him. He was also one smart cookie and he and I had become fast friends, especially after we talked and I found out he played ice hockey at Norwich and had found a local pickup league in Naha.

Given that we were peers, more or less, even though he had pinned on Major already and become a field-grade officer, we would alternate driving to play ice hockey together every Thursday night. I enjoyed the conversation on the rides with him almost as much as playing ice hockey. At six-foot-two, two-hundred fifteen or so pounds, Hites looked like a linebacker, but he was an agile skater and good stick-handler. At five-six (on a tall day), I was shorter than most of the Okinawans we played against and I always appreciated playing on a line with a little beef.

When John came in to the office, he looked at Justin. "What's going on? Barney told me your clients got pistol whipped this weekend."

I was "Barney," and John was one of the few people who addressed me by my pilot's call-sign. When I first moved into the office next to his, I put up a framed print of an AH-1W SuperCobra attack helicopter, a going away present, signed by most of my squadron. On the plate was my name, call-sign, and a quote from my fellow pilots: "Shakespeare was Right." I later got a picture nailed to my door in my office on Camp Hansen that was a picture of Fred Flintstone and Barney Rubble, with "Hitesman" and an arrow pointing to Fred and "Saran" and an arrow pointing to Barney.

"Sir, I don't know if Captain Saran told you, but something weird happened this weekend with my clients and I'm not sure what to do about it." Justin relayed the story quickly and Hites listened with his hands laced in front of his face, moving his head only to spit some tobacco juice from the wad occupying the left side of his mouth, into a Styrofoam cup.

"Well, I'll play devil's advocate, here. Why can't a C.O. call in one of his Marines and talk to him? What's wrong with that?"

Justin seemed a little put off by the question. I was, too. "I'm not sure," he began, "that's why I asked."

"I can think of a few," I piped up. "He's already represented, there are charges pending, he's the Convening Authority's direct superior, and it all around stinks."

Hites barely looked up at me. "I might agree, but what kind of relief are you going to get? I mean, how do you frame this in a motion and what do you think one of our judges is going to say? What would you ask for?"

Hitesman's pragmatism stung me into silence. He was right. There was a long pause.

"I suppose you could write a letter to the SJA's state bar because I think there is an ethical problem that she should know about with her being in there and allowing the C.A. to question your clients. But then again, the JAG Instruction is only for attorneys, not to commanders, and same for the rules of professional conduct. And why wouldn't a commander have his attorney in there as a witness?" Hites turned to Justin. "Did she ask any questions of your clients?"

"No, sir, I don't think so. I think she was just in there." Justin stood against the wall with his hands behind his back looking at the rug. I was still mulling over John's point. Something about it didn't smell right, particularly given the fact that Sergeant Terveen, one of Justin's clients, had changed his mind under what seemed like pretty coercive conditions. Terveen, Justin had told me, had less than a year before he was getting out and decided the hassle wasn't worth it. The other two, a Lance Corporal and a Private First Class, had stuck to their guns. That was probably more impressive than anything else about the story.

"The only other issue is whether or not they were warned of their rights." Justin shrugged his shoulders. "If they weren't warned, none of their statements are coming in at court, but the prosecution probably won't use them anyway and doesn't need them. I'm sure they can prove they were given the order, didn't take the shot, and don't need any subsequent statements your guys might have made in this meeting. Arguably, they knowingly violated his rights if they didn't read him his rights and that's an offense under the UCMJ, but that's a stretch."

Hites waited a minute and then took a step toward the door.

"It's just so fucked up, though," I said. "I mean, how coercive an environment is that? The C.G. himself is there telling you that everyone else is full of shit, along with the Sergeant Major, the C.O., the Doc. And then the guy caves and he's immediately given the shot while he's still in friggin' tears. Something somewhere tells me that's not right." I wasn't sure where I was going, but it just didn't sound right.

"It sucks, gents, but welcome to criminal defense in the USMC on the island of Okinawa." Hitesman slapped me on the shoulder as he went by. "See ya Thursday, Barn. You driving this time?"

I nodded a couple of times in response and murmured, "Mm hmm."

Justin looked at me after John was gone. He let out a long breath. "God, I love the Marine Corps," he said in a drill instructor voice. I was bothered by it all, but I didn't have any answers. "Well, how's Petty

Officer Ponder's case going?" Justin asked. "Did his C.O. ask him to come in and have a chat?"

I chuckled lightly. Suddenly an idea came to me. "Hey, you know what. I've got a bunch of anthrax info from Sonnie Bates's attorney that I'm supposed to look through. Why don't you have one of your guys submit an Individual Military Counsel request for me? Then, we can put our heads together on one case and use what we do there on the other two cases individually?"

Justin nodded. "Sure. Is any of the information helpful?"

"Yeah, it looks pretty good, but I'm not going to get my hopes up yet. I have to figure out what an 'investigational drug' is and research this statute, but it worked for Sonnie Bates, so … maybe it'll work for our guys."

"Sure it will," Justin deadpanned.

This time I couldn't tell if he was being sarcastic or earnest.

CHAPTER 4
JUDICIAL REMEDIES?

The bar created by *Chappell*—a judicial exception to an implied remedy for the violation of constitutional rights—surely cannot insulate defendants from liability for deliberate and calculated exposure of otherwise healthy military personnel to medical experimentation without their consent, outside of any combat, combat training, or military exigency, and for no other reason than to gather information on the effect of lysergic acid diethylamide [LSD] on human beings.

No judicially crafted rule should insulate from liability the involuntary and unknowing human experimentation alleged to have occurred in this case. Indeed, as Justice Brennan observes, the United States military played an instrumental role in the criminal prosecution of Nazi officials who experimented with human subjects during the Second World War, and the standards that the Nuremberg Military Tribunals developed to judge the behavior of the defendants stated that the "voluntary consent of the human subject is absolutely essential … to satisfy moral, ethical and legal concepts." If this principle is violated the very least that society can do is to see that the victims are compensated, as best they can be, by the

> perpetrators. I am prepared to say that our Constitution's promise of due process of law guarantees this much.[1]

There are both moral and legal arguments to be made for the proposition that the actions detailed in Chapters One and Two should be allowed. To be explicit, I am speaking of the idea that the Government—the State—has (1) a right to the compelled obedience of its citizens, and (2) the right to the lives of its citizenry in defense of the State. This has been the default state of affairs for most of human history. From Africa to Asia to Europe to South and North America, the general organization of human beings has almost always involved a leader, chosen usually by some combination of martial prowess and/or political savvy, with rule enforced upon the rest of the tribe/culture/society through several mechanisms including cultural/social pressure and force. People were always deemed to owe allegiance to the ruler and the larger culture. They could be conscripted to fight in the King's/Pharaoh's/Queen's/Caesar's/Czar's/Napoleon's/ Comrade Stalin's Armies against any enemy of the homeland, forced to march to their certain death. The unthinkable, but unassailable, logic follows that if the State can order you to your likely death, or maybe just a group of you, for the benefit of others, why can't it make the same calculus by doing some experiments on you? If you can be ordered into battle as a soldier where you could die, or even be subjected to the enemy's chemical weapons, then why can't the military hierarchy sacrifice *some* of you good chaps for the sake of others, eh? Isn't this what military commanders do in battles all of the time?

The political systems under which this is *still* the *modus operandi*—today—are too numerous to mention.

Fortunately for United States citizens, the entire idea was explicitly rejected in the American Revolution, that is, the great moment of

---

[1] *United States v. Stanley*, 483 U.S. 669, 709-10 (1987) (O'Connor, J., dissenting) (some citations omitted).

"American Exceptionalism." The Declaration of Independence's most trenchant historical observation is coupled with its boldest claim: "that governments are instituted among men, [and] deriving their just powers from the consent of the governed." Governments are not extensions of the Divine Will; political power does not derive through familial claim (inheritance), religious authority, or other "farcical aquatic ceremonies." It was—and remains—among the most radically egalitarian ideas ever proposed, on a par with Martin Luther's heresy to the Catholic Church's authority. It stripped all of the mysticism and power away from government agents of every kind: All of the King's Men were declaimed as equal to even the lowest yeoman farmer, dock worker, deckhand, or wheelwright.

This is also what seems to have gone missing in our culture, and why even in the United States there are still people in respectable circles who feel that soldiers give up their rights when they join the military and therefore, have no grounds to complain of their treatment. This is not confined to those outside of the military, either; it is a common misperception, even among active service members. If service members enjoy less than the full rights that other U.S. citizens enjoy—diminished First Amendment protections, for example, because they can't protest their Commander's decisions, or lower "expectations of privacy" in the Fourth Amendment context (see mandatory drug testing)—then the logic *somewhat* follows that perhaps service members can be experimented upon without having any grounds for relief.

Unfortunately for service members, these arguments get additional fuel because they have more than a slight legal basis. There is a specific exemption in the Fifth Amendment of the U.S. Constitution for "those serving in the land or Naval forces." There are legal scholars who argue that service members do not enjoy the same Constitutional rights as ordinary citizens because of that specific exception to the Fifth Amendment's grand jury requirement for an indictment. There is still some debate over whether the founders intended all other protections to apply to service members or if that exemption was a recognition that service members were less than full citizens while in uniform. The Supreme Court has never issued a definitive ruling on whether the Bill of Rights applies to service members wholesale.

There are also two Supreme Court decisions that hold that service members have no right to a trial by jury. These decisions are particularly odd because neither of the cases involved service members at all. In one case, at the close of the Civil War, a man living in Indiana was tried and convicted by a military commission and sentenced to be hanged. A local grand jury found no evidence against him and the case was dismissed without an indictment being laid. While in jail he petitioned for a writ of habeas corpus that eventually went to the Supreme Court. The opinion, in eloquent language, extols the virtue and necessity of the trial by jury and then in one backhanded sentence mentions that every U.S. citizen, except service members, enjoys that right.[2]

The second decision, handed down in World War II, involved German saboteurs caught sneaking into the U.S. to commit espionage. Once again, while having nothing to do with the case, the Court manages to mention that only service members have no right to a trial by jury.[3] Ultimately, Congress fixed this with the comprehensive Uniform Code of Military Justice, which gives service members the right to a trial by jury, albeit a somewhat different method of jury selection than in civilian courts. Nonetheless, these kinds of decisions and the impression they convey is that service members are on a different constitutional footing than other U.S. citizens, at least while they are on active duty.

The Court of Appeals for the Armed Forces (CAAF), the highest military appeals court (subordinate only to the Supreme Court of the United States in military cases), has, in many cases, spoken in broad terms about the protections afforded to military members and has

---

[2] See *Ex parte Milligan*, 71 U.S. 2 (1866).

[3] *Ex parte Quirin*, 317 U.S. 1 (1942).

rejected the notion that particular Constitutional rights do not apply *per se* to military members. The court has instead held that a particular right such as the Fourth Amendment's protections, for example, apply "differently" in the unique circumstances of the Armed Forces.[4] In a 1995 case, CAAF noted that

> The administration of military justice is rooted in inherent fair play and justice that prevail under the Anglo-American system of law. "In defining the rights of military personnel, Congress was not limited to the minimum requirements established by the Constitution, and in many instances, it has provided safeguards unparalleled in the civilian sector." The broad constitutional rights that service members enjoy spring from the fundamental principle that they do not lay aside the citizen when they assume the soldier.[5]

These kinds of statements would tend to indicate that service members may enjoy the same rights as any citizen, perhaps even more, depending upon what Congress has granted … or those statements could simply be propaganda, legal pablum for judge advocates and the small legal community around the military that even cares about such arcana.

The fine legal question for service members, relevant to the issue about the anthrax vaccine program, is whether or not there is a Constitutional right, or other right given by Congress, to be free from forced vaccination with an unlicensed or experimental drug. The more general question of whether or not a servicemember can be punished if he refuses a mandatory routine vaccination was answered in *United States*

---

[4] Both the Supreme Court and the Court of Appeals for the Armed Forces have mentioned this "different" application of Constitutional rights. See, e.g., *Greer v. Spock*, 424 U.S. 828 (1976); *U.S. v. McCarthy*, 38 M.J. 398 (C.M.A. 1993).

[5] *U.S. v. Manuel*, 43 M.J. 282, 286 (C.A.A.F. 1995).

v. Chadwell in 1965. In that case a Marine refused to take the smallpox, typhoid, paratyphoid, and influenza vaccine, on religious grounds. The court found against him and found the order lawful. Some people therefore conclude that that the anthrax vaccine program is perfectly valid, end of story, close the book, and let's all go home.

Let's not be done with it so fast, however. First, there are a number of important differences between that order and the current anthrax program. Part of it has to do with the routine nature of that vaccine, meaning that it was already being administered to the entire U.S. population, while the anthrax vaccine had not been so administered. Second, the Marine in that case refused to take the routine shot for religious reasons. Almost none of the service members refusing the anthrax vaccine were relying upon religion as the legal grounds for refusing the anthrax vaccine. A third important difference was that the smallpox and other vaccines were not being administered as pretreatments against chemical warfare; they were being given for the same reasons as they were being given to the nation at large.[6] Finally, there was—and still is—a massive lesson that was learned as a result of the Gulf War in 1990-1991 that changed the legal landscape around the issue of the military administering drugs and biologics to soldiers as a prophylactic against chemical or biological warfare.

Prior to the Gulf War, there had never been an attempt at mass inoculation of the military as a treatment against chemical warfare.[7] The current anthrax vaccine is part of the new era of chemical-biological defense. In prior instances, noted in Chapter One, when military members were harmed by the actions of other soldiers, either military doctors or their commanders, if the military would take no action to redress the wrong, private legal action appeared the only way to go.

---

[6] In an interesting aside, the Supreme Court has found that the state can compel ordinary citizens to take a vaccine in a case called *Jacobsen v. Massachusetts*, 197 U.S. 11 (1905).

[7] I cover this history more fully in Chapter Six.

Service members who learned that they had been given experimental drugs sued the government for monetary damages for their health complications as a result of the experiments performed upon them. These types of suits are called *tort* suits. *Tort* is the French word for "wrong" and under Anglo-American law, it is one means of legal redress for harms suffered by a citizen. Juries may award actual damages for the harm suffered and punitive damages as a punishment to the wrongdoer and as a deterrent to others who would do the same.

A U.S. citizen can also file for damages for a violation of their rights pursuant to a Supreme Court case named *Bivens v. Six Unknown Named Agents*, 403 U.S. 388 (1967). In that case, Bivens alleged that FBI agents came into his apartment without a warrant or probable cause, searched his house from one end to the other, arrested him, and ultimately charged him with narcotics violations. He sued in district court for damages for the violation of his constitutional rights. The courts below dismissed his suit on the grounds that he had no cause of action, but the U.S. Supreme Court ultimately held that he could sue government agents for the violation of his civil rights. Today, there is a specific statute that allows citizens to sue government agents who commit violations of their constitutional rights.[8]

There would at least appear to be a number of legal remedies available to citizens, including service members, if they can prove some legal harm either in a regular civil suit with injunctive relief or damages, or if there is a Constitutional violation under *Bivens* or §1983. This would be true *but for* a legal concept known as sovereign immunity and the *Feres doctrine.*

The *Feres doctrine* is named for a Supreme Court case[9] and relies upon a concept in British law known as sovereign immunity. The syllabus at the beginning of *Feres* explains the concept this way:

---

[8] See 42 U.S.C. §1983.

[9] *Feres v. United States*, 340 U.S. 135, 139-40 (1950).

> While the political theory that the King could do no wrong was repudiated in America, a legal doctrine derived from it that the Crown is immune from any suit to which it has not consented was invoked on behalf of the Republic and applied by our courts as vigorously as it had been on behalf of the Crown. As the Federal Government expanded its activities, its agents caused a multiplying number of remediless wrongs—wrongs which would have been actionable if inflicted by an individual or a corporation but remediless solely because their perpetrator was an officer or employee of the Government. Relief was often sought and sometimes granted through private bills in Congress, the number of which steadily increased as Government activity increased.[10]

In short, the general principle was that no one could sue the Crown because the government *creates* or *grants* the rights of its citizens. Despite our Revolution to be free of British rule, in the earliest years of our republic, our courts took their cue from decisions in the British courts. A simple way of explaining this is that if an ordinary citizen ran over a child due to his own negligence, he would be liable in tort law, and perhaps criminally. Contrariwise, if a government agent driving a government truck did the same thing, there would be no relief for the parents if they sued in court. The only way to get relief in the early years was for a citizen to get his or her representative to put a private bill before either the state or federal legislature and for that body to consent to be sued. Eventually, the United States Congress passed the Federal Tort Claims Act as a comprehensive response to some of the arbitrary and unfair results produced when government agents caused serious harm to citizens, and sought to relieve some of these inequities. It spells out who

---

[10] *Id.*

can sue the federal government and under what circumstances. In some cases, it even delineates what the maximum amount is that can be received for certain harms.

The *Feres* decision actually involved three distinct cases, but the Supreme Court combined them for one decision, named after the lead case. In one of the cases, a soldier in the army had abdominal surgery. Eight months later, an additional surgery removed a 30-inch by 18-inch towel labeled "Medical Department U.S. Army" from his stomach. His suit against the Army doctor for negligence was denied by the Supreme Court, whereas it would have been what lawyers affectionately call a "slam dunk" if it had been in the civilian context of a medical malpractice suit. The *Feres* case held that military members were not within the class of persons covered by the Federal Tort Claims Act. This means, in short, that military members cannot sue the government for harms suffered while on active duty by the tortious conduct of other service members, no matter how egregious the wrongdoing.[11]

There have been many subsequent cases, law review articles, and much philosophical debate questioning both the logic and the viability of the *Feres* doctrine. In fact, there have been a number of bills introduced in Congress to overturn the *Feres* doctrine.[12] The case quoted at the opening of Chapter Two, *United States v. Stanley*, is worth reconsidering, as it addresses both the *Feres* doctrine and the ability of service members to sue for civil rights violations (a *Bivens* claim in the military context, first announced in a case called *Chappell v. Wallace*).

The *Feres* case, like most cases, is subject to either a broad or narrow interpretation and can be differentiated on a factual basis or on the basis of its legal *holding*, that is, the legal principle which applies to the given set of facts. The *Feres* court held that "the Government is not liable under

---

[11] *Id.* The soldier's name was Jefferson.

[12] Funk, Deborah. "Bill Would Let Service members Sue Over Medical Malpractice." *Marine Corps Times*, 27 August 2001, p. 20.

the Federal Tort Claims Act for injuries to servicemen where the injuries *arise out of* or are *in the course of* activity incident to service."[13] The legal justification for this was that service members were not within the class of persons allowed to sue under the Federal Tort Claims Act. In *U.S. v. Stanley*, though, Master Sergeant Stanley was experimented upon, given LSD without his knowledge or consent, and these experiments were subsequently covered up by those in the Army who had administered the drug to him. Being slipped a mickey, as the old saying goes, doesn't seem to quite fall within "arise out of" or "in the course of" activities of the military. Notwithstanding the 1977 hearings, during which members of the Senate noted that "the Justice Department and the Courts have their proper role to play," a bare 5 to 4 majority of the Supreme Court found that MSgt Stanley had no grounds for relief, either under the Federal Tort Claims Act or under a *Bivens* claim for violations of his Constitutional (civil) rights. The Court held that

> the reasoning ... that the special factors counseling hesitation—the unique disciplinary structure of the Military Establishment and Congress' activity in the field—extend beyond the situation in which an officer-subordinate relationship exists, and require abstention in the inferring of *Bivens* actions as extensive as the exception to the FTCA established by *Feres* and *United States v. Johnson.* We hold that no *Bivens* remedy is available for injuries that "arise out of or are in the course of activity incident to service."[14]

And yet, there it is, stated as if it were a fact, that being unknowingly experimented upon is now an activity "aris[ing] out of or ... in the course

[13] *Feres*, at 136.

[14] *Stanley*, at 688-89 (internal citations omitted).

of" one's service; the *Feres* doctrine barred MSgt Stanley's tort action and his claim for the violation of his civil rights.

The fact that the Court found against MSgt Stanley on the tort claim is perhaps not surprising given previous cases involving the *Feres* doctrine. What is especially shocking is that *Chappell v. Wallace* involved fairly clear racial discrimination and the Supreme Court had no trouble finding that racial discrimination was so terrible that the Court would intervene and allow relief from the courts—but being experimented upon without one's consent, like a lab animal, like the Nazis did to the Jews? *No problem and no relief at all!*

The fact that the Supreme Court found that MSgt Stanley had no (military) *Bivens* claim is tragic because it means that service members' most fundamental rights may be violated wantonly and they have no redress in the civil courts of this country.[15] This holding does have one further point to it: The Court, in finding that there were 'special factors counseling hesitation', apparently believed that the right of *informed consent* is of a Constitutional stature. Logically speaking, this is a necessary prerequisite for a *Bivens* claim: that there had to have been the violation of a Constitutional right. If not, there would have been no *Bivens* claim at all and MSgt Stanley's claim would have been summarily dismissed, which is not what the Court did. Instead, the Court found that the *Bivens* claim could not go forward because of the "special factors" that give the Court pause—namely, military discipline—but not that there was no *Bivens* claim stated.

Justice Sandra Day O'Connor, in her dissent in *Stanley*, took a different approach and found, quite simply, that "conduct of the type alleged in this case is so far beyond the bounds of human decency that as a matter of law it simply cannot be considered a part of the military

---

[15] The Supreme Court left open the very slight possibility of injunctive relief or declarative judgments for service members, an important point in current military-legal affairs.

mission."[16] Unfortunately, what Justice O'Connor and the American doctors at Nuremberg recognized as "conduct beyond the bounds of human decency" now had a new get-out-of-jail-free card in the majority's lens: as long as it could be tied back to the *military mission* there would be no redress even for medical experimentation on servicemembers. Less than three years later, on the eve of the Gulf War, it was to be repeated on a larger scale, this time not only with the aid of doctors, but also with lawyers replete with waivers, lobbyists flush with cash, and in the 1990s, public affairs officers with propaganda to sell the whole thing to the military members and the American public, too. With decisions such as *Feres* and *Stanley* in hand, servicemembers would again be prevented from turning to the courts for relief and the law of unintended consequences would again rear its ugly head.

[16] *Stanley*, at 709.

CHAPTER 5
THE FDA, DHHS, & VACCINES: ANTHRAX SLIDES BY

> The quality of a vaccine is closely linked to its manufacturing process, which must be rigorously controlled to ensure that batches of vaccines produced on different occasions are of reproducible and consistent quality. In general, quality is achieved by applying the current good manufacturing practice [CGMP] [...] Such principles also apply to the facilities and equipment in which products are manufactured. Accordingly, vaccine production is very highly regulated to ensure that the products are of consistent quality and safe and effective for the purpose(s) for which regulatory approval was granted.[1]

Before 1962, vaccines, drugs, and other such products did not undergo nearly the kind of scrutiny that they do today in order to become licensed. It wasn't until the thalidomide disaster of the 1960s that federal regulation of drugs came to be what it is today. As of 2003, the DHHS is "United States government's principal agency for protecting the health of

[1] GAO Report T-NSIAD-99-148 29 April 1999.

all Americans and providing essential human services, especially for those who are least able to help themselves."[2] This is a monumental undertaking and it is why the DHHS is one of the largest government agencies, with over 63,000 employees, an annual budget of $429 billion, and a number of sub-agencies with their own areas of responsibility, such as the Food and Drug Administration (FDA). The history of these organizations bears some consideration because it is between the historical cracks in legislation and regulation that the current anthrax vaccine would slip.

In 1906, the first Food and Drug Act was passed, authorizing the federal government to monitor the purity of foods and safety of medicines. The 1906 Act was fairly light, even inadequate by most standards. False statements made about a drug by its manufacturer (i.e., public advertising) were not considered as misbranding by the courts. Additionally, the Act did not grant authority to ban unsafe drugs. For a drug to be legal under the 1906 law, it only had to meet the standards for composition of the United States Pharmacopoeia or the National Formulary. The Bureau of Chemistry—the forerunner to the modern FDA—enforced this law.

It wasn't until 1938 that the FDA received broad statutory authority to regulate interstate shipment of unapproved new drugs for investigational use. This kind of federal regulation was a direct result of President Franklin Delano Roosevelt's policies and the Great Depression. Prior to the Great Depression, the federal government exerted nothing even approaching the kind of regulatory authority that it does today.

The Sulfanilamide Disaster of 1937 brought the first modification to the 1906 act. Soldiers originally used sulfanilamide as a treatment for wounds. In powder form, it was sprinkled over a wound as an antiseptic

---

[2] Quote from the DHHS website, hhs.gov/about/strategic-plan/introduction/index.html, last accessed 29 April 2020.

to prevent infection.[3] A manufacturer decided to expand the anti-infective use of the drug by mixing sulfanilamide with diethylene glycol, a substance that currently enjoys a more popular following among American consumers as antifreeze in car radiators. The manufacturer marketed the mixture of glycol and sulfanilamide as an elixir for sore throats. No clinical tests were performed prior to marketing. There were 107 reported deaths from this product.

Subsequently, the Federal Food, Drug, and Cosmetic Act (FDCA) of 1938 was enacted, expanding the government's control to include advertising and labeling of products. More importantly, it authorized the FDA (for the first time) to establish a regulatory system for obtaining pre-marketing clearance of an Investigational New Drug. Manufacturers were now required to submit a new drug application (NDA) containing evidence that a drug was safe for its *intended use.* Despite this grant of authority, the FDA was fairly "light" (by modern standards) in its regulation. These regulations, which remained in effect without change until 1962, left the protection of human subjects almost entirely to the discretion of sponsors and investigators. For example, it did not require a notice for conducting investigational trials to be submitted to the FDA; it did not require pre-clinical safety studies prior to administration of a drug into humans; and, notwithstanding the Nuremberg Trials, *the 1938 Act did not require informed consent of test subjects.*

In 1962, thalidomide, a sleeping pill developed and widely used abroad for several years, was being studied for use in the United States. The FDA did not approve this drug for marketing in the U.S. because of the requirements in the Federal FDCA, and because of the refusal of an FDA medical officer, Dr. Frances Kelsey, to clear the drug on what she believed to be inadequate safety evidence provided by the manufacturer. Notwithstanding this, and even though the drug was restricted to

---

[3] This is one of the substances the Nazi doctors used in experiments named in the indictment at the Nuremberg Trials, thus their defense that what they did differed little from previous U.S. experiments.

investigational use in the U.S., the sponsoring pharmaceutical company widely distributed it to doctors for their use.[4] Later, of course, thalidomide was learned to be a human teratogen that caused malformations in many European children. Children were being born without arms or with other severe deformities. A series of lawsuits demonstrated that, in general, prescribers of drugs had been relying on manufacturers for information pertaining to the drugs, and that this information in some instances had been based on inadequate testing or even on deliberate falsification and deception. The Kefauver-Harris amendments of 1962 were finally enacted as a result of this incident.

These amendments contained several important new provisions to the FDCA. First, it required that all clinical testing of investigational drugs be conducted under applications submitted to the FDA, called Investigational New Drug (IND) applications. Additionally, sponsors were required to submit reports of pre-clinical studies to justify their proposed clinical testing in humans, obtain informed consent from test subjects prior to their entry into a study, and report all findings resulting from the investigational studies to the FDA. Second, Good Manufacturing Practices (GMP) were established. Any drug not produced in accordance with CGMP would be considered adulterated. Prescription drug advertising was also placed under the supervision of the FDA.

Finally, the 1962 amendments required that all new drugs, in addition to being safe, must be shown to be effective *for their intended use* prior to marketing. The standard for scientific evidence acceptable for demonstrating substantial effectiveness was defined by Congress as:

> adequate and well controlled investigations, including clinical investigations, conducted by experts qualified by scientific training and experience to evaluate the

[4] This practice continues to this day by some drug manufacturers.

> effectiveness of the drug involved, on the basis of which it could be fairly and responsible be concluded by such experts that the drug will have the effect it purports or is represented to have under the conditions of use prescribed, recommended, or suggested in the labeling.[5]

The FDA had actually proposed new regulations before the 1962 amendments were enacted, and it issued final rules three months after the new law took effect. These regulations are the broad outlines of the investigational drug regulatory system that remains in effect today.

The former Division of Biologics Standards (DBS), currently the Center for Biological Evaluation and Research (CBER), was involuntarily transferred to the FDA from the Public Health Service (PHS) in 1973. Its transfer was triggered by the failed polio vaccine release on the grounds that old-world style management encumbered it. The DBS was viewed as incapable of protecting the public health because it was too closely involved with the industry it was supposed to regulate—so-called "unholy marriages" between industry and government regulation. This was the same problem that existed with a number of industries and agencies, including the AEC, when a single agency was tasked with both promoting and regulating a given industry. The AEC was partly responsible for radiation exposure experiments on troops in the 1940s, during which AEC regulators actually wore protective suits during experiments while soldiers were completely exposed to the radiation from atomic bomb detonations.

An important slip occurred between passage of the Kefauver-Harris Amendments and the transference of the DBS from the National Institute of Health (NIH) to the FDA, charged with enforcing the FDCA and passing regulations to do so. A certain class of drugs, biologics (which includes vaccines and other blood products), were under the

---

[5] 21 U.S.C. §355(i) (2000).

auspices of the DBS, which was under the PHS. Unfortunately, because of the hodgepodge manner in which agencies had sprung up, the DBS—which saw itself as controlled by the Public Health Service Act (PHSA) and also sought to promote the industry it was regulating—did not require efficacy data for approval of its products—specifically, vaccines. Thus, it was not until some 10 years later when the DBS was transferred to the FDA and became the Center for Biological Evaluation and Research (CBER) that vaccines were truly required to show efficacy data—notwithstanding a law requiring it some ten years earlier.

When DBS (re-named CBER) finally came under the auspices of the FDA, all of the previously licensed vaccines that had been given without the required efficacy data would be reviewed and placed into categories. Category I products were considered safe, effective, and not misbranded. Category II products were unsafe, ineffective, or misbranded. Category III products were split into A and B. Category IIIA products had inconclusive data, but the product would remain on the market pending further study. Category IIIB drugs showed inconclusive data, and the product was to be removed from the market. This review would take an incredibly long time, and the review of the anthrax vaccine, licensed in 1970 without any efficacy data, would not be done until 1985.

With the creation of so many federal agencies came an increase in the administrative regulations over the industries the agencies were set to watch. The Supreme Court repeatedly deferred to these agencies' decisions and upheld their regulations. Agencies such as the Equal Employment Opportunity Commission (EEOC) and the FDA had increasing roles in their respective areas of concern. As part of the passage of regulations in its area of concern, the agency first proposes a rule in the federal register for a period of time and invites comment on the proposed rule. The rule is then viewed in practice and left open for comment; then, if necessary, the rule is amended and a final proposed rule is ultimately published. While these regulations do not have the same force and effect as law, if they do not conflict with any preexisting laws and are not inconsistent with the agency's charter, in effect, these rules become law because they are binding upon persons, corporations, or agencies operating in the particular agency's area of concern.

The rule regarding testing on human subjects passed with little, if any, comment. Who could disagree with the principle that "no investigator may involve a human being as a subject in research [...] unless the investigator has obtained the legally effective informed consent of the subject[.]"[6] In fact, almost every federal agency adopted the same or similar version of the regulation regarding human subjects and informed consent. This rule was passed by the DHHS in 1981. The full version of the FDA's regulations is virtually identical to the full DHHS ones. They read that

> no investigator may involve a human being as a subject in research covered by these regulations unless the investigator has obtained the legally effective informed consent of the subject or the subject's legally authorized representative. An investigator shall seek such consent only under circumstances that provide the prospective subject or the representative sufficient opportunity to consider whether or not to participate and that minimize the possibility of coercion or undue influence. The information that is given to the subject or the representative shall be in language understandable to the subject or the representative. No informed consent, whether oral or written, may include any exculpatory language through which the subject or the representative is made to waive or appear to waive any of the subject's

[6] 45 C.F.R. 46.116 (2000).

> legal rights, or releases or appears to release the investigator, the sponsor, the institution, or its agents from liability for negligence.[7]

Even the DoD adopted regulations with much the same lack of fanfare in 32 CFR 219.116-117. These regulations state, just as above, that "[e]xcept as provided elsewhere in this policy, no investigator may involve a human being as a subject in research covered by this policy unless the investigator has obtained the legally effective informed consent of the subject or the subject's legally authorized representative." The 2003 version of the DoD regulations are identical to the FDA's. Everyone seemed to agree that when it comes to experimenting on human subjects, consent was a prerequisite. As an important corollary, DHHS also published some definitions of what research would be covered by the informed consent requirements. It is an extremely broad definition.

> Research means a systematic investigation, including research development, testing and evaluation, designed to develop or contribute to generalizable knowledge. Activities which meet this definition constitute research for purposes of this policy, whether or not they are conducted or supported under a program which is considered research for other purposes [...] Research subject to regulation, and similar terms are intended to encompass those research activities for which a federal department or agency has specific responsibility for regulating as a research activity, (for example, Investigational New Drug requirements administered by the Food and Drug Administration).[8]

---

7 21 C.F.R. 50.20 (2000).

8 45 C.F.R. 46.12 (2000).

This last "for example" is critical, as it repeats and reinforces the FDA's requirements that using Investigational New Drugs (IND) for the purpose stated in the NDA is research requiring informed consent. This deserves some explanation, as it is crucial to understanding one of the reasons why the anthrax program was illegal.

The FDA regulates the manufacturers of drugs through the licensing and regulatory process, but it does not control the end-user of the product—i.e., a doctor, or in this case, the DoD. Vaccines are subject to the requirements of the FDA under the FDCA (Title 21, Chapter 9) as prescription drugs and the requirements of the PHSA (42 U.S.C. 262) as a biologic. The two acts are not exclusive, but complementary. Typically, a manufacturer submits a proposed NDA with the FDA setting forth what "clinical protocol" or experiment it is going to do in order to demonstrate the efficacy of its drug. At the same time, the manufacturer also must comply with FDA regulations for how its manufacturing process takes place. Normally, an approved drug must have a dual part license, a Product License Amendment (PLA) for the drug, and an Establishment License Amendment (ELA) for the facility. This ensures that the product meets the four necessary prerequisites for licensing: sterility, safety, potency, and efficacy.

The ELA helps ensure that the drug/biologic is sterile in its manufacturing process and potent. The FDA regulates this process in the facility by enforcing Current Good Manufacturing Practices (CGMP). These practices are industry standards surrounding such procedures as sterility of the filtering systems, handling of the material, and random testing of the finished product to ensure uniformity from batch to batch. Potency is a good measure for quality control and to ensure efficacy of the manufacturer's claims and proposed advertising. If random samplings of different batches reveal widely differing potency levels, it calls into question the consistency of the manufacturing process (a quality issue) and whether the drug can support the claims of efficacy. FDA inspectors, supposedly experts in the field, go check the facility to ensure compliance.

The PLA sets forth the clinical protocol for the product. This includes what studies and data the manufacturer will use to demonstrate effectiveness. In other words, a company cannot simply claim they made a product cleanly and safely (which fulfills one half the ELA), they must also show the product does what it is advertised to do. This will set forth how the product will be used (or has already been used) and the data from those controlled studies. Initially, in most cases, animal studies and basic research will be used to gather data. The company will then submit an NDA for completely new drugs or an IND application for drugs already licensed that the company is seeking to modify. The PLA, and ultimately the license for a drug, is so specific that any change requires a modification to the existing license. The PLA gives the company an "indication" for using the drug. The "indication" in the license will include the route of administration of the drug (e.g., taken by injection or by mouth), the number of shots or pills to be taken (e.g., twice daily or once a month), what form it will be in (e.g., pills, liquid, caplets), dosage (e.g., 20, 30 or 40 mg), and what exactly the drug is designed to prevent, cure, or ameliorate.

In the typical course of business, the drug will have advanced from the "experimental" stage to the IND stage whether it is a new drug or an existing licensed drug, where some animal studies or other data exists indicating the drug's likely effect. At this point, in order to gain licensure and prove efficacy in human beings, there *must be two well-controlled human studies to prove efficacy of the drug.* This point cannot be overstated: Before a manufacturer can prove efficacy of a drug for its licensed indication, it must have two human studies. This means that no company manufacturing a drug as a pretreatment for chemical warfare can ever get beyond the Investigational stage. As two Army doctors pointed out in an article in 1992,

> For products designed to protect against chemical and biological agents, a clear demonstration of efficacy would require exposure to humans to these lethal agents. Since

> this practice would be unethical and immoral, these products never advanced beyond the investigational stage.[9]

This requirement proved to be the insuperable obstacle for any DoD contractor trying to make a vaccine as a pretreatment for biological warfare agents—because it would be unethical to test drugs on human beings as pre-treatments for chemical warfare. *However*, if there were an extant vaccine that could be used as a pretreatment for a chemical or biological agent and it was licensed for some other purpose, the DoD could use that without being subject to FDA regulation.

This brings us full circle to the question of what agency the FDA regulates.

The FDA requirements apply above all to *manufacturers*, not the end user. Thus, as an example, let us suppose that there is a drug we will call PB that is used to block a particular chemical from being produced by the brain in patients with a certain disease we will name MG. Let us suppose this has been licensed for many years and shows no side effects on these patients in the dosages they take for 35 years of licensed use. Now, let us suppose that the DoD gains knowledge about a certain nerve agent named SM that, as its mechanism of attack, causes the brain to massively produce the same chemical that our licensed drug, MG, blocks production of. The agent is usually delivered in bombs in aerosol form. The DoD could, it would appear, buy large quantities of this drug and give it to troops in order to prevent the effects of the nerve agent SM. This use of the drug is considered *off-label* and *investigational.* This is because the drug is normally used (and has been licensed) to fight a particular disease, not be a prophylaxis against a nerve agent, and so there is no licensed indication for such use and certainly no proof of efficacy. Thus, the manufacturer could certainly not advertise the product as a pretreatment for the hypothetical SM without incurring the regulatory

[9] Col. Garland E. McCarty and Lt. Col. Gregory P. Berezuk, *Military Medicine*, Vol. 157, August 1992, p. 404.

wrath of the FDA, but what about the DoD? The DoD could use the drug in such a fashion, *provided it obtained informed consent from the individuals it was giving the drug to.* While the FDA would have no way to regulate an end-user relationship normally, the FDA is responsible for monitoring IND applications and clinical trials under an IND application. If the above drug were not licensed fully and the DoD intended to use the drug and track to whom it was given, when, how many times, and record that in service members' record books, that would be research as defined under FDA, DHHS, and even the DoD's own regulations. Since research requires informed consent, such administration of the product, vaccine or drug, would have to be performed under an IND clinical protocol.

On the eve of the Gulf War, the DoD was up against the regulations requiring informed consent, with the concomitant intelligence and history showing that Saddam Hussein (a) possessed such agents and (b) had previously used chemical and, perhaps, biological weapons on minorities in his own country. The DoD therefore lobbied the FDA for a waiver from the requirements of Rule 50.23(d) of the FDA's regulations.[10] This would happen for a number of licensed, investigational, and even experimental products, with service members having no say in the matter.

[10] 21 C.F.R. 50.23(d) (1990).

CHAPTER 6

THE GULF WAR DRUGS

The current regulations do not permit a determination that obtaining informed consent is otherwise not feasible or is contrary to the best interest of the subject ...

II. DoD's Request

... FDA assistance is also needed on the issue of informed consent. Under the Federal Food, Drug, and Cosmetic Act, the general rule is that, regardless of the character of the medical evidence, any use of an IND, whether primarily for investigational purposes or primarily for treatment purposes, must be preceded by obtaining informed consent from the patient. The statute authorizes exceptions, however [...]

Our planning for Desert Shield contingencies has convinced us that another circumstance should be recognized in the FDA regulation in which it would be consistent with the statute and ethically appropriate for medical professionals to "deem it not feasible" to obtain informed consent of the patient—that circumstance being the existence of military combat exigencies, coupled with a determination that the use of the product is in the best interest of the individual [...]

> In all peacetime applications, we believe strongly in informed consent and its ethical foundations. In peacetime applications, we readily agree to tell military personnel, as provided in FDA's regulations, that research is involved, that there may be risks or discomforts, that participation is voluntary and that refusal to participate will involve no penalty.[1]

In the late 1980s, the DoD had a problem. It was anticipating the need for better means to combat chemical and biological agents and, to the point, the U.S. was way behind the Soviet Union in its chemical and biological warfare preparedness. Protective suits and gas masks are the primary means of biological and chemical defense, and different garments are worn depending on the threat level. This is referred to as Military Operational Protective Posture (MOPP) level, and in military slang, the garments are referred to as MOPP gear. Revelations circa 2000 made it clear that the protective suits and gas masks issued to troops were defective in large numbers.[2] The DoD made assertions initially that the defects were not serious and not widespread, but a subsequent inspection revealed failures of entire lots, and the DoD eventually sued the manufacturer.[3]

Besides protective suits and gas masks, the DoD's assertion was that the only way to defend against many chemical and biological agents is through the use of drugs and vaccines. Drugs are typically administered after a person has been exposed to a particular agent in order to

---

[1] Informed Consent for Human Drugs and Biologics; Determination That Informed Consent Is Not Feasible, 55 Fed. Reg. at 52814.

[2] See, e.g., http://media.defense.gov/2019/Aug/08/2002169259/-1/-1/0/CPC%20OUTREACH%209.pdf, last accessed 14 July 2020.

[3] See GAO Report 01-667, p. 8-11: "In September 1999, officials from one manufacturer pleaded guilty to selling 778,924 defective suits to the government."

counteract the agent's effects, to the extent those drugs can. Vaccines, in the case of biological agents, theoretically may provide some prospective protection if the particular vaccine produces the proper response to the agent or disease to which the soldier is exposed. The process obviously involves a lot of guesswork, from the perspective that in the first instance, we never know definitively what agent the enemy will use and, in the second instance, no one knows for certain what any individual's immune response will be to the vaccine, especially with the introduction of some weaponized disease, gas, or other agent. These uncertainties were never more apparent than in the Gulf War.

Let us return to the example of our hypothetical drug PB that combats the hypothetical illness MG.

Pyridostigmine bromide (PB) had been licensed since 1955 as a treatment for terminally ill patients with a disease called myasthenia gravis (MG), a degenerative neurological disorder. Prior to the Gulf War, after receiving an informed consent waiver from the FDA, the DoD issued troops PB in pill form as a pretreatment for a certain nerve agent, *soman* (SM in my example) that the U.S. government believed Iraq might use against U.S. troops. Eventually we learned that Iraq had no such agent, but instead had a different agent called *sarin*—yes, *that* gas. The PB that the U.S. had issued to its troops would almost certainly have *aggravated* the effects of sarin on U.S. troops, not ameliorated it, due to the underlying chemical mechanisms in the brain.[4]

Vaccines are no better because of the specificity with which the body develops an immune response. For example, there is no vaccine against the common cold because, like most viruses, it mutates constantly, thus defying the immune system's "memory," its capability to reproduce antigens to fight diseases that it already recognizes. The anthrax bacteria has dozens of strains (some have numbered it at 33) that are produced as

[4] GAO Report T-NSIAD-98-104, p. 7-8 (and footnote 19); Available at gao.gov/archive/1998/ns98104t.pdf, last accessed 14 July 2020.

a biological weapon. The current anthrax vaccine is based upon one of the weaker strains of anthrax that is passed by skin contact with a spore-laden animal pelt. This is to say nothing of genetic manipulation of strains, which would make them completely resistant to any antigen produced by the body. Thus, any vaccine, no matter which one, necessarily relies upon the hope that the agent to be used by the enemy will be the exact one for which the body has an immune response. There are additional considerations, such as the risk of adverse reactions that any vaccine or drug carries with it, which is a very real possibility when vaccinating a population the size of the entire U.S. Armed Forces—several million people.

In 1989, the Assistant Secretary of Defense Robert Barker sent a letter to Senator John Glenn in answer to questions from the Senate Governmental Affairs Committee regarding the escalation of the biowarfare threat. In the letter, Barker expressed the limitations of vaccines as a pretreatment for chemical and biological weapons. Interestingly, he specifically noted the limitation of the anthrax vaccine as a pretreatment for chemical warfare, a position evidently reversed by the DoD a short time later during its lobbying effort with the FDA.

Current vaccines, *particularly the anthrax vaccine*, do not readily lend themselves to use in mass troop immunization for a variety of reasons: the requirement in many cases for multiple immunizations to accomplish protective immunity, a higher than desirable rate of reactogenicity, and, in some cases, lack of strong enough efficacy against infection by the aerosol route of exposure."[5]

Notwithstanding all of these limitations, as the Gulf War approached, the DoD began a concerted effort to get the FDA to allow the DoD to use investigational, and even experimental, drugs either as pretreatments for chemical-biological agents or in response to such an exposure. The

[5] Letter from former Assistant Secretary of Defense Robert B. Barker to former U.S. Sen. John Glenn, chairman of the Senate Governmental Affairs Committee, 24 August 1989, transcript of Senate Hearing 101-744. The letter and quotes from Barker to Glenn are on pages 474 and 480 (emphasis added).

DoD was seeking a waiver from Rule 50.23(d)'s strict requirements of obtaining informed consent from service members prior to treating them with a number of agents. The DoD was turned down on a number of these requests because the drugs were so experimental. Then-commissioner of the FDA, David Kessler, explained before a house committee in 1996 that

> I had just become Commissioner. Desert War broke out immediately thereafter. There were INDs available for certain drugs to treat both anthrax and botulism toxin. In fact, one of them was not just—there was no interest in a manufacturer producing them but had been used for many years.
>
> The Army came and said we have soldiers going into battle. Only years later did we learn that Saddam really did have stockpiled some of these biological agents. And in the midst of that crisis, I made the decision that we needed to make sure that we knew everything possible about these drugs.
>
> In fact, one drug they wanted to use was a skin cream to prevent nerve gas. We went up to the plant and inspected the plant, and we found that before it was released it caused blisters on the arms.[6]

Even the licensed drug PB was considered investigational because the DoD was going to use a different dosage than the licensed indication and was going to use it as a pretreatment for a nerve agent, rather than as a treatment against the disease myasthenia gravis. The FDA expressed reluctance to give the DoD a complete blanket waiver from Rule 23(d)'s

[6] Testimony on 12 March 1996 before the House Committee on Appropriations' Subcommittee on Agriculture, Rural Development, Food and Drug Administration, and Related Agencies.

requirements, so a compromise was reached. A Senate Committee looking into this in 1994 summarized the events well.

> In August 1990, the DoD contacted FDA to review regulatory restrictions of DoD's plan to use pyridostigmine and botulinum toxoid for U.S. troops in the Persian Gulf. The major focus of the meeting was informed consent. The DoD sought a waiver of requirements for informed consent for the use of pyridostigmine bromide and botulinum toxoid, arguing that these investigational products had well-established uses and were safe. They also claimed that there were no reasonable alternatives. According to minutes of the meeting, "FDA expressed some concern about liability and the need to comply with the regulations," and FDA's Deputy Director for Drug Review "pointed out the need to establish an appropriate investigational framework to collect observational data and evaluate the military medical products in question."[7]

One wonders if DoD officials had the same concerns about liability and lawsuits that the FDA did. As has already been shown, the tendency of courts, including even the United States Supreme Court, to shy away from questioning military decisions because of the inherent lack of expertise of judges in matters martial was certainly known to DoD officials and lawyers. In these discussions between the FDA and the DoD, despite the fact that the FDA is the federal agency given the statutory authority to regulate drugs and biologics, the DoD insisted that it could administer the drugs if it so chose to, in complete defiance of the

---

[7] Staff Report Prepared for the Committee on Veterans' Affairs, Senate Report 103-97 (1994) (citing a Memorandum for Record, 30 August 1990, submitted by Craig R. Lehmann, Lt. Col., USAF, BSC; in Committee files).

Nuremberg Code or the Helsinki Declaration, or the regulatory authority of the FDA.

> [...] DoD informed FDA that they did not want to abide by informed consent regulations, and FDA officials pointed out that pyridostigmine and botulinum toxoid were investigational and that there are laws regulating how they can be used. DoD claimed that "under the DoD directive the Secretary of Military Departments [could] dictate the use of unapproved FDA regulated products" in the Persian Gulf, but "DoD's current position is that this not their primary choice at this time."[8]

Exactly what DoD directive Defense officials were relying upon is not clear. How that DoD directive could trump the FDA's regulatory authority over drugs and biologics is not clear, either. How an Armed Services Secretary could decide all alone that he/she would ignore 45 years of law is not only unclear, it boggles the mind. International law in the form of the Nuremberg Code and the Helsinki Declaration, and by 1990, a United States statute that made the Nuremberg Code a part of federal law, 50 U.S.C. §1520a, all said this was a human rights violation. The U.S. put people to death for violating this principle, yet here is concrete evidence—if what happened to MSgt Stanley and Nathan Schnurman was not proof enough—that the DoD felt it was free to disregard any law in pursuit of the military mission, in this case, the war with Iraq. We can leave aside the issue of whether or not the war served any useful or legitimate purpose; we should not forget, however, that there was never any Congressional declaration of war.

---

[8] Staff Report Prepared for the Committee on Veterans' Affairs, Senate Report 103-97 (1994) (citing an FDA memorandum from Richard Klein and Ann Graham to Stuart Nightingale, 7 September 1990; in Committee files).

There is a Latin maxim that *inter arma leges silentae sunt*: "Amid the clash of arms the laws are silent." This might be acceptable for a nation engaged in a civil war or threatened with invasion, and can perhaps (if one is generous) explain the actions of military governors post-Civil War or possibly the internment of Japanese during World War II. In no way, however, could the Gulf War possibly justify the DoD's defiance of plain U.S. and international law for an "optional," undeclared war halfway around the world: But there it was and is. If the DoD's actions do not speak clearly enough, a memo by Deputy Secretary of Defense John Deutch to a Senate committee after the war sums the DoD's position up succinctly: "Although pyridostigmine and botulinum toxoid were classified as investigational drugs as required by FDA regulations, they were not used for experimental purposes in [Operation Desert Storm] and the military personnel who received these products were not experimental subjects."[9] Mr. Deutch felt that "these drugs were used for *treatment purposes*, not research purposes," and additionally had been "specifically approved by the courts in litigation challenging the governments [sic] actions." The DoD's position was that because they didn't really *intend* for the use of these drugs to be research, it therefore wasn't research. Moreover, because they won in court in a suit filed by a soldier in federal district court,[10] the DoD now had "specific approval" from—of all branches—the courts! The Senate committee's comment on this letter in its report cuts to the heart of the problem with that logic: "Once again, it appears that the DoD confuses the goals of using these

---

[9] Letter from John Deutch, Deputy Secretary of Defense, to Sen. John D. Rockefeller IV, Chair, Senate Committee on Veterans' Affairs, 17 November 1994; in Committee files.

[10] The case *Doe v. Sullivan*, 756 F. Sup. 12 (D.D.C. 1991) is interesting because the judge, Stanley Harris, made it clear that he was no expert in military matters and therefore the "DoD's decision to use unapproved drugs is precisely the type of military decision that courts have repeatedly refused to second-guess." *Doe* at 13. The judge also believed that the "primary purpose of administering the drugs is military, not scientific." *Doe* at 15-16. The Nuremberg Code is not mentioned anywhere in his opinion, nor the federal statute codifying it.

medical products with the process, which was clearly considered investigational by FDA."[11]

My position is neither anti-war nor anti-national security; rather, it is pro-law and pro-ethical principles. Either the United States is a nation of laws protected by an Armed Force committed to the same, or it is not. We cannot be dedicated (selectively) to "principles"—and only when convenient. Situational ethics is an oxymoron; ethical principles are not situational. This commitment to principle is not mere naïveté, but an important aegis that serves to protect our troops, our citizens, and even our enemies. If we are not committed to these principles, particularly when they are a pain for us to follow or when we can invoke mantras like "national survival," then things like MKULTRA, the Atomic Energy tests, Nathan Schnurman's mustard gas experiences, the internment of Japanese citizens, and other more unspeakable tragedies are inflicted upon the innocent. It is too easy to dismiss these incidents as anomalous or products of their time rather than facing the legal, moral, and ethical reality that these repeated incidents are a product of a cultural mindset that values results—mission completion—over all else, including the rights of soldiers and citizens.

After some lengthy debate surrounding the issue of rule 23(d) waivers between the FDA and DoD, an agreement was finally reached on 13 December 1990, about how these products would be administered to U.S. troops. According to the minutes of that meeting, "DoD officials agreed that the botulism vaccine would be administered by trained individuals with a health care background, and that information would be provided orally 'at minimum, and in written form if feasible, to all personnel receiving the vaccine.'"[12] The essence of the agreement was that the DoD assured the FDA that although informed consent would not be sought

---

[11] Staff Report Prepared for the Committee on Veterans' Affairs, Senate Report 103-97 (1994).

[12] Id. (Draft of minutes, meeting between officials of DoD and FDA, 31 December 1990, provided by FDA to Committee; in Committee files.)

from each individual, the DoD would ensure "that at least verbal [sic] information would be provided to each person receiving the vaccine."[13]

There were some additional issues that were raised at these meetings regarding vaccines and drugs being given to pregnant women. With the introduction of women into military roles closer and closer to front-line combat has come the necessary consideration of gender differences and pregnancy among troops. The FDA's Informed Consent Waiver Review Group recommended that

> pregnant women be excluded from receiving the vaccine and that information about the vaccine be "posted at places where vaccine is administered." However, DoD argued that pregnant women would be at greater risk from exposure to botulism toxins than to the vaccine, and FDA agreed that instead of excluding pregnant women, a statement would be added to the information sheet stating that, "If you are pregnant, it is not known if this vaccine will hurt the unborn baby, however, most vaccines do not."[14]

Unfortunately, notwithstanding these assurances by the DoD, inquiries by Congress and the DoD itself after the war showed that the overwhelming majority of service members were told little or nothing about the drugs and vaccines they received.[15] As the Committee on Veterans' Affairs noted in 1994:

> DoD had promised to provide extensive information about potential risks orally and in writing. In addition to

[13] Id.

[14] Id.

[15] Staff Report Prepared for the Committee on Veterans' Affairs, Senate Report 103-97 (1994).

> being ordered to take an investigational product without informed consent, most Persian Gulf War military personnel surveyed claim they received no oral or written information about the drug or vaccine, despite the DoD promises to FDA to provide information about potential risks. These claims are supported by a survey conducted by the DoD following the Persian Gulf War.[16]

This lack of promised information was not an isolated incident where a few people were not told. The post-war surveys conducted by both Congress and the DoD showed that the medical personnel administering the shots in most cases had no idea what they were administering, what the side effects were, or any possible adverse effects.[17] Eight or nine out of every 10 service members surveyed were told nothing or that they simply *had* to take the given drug. In one DoD survey, 16 of 23 corpsmen administering the PB tablets provided no information to service members. The history of this particular "hypothetical" drug bears some close examination as its procurement and use by the DoD bears a striking resemblance to the anthrax vaccine.

A brief chemistry lesson is necessary to understand just how bad the DoD got this. Nerve agents come in two types, carbamates and organophosphates (OP). The best-known OP agents, developed by the Germans in the 1930s and 1940s and still in use today, are tabun, sarin, soman, and VX gas. These agents all operate basically the same way: The agents bind to an enzyme, acetylcholinesterase (AChE). This enzyme is responsible for "turning off" the neurotransmitter acetylcholine (ACh), which sends nerve impulses to the muscles. When these agents bind to

---

16 Id.

17 Id.

the enzyme, AChE, they prevent the enzyme from turning off the muscle impulses. If ACh continues to produce uncontrolled muscle stimulation, it results in twitching, loss of muscle coordination, weakness, and ultimately, can produce death. In graphic language, it turns a man into a twitching, frothing, writhing mass of flesh until he dies.

Pyridostigmine bromide (PB) is a drug licensed by the FDA and used to treat myasthenia gravis patients. It was first licensed in 1955.[18] Myasthenia Gravis is a degenerative neurological disease that is characterized by extreme weakness. It is caused by the production of antibodies that interfere with the uptake of the enzyme, acetylcholine (ACh) at the neuromuscular junction. Pyridostigmine is actually a nerve agent itself, but it is a carbamate. PB acts similarly to OP agents in that it inhibits production of AChE also, but it limits the production to about 40% and its effect is reversible. Thus, in high quantities, PB produces an increase in the production of AChE that overcomes the blockage of antibodies at the neuromuscular junction.

The theory behind using PB as a pretreatment for the nerve agent soman is that it would limit the level of AChE production to 40%, thus negating the (threatened) OP agents' *complete* inhibition of AChE. Further, PB is used in conjunction with two other agents found in the standard Nuclear, Biological, Chemical (NBC) treatment kits, 2-PAM-chloride and atropine. 2-PAM-chloride reverses PB's inhibition of AChE and the atropine theoretically counteracts any overstimulation due to the accumulated acetycholine (ACh) at the neuromuscular junction.

Of course, it bears repeating that PB has never, ever been tested in such a fashion. The theories on the chemistry above are just that, *theories*, based upon the current understanding of PB upon myasthenia gravis patients and the known properties of OP nerve agents. Complicating matters even more was the dosing problem: The DoD gave soldiers two 30 mg tablets to take every eight hours, likely as a concession to safety.

[18] See, e.g., 30 FR 6662, correcting scrivener's error to dosing.

The dosage for myasthenia gravis patients can reach as high as 120 mg every three hours. Thus, not only was the use of PB for a different purpose, it was used in a different dosing, both in schedule and amount, than its licensed or prescribed use, making it an *experiment* by any reasonable definition of the word.

Finally, and unfortunately, because of the intricate chemistry in our brains, it is believed that PB would actually be less effective against sarin and might make one more susceptible to its effects. At the close of the Gulf War, we would learn that Iraq stocked sarin, not soman. While the DoD denied for 6 years that there were any exposures of U.S. troops to nerve agents, it finally admitted in 1997 that some 100,000 service members may have been exposed to the nerve agent sarin when the U.S. destroyed an ammunition supply dump at Kamisiyah at the close of the war. The DoD covered this information up for years, causing some to call for the DoD to lose its authority to investigate the possible causes of Gulf War Illness.[19]

This does not end the story, though. Quite possibly more damning than any of the legal requirements is the scientific evidence of the effects of PB that the DoD had collected in its own studies before applying for the waiver of informed consent. It makes their claims of safety to the FDA ring deathly hollow.

The DoD conducted a number of different studies on pyridostigmine bromide in the late 1980s. Almost none of those studies included women, which is problematic for two reasons. First, there is some data to suggest that women have differing levels of AChE than men. Women on birth control certainly have differing levels of AChE than men, as do women in different stages of their reproductive cycles. Second, dosing is based upon weight, so there should be some consideration for the

---

[19] Waldman, Amy. "Credibility Gulf: The Military's Battle Over Whether to Protect Its Image or Protect Its Troops," *Washington Monthly*, December 1996, p. 28-29.

differing physiologies of men and women, i.e., the average man weighs significantly more than the average woman.

In these 1980s studies, the DoD had concerns about the safety of PB, so the studies screened out persons who might be hypersensitive to PB, or to bromide more generally, or people who might be taking certain medications, such as propranolol, birth control medications, or anti-malaria medications. Smokers were ruled out of certain studies and participants in some were told not to drink alcohol. People with blood pressure abnormalities, asthma, glaucoma, hyperthyroidism, GI disorders, or, probably most directly of concern, people with low serum AChE levels were kept out of some of the studies.[20]

Notwithstanding all of these concerns and safety measures taken by DoD in its own PB experiments, some test subjects still had severe reactions to PB. For example, during one study, PB was given to "a group of 28 active duty Air Force pilots. One pilot experienced respiratory arrest 91 minutes after swallowing the third in a series of three 30-mg pyridostigmine tablets. This pilot had shown no sensitivity to the test dose of pyridostigmine prior to the study."[21] In another study of 32 males, one person "lost consciousness following vision problems and headache."[22] In still other studies, "abnormal liver tests, unusual electrocardiograms, gastrointestinal disturbances, and anemia were reported."[23] Most interesting from a scientific perspective, and perhaps from an ethical perspective as well, was that some of these same studies "showed that pyridostigmine impaired performance, including tasks which require short-term memory, and prevented a number of test subjects from exercising in hot environments during the second or third

---

[20] S. Rep. No. 103-97 (1994), note 114.

[21] IND Amendment, 28 March 1988, IND 28,480.

[22] IND Annual Report, 1987-1988, IND 23,509.

[23] See Senate Report No. 103-97 (1994), notes 117, 118, 119.

day of treatment."[24] With hundreds of thousands of soldiers in the desert of Saudi Arabia, where temperatures routinely reach the hundred-degree level, the DoD had in its possession clinical data that suggested that some people were affected differently by PB under hot conditions. No one had ever considered that all of the data previously obtained from myasthenia gravis patients was in the relatively aseptic environment of a hospital. This area of scientific inquiry would produce additional troubling data after the Gulf War, which will be addressed at the end of the book.

In August 1990, as U.S. troops were preparing to go to the Gulf, the DoD's scientists requested approval for a four-man study that would "evaluate the effects of pyridostigmine on vision."[25] This study was quickly approved because of the urgency of events in Kuwait and Saudi Arabia. This study included extensive safety precautions. Each man was given a medical exam before receiving the PB. There were restrictions on the subjects—they could not have "bronchial asthma, peptic ulcer, liver, kidney, heart disease, or hypersensitivity to pyridostigmine or related drugs."[26] Volunteers were informed that possible adverse side effects included "nausea, vomiting, slow heart rate, sweating, diarrhea, abdominal cramps, increased salivation, increased bronchial secretions, and pupil constriction." The scientists also warned the subjects of other possible adverse effects, including "weakness, muscle cramps, and muscle twitches." Because of these possible side effects, "all subjects will be admitted to Lyster Army Hospital as in-patients so that they will be medically monitored during evening periods of non-testing. A drug will be available at the test site to counteract the possible adverse side

[24] Id.

[25] Abbreviated Protocol, signed by Roger W. Wiley and Darcelle Delrie, and other documents regarding "The Effects of Pyridostigmine Bromide on Vision"; attached to a cover letter from Martha H. Myers, Acting Chief, Human Use Review and Regulatory Affairs Office, Department of the Army, 15 August 1990. Documents are in Committee files.

[26] Id.

effects."[27] Finally, the Human Subjects Committee reviewing this study gave some thought to adding a clause to the consent form explaining that there was a "possibility of pyridostigmine causing death [...] after some discussion, it was decided that such a warning was unnecessary since death was unlikely."[28]

These extensive precautions were being taken at the exact same time, in August 1990, that the DoD was simultaneously urging the FDA to waive the requirements of Rule 23(d) and informed consent for the *exact same drug*—and the FDA granted the request in December 1990. This was despite the data from the previous studies and the data being collected in the August 1990 study. Months later, DoD would be giving PB to some 400,000 U.S. soldiers, including approximately 28,000 women and others who were not screened for any diseases, sensitivity to PB, or any other possible at-risk factor for PB.

Nerve agents are very similar chemically to modern pesticides, and because of this, in 1993, Dr. James Moss at the U.S. Department of Agriculture (USDA) conducted studies on cockroaches using pyridostigmine bromide in conjunction with several different pesticides. These common insect repellants such as DEET (Diethyl-meta-toluamide), a very popular repellant available in almost any Post Exchange, and permethrin, a chemical that was used to treat the uniforms of Gulf War soldiers, had increased levels of toxicity when used in conjunction with PB. DEET is more toxic by a factor of seven and permethrin twice over when used in conjunction with PB. Likewise, PB was found to be four times more toxic when used in conjunction with DEET. These studies also showed increased toxicity for other substances, such as lindane, a treatment for lice used during the Gulf.[29]

---

27 Id.

28 S. Rep. No. 103-97 (1994).

29 Id.

George Santayana once trenchantly observed that "those who cannot remember the past are condemned to repeat it." The history of pyridostigmine bromine's use during the Gulf War is instructive because of what it portends for service members in the new era of biological warfare. Will service members' bodies become the new battlefield, with each new biological threat giving rise to a new prophylactic countermeasure—a new drug, vaccine, or antibiotic? More importantly, will the safety data be timely enough to protect service members' health? As of 2003, there were an estimated 100,000 veterans of the Persian Gulf War suffering from some symptoms that defy classification, but are undeniably, objectively real, notwithstanding DoD's claims (which have gradually changed over time and investigation) that the diseases are nothing more than PTSD—post traumatic stress disorder. Studies have shown several potential causes, including the anthrax vaccine, nerve agents in the Gulf, and PB and/or its interaction with the heat and other chemicals. If the lessons of the Gulf were not learned, they might be repeated, resulting ultimately (if one chooses to be a hardline pragmatist) in cost to the taxpayers for skyrocketing veterans' disability claims.

PB's history has some important parallels to the current anthrax vaccine program and for future biological warfare programs. DoD claimed that PB was a "licensed product" by the FDA many years ago with supporting claims of long-term safety anecdotally, although there were certainly no epidemiological studies regarding its administration to healthy individuals. It was claimed that scientists had enough knowledge about how PB worked and the chemistry involving nerve agents to infer a particular result for the effectiveness of PB against a particular agent. PB's use was clearly investigational, as the DoD acknowledged by asking for Rule 23(d) waivers and by its submission of a New Drug Application and a clinical protocol for PB. Over the course of time, however, the DoD's position varied from (a) we can do this if we want to ultimately … but it is our choice to follow the procedures at this point, to (b) this was not "research" but "treatment" because of how we intended to use these things, so no informed consent was necessary, to (c) we won in court when someone tried to get an injunction, so therefore this is legal. This position changed each time Congressional inquiry yielded more and more information (to paraphrase the Nixon impeachment hearings) about "what the DoD knew and when they knew it." Leadership in Congress, frustrated by the DoD's intransigence and dissembling, swamped by calls from constituents and veterans with Gulf War Syndrome/Gulf War Illness, and bemused by investigative journalism that revealed continued DoD cover-ups, would finally decide to act in 1997.

So would the DoD.

CHAPTER 7

CONGRESS ACTS: 10 U.S.C. §1107

> More can and must be done, however, to rebuild trust, to avoid repeating past mistakes, and to prevent future health consequences similar to those experienced during and after the Gulf War. Our troops must be assured that when we send them into battle, they will be protected by the best military technology, the best leaders, and the best medicine. Protection also means proper education and training, as well as provision of critical information, including information about investigational new drugs that may be administered to our troops for their protection against chemical and biological threats.[1]

In 1997, at the end of many hearings on Gulf War Syndrome and at the close of many inquiries into the DoD's use of experimental and investigational drugs during the First Gulf War, Congress (finally) decided that enough was enough. Representative Patrick Kennedy (D-RI), introduced a bill on the floor of Congress to provide some small measure of protection for service members. In its original form, the bill imposed three requirements on the DoD: Either prior to, or within 30

[1] 143 Cong. Rec. E 637, 10 April 1997 (remarks of Representative Patrick Kennedy of Rhode Island).

days of, administering an investigational new drug, the DoD would have to inform military members that

1. The drug being administered is investigational;
2. The reasons why the drug is being administered;
3. The potential side effects of the drug, including side effects resulting from interactions of the drug with other drugs or treatments being administered to the individual.

Representative Kennedy's remarks made it clear that the bill was the direct result of inquiries into the Gulf War and what he perceived as a DoD cover-up of possible chemical exposures of U.S. troops. He noted that the trust between soldiers and the government

> … has been called into question. One need merely read newspaper articles surrounding the Persian Gulf War to see what I mean. On February 28, the *New York Times* ran an article entitled: "Pentagon Reveals It Lost Most Logs on Chemical Arms"; "Missing From Two Sites: Gulf War Veterans Now Raise Questions of Cover-Up or Criminal Incompetence."[2] Mr. Kennedy went on to cite another article that revealed that the Army had been warned by the CIA five years prior (to the article) about the possible exposure of troops to chemical agents and that the DoD had claimed that it only became aware of the exposures the prior year. Additionally, Kennedy referenced the DoD and FDA negotiations that took place prior to the Gulf War regarding a waiver of informed consent. He

[2] Id. See also nytimes.com/1997/02/28/us/pentagon-reveals-it-lost-most-logs-on-chemical-arms.html, accessed 30 April 2020.

> criticized the DoD for failing to comply with the conditions the FDA had set forth in order to grant the waiver of informed consent that the DoD legally needed and had negotiated in order to use both pyridostigmine bromide and botulinum toxoid on troops. Oddly enough, however, Kennedy then seemed to concede that the DoD could now use investigational drugs without informed consent because "[u]nfortunately, for our troops, the threat of chemical and biological weapons have become an increasing reality[.]" Mr. Kennedy seemed to believe that, at the least, "the men and women who served in the Gulf War had a right to know that the vaccines administered to them were investigational" and that "[t]he same service members had a right to know about the side effects of the investigational drugs."[34]

To his credit, however, Kennedy did introduce the bill in order "to ensure that in the future our troops are informed of investigational drugs, and to help ensure that our service members can and will trust their government."[5] The legislation received some discussion on the floors of both the Senate and the House, always with reference to the Congressional investigations surrounding Gulf War Illness and the mistakes made with pyridostigmine bromide.[6] Finally, as part of the National Defense Authorization Act for fiscal year 1998 (from October

---

[3] Id.

[4] I feel compelled to add that Representative Kennedy did swear an oath to "defend the Constitution of the United States of America against all enemies foreign and domestic" and "to bear true faith and allegiance to the same," which can only mean that either (a) Kennedy believed that it is perfectly fine for the U.S. government to experiment on its troops or (b) he doesn't know very much about the Constitution. ("Both" is also an acceptable and likely answer.)

[5] Id.

[6] See, e.g., 143 Cong. Rec. H. 9137 (23 October 1997), Section 766 of the National Defense Authorization Act for fiscal year 1998 contained this bill under the subtitle Persian Gulf Illness (Subtitle F).

1997 to October 1998), Mr. Kennedy's proposed bill became 10 U.S.C. §1107. In something that couldn't be made up, within a year of this bill being approved and becoming law, Secretary of Defense William Cohen announced that he would begin the inoculation of all U.S. military personnel with the anthrax vaccine.

As this vaccination program was kicking off, the Senate Armed Services Committee was already calling high-ranking DoD officials to explain how the program was going to work in light of the Persian Gulf experience and even the then-recent deployment of troops to Bosnia. In fact, members of the committee pointed to the Presidential Advisory Committee's review of the DoD's efforts in Bosnia and pointed out that they were deemed "an abysmal failure."[7] This committee even addressed the issue of how the DoD proposed to handle the administration of clinical protocols in accordance with FDA regulations. It is important to note that here the DoD was acknowledging that it had to comply with clinical protocol requirements of the FDA if it administered a drug in such a way as to render it an investigational new drug. An FDA official opined that "we [the FDA] believe that they [DoD officials] understand [...] [the need to comply with IND procedures]. We believe that they have the capability of complying with all of our IND rules and regulations. As to whether they will comply in the next deployment situation, obviously we can't predict that."[8]

The Acting Secretary of Defense for Health affairs, Gary Christopherson, tried to assuage the concerns of committee members by admitting that though the Bosnia experience[9] was a "situation where we believed we ought to be able to do an IND and do it well, it still did not

---

[7] U.S. Senate Committee on Veterans' Affairs Holds Hearings on the Nomination of Togo West to be Secretary of Veterans' Affairs and U.S. Biologic Vaccines for Gulf War Veterans. Statement of Senator Rockefeller. 17 March 1998.

[8] Id. Testimony of Mr. Randolph Wykoff, Associate Commissioner for Operations, Food and Drug Administration.

[9] In the Bosnia deployment, the DoD vaccinated troops against a tickborne encephalitis with an investigational drug.

come off 100 percent. It did not meet their standards. It did not meet our standards in there."[10] He went on to add that the DoD and the FDA were engaged in a "conversation" to improve their compliance with the FDA's regulations. In a bit of backpedaling, Mr. Christopherson implied that there was some kind of agreement between the FDA and DoD that there would not need to be full compliance with the requirements of the Nuremberg Code, the FDA's regulations, or the DoD's own internal regulations. He offered that "[t]he one thing that I think both FDA and we have come to somewhat—not necessarily a conclusion, but close to—is that in real combat situations it's very difficult if not impossible to do a full investigative new drug protocol." This did not seem to arouse much comment from any of the Senators, despite the clear implication that DoD was not going to comply with the requirements for informed consent for an IND procedure. One other question not raised (of course) was how combat would be defined. Even if the DoD were granted a waiver for combat exigencies, would Bosnia and other peacekeeping operations fit the justification given for the Gulf War?

At the same time that the Senate hearings were going on and the Anthrax Vaccine Immunization Program (AVIP) was going forward, the FDA was also trying to determine if the interim rule that it had published to allow DoD to use investigational drugs without informed consent should become a final rule. That rule, granting the DoD waiver, was still "on the books" as the interim rule pending finalization. The FDA was soliciting comments by 29 October 1997. This meant that (legally speaking) as late as autumn 1997, the DoD still had a waiver from the FDA's requirements of informed consent. The language of the rule was broad and did not specifically exempt just those two products, although that was the agreement reached in 1990. Now, as the DoD was preparing to use another investigational drug in Bosnia and not doing it particularly well, the FDA was asking whether or not the DoD should be allowed to

[10] Id. Testimony of Mr. Gary Christopherson.

maintain the waiver. This produced some interesting exchanges in committee hearings in Congress. In 1996, the Director of the FDA brought forward Ms. Mary Pendergast, a doctor at the FDA's Center for Biologics Evaluation and Research (CBER), to answer the question about this rule.

> **REP. NETHERCUTT:** So your conclusion five years later is that waiving the Informed Consent requirements is acceptable?
>
> **MS. PENDERGAST:** Yes, basically. It's not the preferred option, but there are some products that you cannot ethically test …
>
> **REP. NETHERCUTT:** Okay. I'm trying to get to now … as to why you feel it's acceptable to do that.
>
> **MS. PENDERGAST:** If there is another war—
>
> **REP. NETHERCUTT:** Which is prospective.
>
> **MS. PENDERGAST:** Yes. If there is another war and if there is a circumstance where the military might need to give prophylactic treatment to its troops, then we would create simply the framework that would give them the opportunity to come to the FDA to ask for permission to waive informed consent.
>
> It's not saying that we would waive it during peacetime; it's not that we would automatically waive it, rather, we would create a framework that would permit them to ask for permission.

DR. KESSLER: I think the presumption is, if it is at all possible, you get informed consent. That certainly is my personal position.[11]

In this exchange, the head of the FDA, Dr. David Kessler, asserts that informed consent would not be waived during peacetime at the same time that the FDA has on the books an interim rule that allows the DoD to waive informed consent, not just for combat, but also for the "the immediate threat of combat."[12] How *immediate* would the threat have to be and what level of combat would it have to be? One can only envision that the DoD would get to make both of these determinations; certainly the FDA is not going to question a military officer's determination that combat is imminent or immediate or of sufficient ferocity to be deemed combat.[13] Thus the rule is really no rule at all in terms of limiting the application of when the DoD can waive informed consent.

In a hearing on Bioethics in 1997, this issue came up in two ways. Dr. Arthur Caplan, a professor of bioethics at the University of Pennsylvania, offered that "the handling of the waiver with respect to the troops was unethical."[14] His opinion was that even with the waiver of prior informed consent, the DoD should have informed troops after the fact, if nothing else; that "the Defense Department—and those military agencies have not—did not do what they needed to do to, after the fact, inform people when they were exposed to innovative or experimental substances."[15]

---

[11] Testimony before the House Committee on Appropriations Subcommittee on Agriculture, Rural Development, Food and Drug Administration, and Related Agencies, 12 March 1996.

[12] 21 C.F.R. 50.23(d) (1990).

[13] This is not a game of semantics, either. Our predecessors, veterans, in Vietnam, spending time in the "Arizona Valley" near Da Nang or serving near the DMZ would hardly characterize the role of our troops in Bosnia as "combat", yet any time a bullet flies from a hostile rifle, there is the possibility for death and harm. The FDA is certainly not going to gainsay the military in such matters.

[14] House Government Reform Committee and Subcommittee on Human Resources Holds a Hearing on Biomedical Ethics, 8 May 1997.

[15] Id.

His second point of contention was that "there's still been no formulation of a policy about what we do with respect to research on our troops. We don't have it today. We didn't have it six years ago. And I find it incredible that we have not had more than an interim rule to guide us with respect to research in the military." At the time he said this, the FDA's interim waiver rule for 50.23(d) was still in effect. Another doctor looked back even further and questioned the underlying assumption of the waiver, which, unfortunately, more people have not done.

> **DR. BENJAMIN WILFOND:** I think I was not convinced this morning that they ever gave a clear reason why it was not feasible to have given—asked for consent in the first place. I mean, presumably if you ask the soldiers: You may be exposed to nerve gas. This medication may help you, but we really don't know and would like to do a project. Would you like to participate? Most of them would probably say yes.[16]

Some discussion ensued and there was the usual deference about the "quick" mustering up of forces, but Dr. Wilfond continued to question the assumption: "My point is that there's still no—it's not clear that they couldn't have done it ahead of time either."[17]

This is an important issue that seems to have been swept away amidst the rhetoric. It is a particularly pragmatic point but deserves some attention. Every member of the Armed forces has, at one time or another, stood in line awaiting some inoculation. There is absolutely no explanation why, if a member of the Armed Forces has to stand in line to get the shot, there would not be sufficient time to obtain the member's informed consent. Even if the requirement for *written* consent were

[16] Id.

[17] Id.

waived, if medical records have to be annotated anyway, how much more difficult would it be for the corpsman or medical personnel to hand a sheet out to everyone as they are standing in line? Or, how hard would it be to include a standard medical brief along with all of the other briefs that service members receive when deploying, during which the ranking surgeon explains that this is the only possible treatment for the known threat. As the two doctors pointed out in their testimony to the Congressional committee:

> **CAPLAN:** We took a lot of testimony at the Presidential Advisory Committee on this matter, and it was summed up fairly well by one of our people who came to testify to us who said, if someone is shooting very large bullets at you which may be filled with biological weapons, the likelihood of your refusing an antidote is zero.[18]

Despite these committee hearings, most of which some representative of the FDA attended and concurred in the recommendations of others, the FDA had still not issued a new rule to replace the interim waiver rule from the Gulf War in late 1998. By this time, Congress had held so many hearings on the issue of informed consent and military members that it moved from the committee level onto the floor of Congress.

Representative Christopher Shays, a vocal opponent to the waiver granted to the FDA, rose as the *speaker pro tempore* in the House on 16 June 1998. He pointed out that there had been 13 hearings in three and a half years looking into Gulf War Illness. During this time, various agencies had testified in order to "try to get a handle on the problems that our Gulf War veterans have faced when they returned home. Out of the 700,000 that have returned, almost 100,000 have had some types of physical problems to deal with and have sought to have their illnesses be

---

[18] Id.

dealt with by the Department of Veterans Affairs."[19] Mr. Shays noted that after 11 hearings, there had been a number of findings and recommendations made, among them that "the VA and the Pentagon did not properly listen to sick Gulf War veterans in terms of the possible causes of their illness[;] [that] there is no credible evidence that stress or Post Traumatic Stress Disorder caused the illnesses reported by many Gulf War veterans[; and] that Congress should enact legislation establishing the presumption that veterans were exposed to hazardous materials known to have been present in the Gulf War theater."[20] Most importantly, Congressman Shays recommended that "*the FDA should not grant a waiver of informed consent requirements allowing the Pentagon to use experimental or investigational drugs unless the President signs off and approves.*"[21] This recommendation would become the cornerstone of a new version of Representative Patrick Kennedy's first modest legislation. Interestingly, all it *really* did was seek a return to the "common rule" set forth in the DoD's own regulations, the DHHS regulations, the FDA's regulations (prior to the waiver), the Nuremberg Code, and the federal statute passed which codified the Nuremberg Code. All of these regulations and laws have *always stated* that "the informed consent of the subject is absolutely essential" and all of them stated a presumption that "informed consent is feasible except … in certain limited circumstances, usually when the subject was incompetent or incapable of giving consent or in a life-threatening situation where the subject could not consent."[22] As an example, the DoD's own regulations state, unequivocally:

> Except as provided elsewhere in this policy, no investigator may involve a human being as a subject in

---

[19] 144 Cong. Rec. H. 4616, 16 June 1998.

[20] Id. Remarks of Congressman Shays.

[21] Id., emphasis added.

[22] 32 C.F.R. 216.107, 46 C.F.R. Part 45, 21 C.F.R. 50.23(d), 50 U.S.C. 1520a and The Nuremberg Code.

> research covered by this policy unless the investigator has obtained the *legally effective informed consent of the subject* or the subject's legally authorized representative. An investigator shall seek such consent only under circumstances that provide the prospective subject or the representative sufficient opportunity to consider whether or not to participate and that minimize the possibility of coercion or undue influence. The information that is given to the subject or the representative shall be in language understandable to the subject or the representative. No informed consent, whether oral or written, may include any exculpatory language through which the subject or the representative is made to waive or appear to waive any of the subject's legal rights, or releases or appears to release the investigator, the sponsor, the institution or its agents from liability for negligence.[23]

The FDA and DHHS regulations are identical, almost word for word. Additionally, the same regulation goes on to assure the subject that the only way that informed consent could be waived is if an appropriate Institutional Review Board, composed of doctors and other experts and members of the given community, determined that

> 1. The research involves no more than minimal risk to the subjects;
> 2. The waiver or alteration will not adversely affect the rights and welfare of the subjects;
> 3. The research could not practicably be carried out without the waiver or alteration; and

[23] 32 C.F.R. 219.116 (2001). These regulations have been in place since 1991.

4. Whenever appropriate, the subjects will be provided with additional pertinent information after particip-ation.[24]

This language is hard to reconcile with the policy in the Gulf War that Mr. Shays noted that "our troops were ordered to take an experimental drug referred to as PB […] It was used […] as an experimental drug to do something it was not designed to do. *Our troops did not have the option to decide whether or not to do this. They were under order. If they did not live by their order, they would be prosecuted by the military.*"[25] Congressman Shays, looking back at that moment, probably had no idea that his words actually foreshadowed what was to come under the anthrax vaccination program that had just begun in April 1998. Notwithstanding his intent to prevent just such matters and the legislation that was to pass later that year, the courts-martial were just beginning for those who would try to exercise the very rights being re-issued to them under the new version of 10 U.S.C. §1107.

The 1998 version of 10 U.S.C. §1107 was passed as part of the National Defense Authorization Act for fiscal year 1999, in October 1998. The differences between the 1997 version and the 1998 version are startling and important to note, not only for their legal effect, but for what they reveal about the rationale for making the changes. The original (1997) 10 U.S.C. §1107 required the Secretary of Defense to provide *written* notice to service members of the use of an investigational new drug or a drug unapproved for its applied use "*unless* the Secretary of Defense determines that the use of written notice is impractical because of the number of members receiving the investigational new drug or drug unapproved for its applied use, time constraints, or similar reasons."[26] This means that the Secretary of Defense had almost unfettered

---

[24] Id.

[25] 144 Cong. Rec. H. 4616, 16 June 1998.

[26] 10 U.S.C. §1107, 1997.

discretion to determine that written notice was not feasible. The only condition or enforcement mechanism was that the Secretary was supposed to provide Congress a written explanation if written notice was not used. The 1998 version, however, in sharp contrast, would strike that language out (from "unless" to the end), thus eliminating anything *except* written notice. The new version would then add one significant paragraph (f), and change the current (f), the definitions section, to (g). The new paragraph, unchanged since 1998, reads as follows:

> (f) Limitation and Waiver.—
>
> (1) In the case of the administration of an investigational new drug or a drug unapproved for its applied use to a member of the armed forces in connection with the member's participation in a particular military operation, the requirement that the member provide prior consent to receive the drug in accordance with the prior consent requirement imposed under section 505(i)(4) of the Federal Food, Drug, and Cosmetic Act (21 U.S.C. 355(i)(4) may be waived only by the President. The President may grant such a waiver only if the President determines, in writing, that obtaining consent—
>
> (A) is not feasible;
>
> (B) is contrary to the best interests of the member; or
>
> (C) is not in the interests of national security.
>
> (2) In making a determination to waive the prior consent requirement on a ground described in subparagraph (A) or (B) of paragraph (1), the President shall apply the standards and criteria

> that are set forth in the relevant FDA regulations for a waiver of the prior consent requirement on that ground.

This portion vests the decision to use or not use investigational drugs with one person and one person alone, the President of the United States. While the President appoints a cabinet member, the Secretary of Defense, to be his representative on military affairs, this law specifically lifted the power to make these decisions out of the Secretary's hands and placed it squarely on the President.

> (3) The Secretary of Defense may request the President to waive the prior consent requirement with respect to the administration of an investigational new drug or a drug unapproved for its applied use to a member of the armed forces in connection with the member's participation in a particular military operation. With respect to any such administration—
>
> (A) the *Secretary may not delegate* to any other official the authority to request the President to waive the prior consent requirement for the DoD; and
>
> (B) if the President grants the requested waiver, the Secretary shall submit to the chairman and ranking minority member of each congressional defense committee a notification of the waiver, together with the written determination of the President under paragraph (1) and the Secretary's justification for the request or

> requirement under subsection (a) for the member to receive the drug covered by the waiver.

The crucial portion of this new law was quite simply that *only the President could waive the requirement for informed consent.* Furthermore, even if the Secretary wishes to request a waiver, he cannot delegate that request, putting him on the hook as well if something were to go wrong. The President could also only grant the waiver in writing and then the Secretary has to submit a copy of the waiver and his justification for requesting it in writing to both the House and Senate Committees involved that have cognizance over military affairs *and* appropriate the money for such operations.

This section thus vests political liability for the decision to waive informed consent with one person, the President. Second, it provides Congress with the weapon to veto the Presidential decision with its mightiest tool—control over the appropriations to conduct such an operation. While there is still an ongoing battle over the two provisions of the Constitution that vest control of the military in two different branches of government,[27] ultimately Congress could win such a battle by denying the funding for any military operation under its plenary power to appropriate money.

Perhaps the most important aspect of the statute that expresses the Congressional frustration with both the FDA and DoD and the intent to do something about it, comes from the enabling public law. The National Defense Authorization Act for FY 1999, which passed and enacted the second version of 10 U.S.C. §1107, contained two notes that would affect any existing waivers of the requirement for informed consent. The first paragraph (paragraph (2) of the 1998 act) explains that the new paragraph

[27] The Constitution, in Art. I, §2, names the President as Commander-in-Chief of the armed forces. However, Art II, sec 8, grants Congress the power to make rules for the land and naval forces, to raise armies, and the power to make all necessary rules in carrying out its duties under Art II.

(f) applies to any new operation involving service members. The second of these two clauses addressed the possible "grandfathering" of any pre-existing waivers and states that

> (3) <10 U.S.C. §1107 note> *A waiver of the requirement for prior consent* imposed under the regulations required under paragraph (4) of section 505(i) of the Federal Food, Drug, and Cosmetic Act (or *under any antecedent provision of law or regulations*) *that has been granted* under that section (or antecedent provision of law or regulations) *before the date of the enactment of this Act for the administration of a drug to a member of the Armed Forces* in connection with the member's participation in a particular military operation *may be applied in that case after that date only if*—
>
> (A) the Secretary of Defense personally determines that the waiver is justifiable on each ground on which the waiver was granted;
>
> (B) the President concurs in that determination in writing; and
>
> (C) the Secretary submits to the chairman and ranking minority member of each congressional committee referred to in section 1107(f)(4)(C) of title 10, United States Code (as added by paragraph (1)—
>
> (i) a notification of the waiver;
>
> (ii) the President's written concurrence; and

(iii) the Secretary's justification for the request or for the requirement under subsection 1107(a) of such title for the member to receive the drug covered by the waiver.

Thus, the statute not only looked forward to future operations, it also reached back and effectively wiped out the existing interim FDA rule and waiver that the FDA still had not changed. The FDA would update its regulations in May 1999, incorporating all of the requirements of 10 U.S.C. §1107, some 7 months after the passage of the act and some eight plus years after it issued an "interim" rule for Desert Storm.

CHAPTER 8
IT'S ILLEGAL!

I didn't even knock on Justin's door. I busted in like Kramer on a *Seinfeld* episode. Justin had a client sitting in front of his desk.

"Sir—" Justin began as a young lance corporal turned around to see who had just come in.

"Oh, shit. Sorry. When you're done, could you come by my office?" I asked.

"Yes, sir. We're almost done." Justin continued to call me "sir" for appearances, but we had already tried a case or two as co-counsel, he was due to pin on Captain soon, and we spent a lot of time off-duty together, playing rugby and roller hockey on the same teams, along with the fact that as a single guy there wasn't a whole lot for him to do off-base in Okinawa. My kids loved him, while he (from Virginia) and my wife (from South Boston) had an ongoing North-South argument that made the Civil War appear just that. I went back to my office to wait.

"What's goin' on?" he asked curiously when he came by a few minutes later. He could see the smile on my face.

"Dude, I got this in the mail." I held up a stack of documents, about 400 pages total, bound together.

"Is that the stuff from Bates's attorney? What was his name?" Justin asked.

"Yes, Bruce Smith and a guy named Lou Michels, who's a partner in McGuire, Battle, and Woods, by the way." McGuire, Battle, and Woods was a fairly well-known law firm outside of Washington, D.C. in Virginia, not far from where Justin went to high school. In addition to being a partner, Mr. Lou Michels was a LtCol in the Air Force Reserves.

"Well, what's in there?" he asked again.

"Listen to this carefully—there is a federal statute, ten U.S. code section one-one-zero-seven, that says the DoD cannot give a service member an investigational new drug or a drug unapproved for its applied use without the service member's informed consent."

"Okay … " Justin waited for the punch line.

"Here, my good man," I brandished a thick sheaf of papers, "I hold in my hand the investigational new drug application from the company that makes the anthrax vaccine." Justin's eyes opened wide. "And," I went on, "here is the cover page for the IND application, in which the DoD asks to join the application and even asks the FDA to hurry up and approve it so they can start testing!"

"No way. Come on."

I handed him the application, which contained the entire clinical protocol.

"And, better yet, the application specifically asks for a change to get the anthrax vaccine licensed for an aerosolized exposure." Justin looked at me quizzically. "You know how all of those radio commercials have been saying that the vaccine has been licensed for thirty years, it's been licensed against anthrax?"

"Oh, you mean the 'education program'—the DoD brainwashing campaign? Yes, I've been taking copious notes since there's only one English-speaking radio station on the island and the Armed forces owns it." Justin's voiced dripped with sarcasm. I laughed. I was sick of hearing about the mandatory anthrax education video, too.

"Well," I plowed on, "you can get anthrax three ways: You can get it through your skin, you can get it intestinally by eating some infected food, or you can inhale the spores—and that's how it would be delivered in combat, in an aerosolized form—"

"—from an artillery round," Justin jumped in.

" … or a sprayer from a crop duster, or bomb of some kind." I finished, "The company that manufactures it and the DoD specifically asked the FDA for a modification of the existing license in order to get it approved for that use."

"What does that mean, though? Was it approved or just ignored?" Justin was still suspicious.

"Neither, it was acted upon, and here's the ace in the hole, the President of the company testified before Congress like six months ago that 'we still continue to hold an IND for the anthrax vaccine.' Dude, it's an IND, hence you can't give it without informed consent, hence the program currently violates federal law. *Quod Erat Demonstrandum*, homes."

Justin looked at me. "I follow everything except the Latin."

"Oh, sorry. Q.E.D. It's what you put at the bottom of a geometry proof when you solve it. It means like 'what was to be shown, was' or something like that. You didn't have to do that in high school?"

Justin looked at me and shook his head. "Proofs, yes. Trivial Latin phrases, no. We had to learn to speak English first," he said, mocking me.

"Backwards Virginia school systems."

"Yeah, right." He sat down. "I can't believe this," he went on, thumbing through some papers. "I mean, how the hell did somebody not find this before? Don't get me wrong, Dale. I think you're a good attorney, and I know I'm great, but these aren't the first anthrax refusal cases. How come it hasn't come up before?"

I had asked myself this same question and done some research. "I think a couple of reasons. First, the law only changed in late 1998 and some of the first cases were at 29 Palms. Second, would you have ever thought to look for a federal statute regarding investigational drugs in order to show the order wasn't lawful?"

"Hmmmm. Yeah, good point. But how come no one in the SecDef's office picked up on this? He must have a host of lawyers working for him."

"Same answer, man. The anthrax program was launched in late 1997 and early 1998, but the law didn't change until late 1998. So, in the

Secretary of Defense's defense, that law wasn't out yet. However, the law actually reached back and so it doesn't grandfather anything. In other words, if the SecDef wants to give troops an IND or a drug unapproved for its applied use, then he has to get a waiver from no one less than the President himself." I sat back in my chair.

I couldn't have been prouder, although in truth I had done very little of the work. My client, Ponder, had actually hounded me to contact Mr. Bruce Smith, who had in turn put me in touch with Michels, who had sent me a pretty nice packet of information. By miraculous coincidence, Ponder was from the same part of Kentucky as Major Sonnie Bates and had followed Major Bates' case in the press pretty closely, as had his wife Jennifer. Eventually, David's wife got in touch with Major Bates' wife Roxanne, who then connected David with some information regarding the law.

"There's one other possibility," Justin murmured. I sat forward. He looked up at me. "They knew about the law and just fucking ignored it." I hadn't thought of that and refused to consider it. It sounded ominous the way he said it. He went back to reading. "This is unbelievable." He said it out loud, but he was talking to himself as he read. I was thinking the same thing.

The anthrax program, on its face, violated a federal statute.

Normally, in an orders violation case, the government enjoys a strong presumption that an order is lawful. Usually, all the government has to do is ask the judge to find as a matter of law that an order was lawful and then, once the judge rules in the government's favor, the prosecutor only has to show that the order was transmitted to the accused and the accused refused to obey it. The defense has a pretty high burden to overcome the presumption of lawfulness … but there I sat with the smoking gun.

The DoD's own signature was on an IND application to amend the existing anthrax license in order to get an indication against aerosolized anthrax, the exact use to which the government was putting the vaccine. I sat there smiling, luxuriating in the feeling. I could tell Justin was, too.

"You know what?" he began, smiling.

"What?" I was smiling back, almost laughing.

"I cannot wait to tell this to Jay tonight at the O club." I burst out laughing. Jay Town was another of our classmates from Naval Justice School. He and Justin were close friends, had attended the Basic School together, a six-month infantry school for all Marine officers, and lived near each other in the Bachelor's Officers Quarters. Unfortunately, however, depending upon one's view, Jay was assigned as the Deputy Staff Judge Advocate for 1st Marine Aircraft Wing. He was the assistant to the General's lawyer. In our parlance as defense attorneys, he was a government "hack" and we taunted him endlessly about it. With a few beers in us all, the Officer's Club on Kadena Air Force Base should supply some laughs in the coming evening.

"Do you think he'll feel obligated as a government weenie to tell someone about this?" I asked, considering whether we should share it. Our anthrax cases had nothing to do with 1st MAW, so Jay was a spectator on this case. Jay was also a good friend, but then again …

"No, he won't care." I nodded agreement. "But that won't stop me from harassing him as the government representative," Justin said, laughing.

"In short, sir, that means that if the defense can show that the anthrax vaccine is an investigational new drug, then the order violates the express terms of … 10 U.S.C. §1107. The statute creates rights, namely the right to informed consent before any servicemember accepts an investigational new drug."

27 June 2000

It was almost three months after our first session of court in April. We had a discovery hearing on 9 June that accomplished nothing, just jousting. I could probably get my hands on anything I needed. Bruce

Smith, Lou Michels, and some of their cohorts, were quick to answer any e-mail and seemed to have an incredible list of contacts. If, for example, I had a question about FDA licensing procedures, 10 minutes later an affidavit from a former high-ranking FDA official, now retired, appeared on my fax machine.

"So," I continued, "it's the defense's contention that under Supreme Court case law, under FDA regulations, and under any of the other applicable standards that have been set forth as to what is an investigational new drug, the defense will put on evidence to show that the anthrax vaccine is an investigational new drug." Okinawa in late June was tropical, so it was hot in the courtroom. I looked over to see Petty Officer Ponder with a sheen of sweat on his forehead, but it might just as well be from nerves. I could feel my white tee-shirt sticking to me under my "Charlie" (service "C") uniform. The air conditioner was on, which made a noise like a 707 engine being turned up. I had to speak loudly.

"Therefore, if it is an investigational new drug and service members are being forced to take it against their will, that violates statutory rights that have been conferred by the Executive Order and the statute, 10 U.S.C. §1107." I felt like I was starting to hit my stride. "And I would note, sir, that in the Manual for Courts-Martial … on page IV-20, at the top of the page, the first full paragraph—it says, 'Relationship to Statutory or Constitutional Rights. The order must not conflict with the statutory or Constitutional rights of the person receiving the order.'" I had set it out as clearly as I could and the judge appeared genuinely interested, or he was doing a good job of faking it.

I sat down and wrote some notes and we debated some discovery issues and eventually the government called the Group surgeon to put some evidence in the record about the threat of anthrax and the general nature of the anthrax program. During the doctor's direct testimony, I made some notes, but I couldn't have cared less about what he was going to say. While the judge was going to allow me to cross-examine the doctor, a Navy Commander, it would be for giggles mostly. He had very limited information on the program. Our case would rise and fall on 10 U.S.C. §1107, not on my cross-examination of a Navy doctor.

Back in my office, I put my air conditioner on full and tried to pull the sticky tee-shirt away from my body. Ponder and Justin were in the room. I turned to newly pinned Captain Constantine.

"Well, how did it come off? Do you think the judge got it?" I was asking for reassurance more than critique. It was lonely in defense and it wasn't often that someone came and watched a case to offer support.

"I was actually looking for pointers on how to present the arguments for Arroyo's case. I thought it went pretty well." Justin represented PFC Vitolino Arroyo, one of three Marines who had all refused the shot together. Justin and I represented LCpl Jason Stonewall together.

"Sir, I thought you did great." Ponder sounded genuinely impressed, with his southern drawl. He was as sincere a person as I had ever met. It was the first time a client had used such words; most clients I had acquitted were less effusive than David was being.

"I just hope he gets it," I mumbled to myself as much as anyone else. On some visceral level, it was crucial for me to convince the judge. I had crossed over the line at some point from mere advocacy to personal entreaty. I believed in 10 U.S.C. §1107 as fervently as my young daughters believed in Santa Claus, probably more so.

I went to the window and opened it. There was a slight breeze stirring the hot, sticky Okinawan air, a few scattered clouds in an otherwise blue sky. I heard a familiar slapping and thudding sound and looked to the right, over the trees toward Marine Corps Air Station Futenma, perhaps a mile straight line distance from where I was on Camp Foster. A Cobra helicopter was in a climbing left-hand turn, the 32-inch-thick blades beating the air as the pilot climbed to what must be the autorotation pattern altitude of 1,000 feet. Those blades were truly awesome in their power, the tips turning at just under the speed of sound, each blade weighing 385 pounds. I had once seen up close what they could do to another aircraft and the human body. In 1996, I had served on an aircraft mishap board for a mid-air collision between a Cobra and a CH-46 Sea Knight, or "Phrog", as it was affectionately known. During that board I had learned that I was selected for the Funded Law Education Program. Sifting through the wreckage, and then having to return home at the end of the day, living a block from the wife and children of one of the dead pilots, had made my decision to either accept or turn down the program a lot easier.

"Beautiful day for flyin'," I said to no one in particular.

"What's that, sir?" Ponder asked.

I turned around and brought my thoughts back to the moment. "Nothing. Hey, don't worry too much about the judge denying our discovery. We're just playing footsy at this point. I can get my hands on everything through 'alternative means', but I was hoping to have the government produce the documents to eliminate any concerns about their authenticity. Even the judge denying our expert, Doctor Nass, isn't a killer. Remember that biology professor I told you about?"

"Yes, sir. Mr. Cohen, is that his name?"

"Yeah. He said he will testify if we can't get our expert here and he may not have the specific knowledge that Dr. Nass does, but he's got a PhD in microbiology and he thinks the program is shitty. So, that gets him there in my book."

Justin laughed.

"What are our chances, sir?" Nobody laughed at Ponder's question. I had thought about this a lot. I had four acquittals; three of them came in bench trials in front of the same judge now hearing the anthrax cases. Some of the prosecutors had needled me that Judge Stone was partial to me. In reality, the cases had not only been shitty for the government, but I believed, no—*knew*—they had come out the right way.

"I don't know, BT3. I mean, there is a federal law that says pretty clearly that you can't be ordered to take the shot without your informed consent. All we have to show is that the vaccine is investigational and we've got the friggin' application. That would seem to sufficiently rebut the presumption of lawfulness, but the judge was saying some weird things in chambers in Stonewall's case. I just hope he gives us our chance to put this on in front of a jury. We sure have a lot of evidence." I nodded toward the box in the corner of my office that was filled with Government Accounting Office reports, briefs, binders, transcripts of other cases, an Inspector General's report on the contractual relationship between the DoD and the manufacturer, and a number of Congressional committee transcripts and reports. And that didn't include the stuff I had at home and on my computer, not yet printed.

"Looks like you're earnin' what I'm payin' you, sir," Ponder cracked.

I laughed. Justin moaned. He was always talking about "getting out" and finally getting paid like a "real lawyer" for the work he did.

"Hopefully you'll still be saying that if the judge loses his mind and things don't go so well."

I was only half-joking.

CHAPTER 9
HISTORY OF THE AVA

The first use of a human anthrax vaccine took place in 1954.[1] The primary purpose, like all vaccines, was to provide some prophylaxis for human beings from contracting the anthrax bacteria, which is typically found in cattle. Those most likely to come into contact with the anthrax spores were livestock handlers and people who might be handling animal hides in leatherworking factories or similar circumstances. The first comprehensive field trial of a human anthrax vaccine was conducted at goat-hair processing mills from 1955-1959 in the northeastern United States by Dr. Philip Brachman. This study has come to be known as the Brachman Study because it is, essentially, the only data available on the subject.[2] In this study, 369 workers in the mill who handled animal hides were vaccinated against the bacteria. The results, while not spectacular, certainly indicated that the vaccine was effective against catching anthrax from handling pelts and hides that had the spores: To be precise, the vaccine trial was designed to provide prophylaxis against contacting anthrax via contact with the skin. The study showed a "high confidence level of 93% effectiveness" and a low of 65%, a fairly significant spread.

The MDPH first produced the AVA under an Investigational New Drug application (DBS-IND 180) in 1966. MDPH filed a license

---

[1] Wright, GG. Et al. "Studies on Immunity in Anthrax." *The Journal of Immunology*. Vol. 73 No. 6 p. 387-391.

[2] Brachman. P.S. et al. "Field Evaluation of a Human Anthrax Vaccine." American Journal of Public Health. Vol. 52 p. 632-645.

application for the manufacture of Anthrax Protective Antigen, Aluminum Hydroxide Adsorbed in 1967. The specification for manufacture is based on U.S. Patent 3,208,909. The license application references an article published in *Applied Microbiology* that details the production process. The license to manufacture AVA, granted in 1970, has two parts. One license is for the facility, the ELA; the other is for the product itself, the Product License Application (PLA). MDPH produced AVA continuously (if in small quantities) from its first contract (PH21-68-2064) in 1968 until 1997 when MDPH split off its biologics division and privatized it into the Michigan Biologic Products Institute. It, in turn, sold the facility and its licenses to BioPort, Incorporated in 1998, a subject to which we will return in detail later.

Bacillus anthracis is a bacteria that survives in its environment by exuding enzymes that break down surrounding compounds, such as fats, proteins, and polysaccharides (complex sugar molecules). The bacteria then absorb these byproducts. In addition to secreting the enzymes, which serve a nutritional gathering function for the bacteria, anthrax also secretes two toxins, or poisons, known as lethal factor (LF) and edema factor (EF). These two toxins only work, however, when combined with a protein known as Protective Antigen (PA). A vaccine will be effective against anthrax if it confers a certain level of antibody response to the PA, thus inhibiting the expression of LF/EF. In other words, if the vaccine causes the immune system to create enough antibodies that will fight and overwhelm the Protective Antigen, it is considered effective.

The anthrax vaccine is unique among vaccines in that there is no step in the manufacturing process for purifying the active fraction of the vaccine. The vaccine is made by growing a non-virulent strain of anthrax in a culture. This culture is filtered to remove the bacteria, but the remainder, including the proteins and enzymes, is absorbed onto aluminum oxyhydroxide. The antigens that are absorbed are then centrifuged out of the solution and, without being "washed", are then resuspended into a saline solution with some preservatives. Because of the way in which the bacteria secretes enzymes and absorbs proteins, the vaccine is

> composed of an undefined crude culture of supernatant adsorbed to aluminum hydroxide. There has been no quantification of the protective antigen content of the vaccine or of any of the other constituents, so the degree of purity is unknown. Standardization is determined by an animal potency test.[3]One would think that this statement must have come from an anthrax vaccine opponent, except that it is from an article authored by Colonel (Dr.) Arthur Friedlander, U.S. Army—as of 2004, the Chief Researcher at the U.S. Army's Medical Research laboratory at Ft. Detrick, Maryland—and Dr. Philip Brachman, head of the *original study* on the previous Merck Pharmaceuticals-manufactured anthrax vaccine. As Dr. Friedlander notes, the antibody titer—the level of antibodies produced by the body in response to the vaccine, measured by a blood test—varies widely from lot to lot of the vaccine and is measured by injecting guinea pigs and measuring antibody response. This variety is due, in part, because the manufacturing process, developed in the 1960s, is antiquated by modern microbiology standards, which now controls how a vaccine is judged for licensing purposes. All of this means that even under ideal conditions, the vaccine is likely to produce significant differences in potency from batch to batch. The problem with the AVA is that it has never been manufactured under anything even approaching ideal conditions.

---

[3] Friedlander, A.M. and P.S. Brachman, *Vaccines*, ed. Plotkin and Mortimer, 1994 edition chapter 26, p. 737.

At the same time that the original Brachman study's results were being published, the development of the anthrax vaccine continued apace. Interestingly, the vaccine used in the Brachman study was originally made by Merck Pharmaceutical, but it was changed in both content and production method by a new manufacturer, the MDPH. This changed vaccine, *not* the original one used in the Brachman study, was patented by the U.S. Army in 1965.[4]

In 1967, an application was submitted to the National Institute of Health's Division of Biologics Standards to get a license for the patented vaccine. A study was conducted at a Talladega mill using the newly patented vaccine.

This study's results have never been published.

There was correspondence between the NIH and the head of the Talladega study indicating that there were problems with the methodology. Dr. Philip Coleman, the head investigator, wrote candidly to the NIH: "As to the efficacy of the vaccine, we have no real method of determining the protection afforded."[5] There were also memos exchanged regarding the scientific validity of the Talladega study. An ad hoc licensing oversight committee sent a memo to a Dr. Margaret Pittman of the Department of Health Education and Welfare (HEW), the forerunner to the DHHS, pointing out that "[t]he lack of cases of anthrax in an uncontrolled population of approximately 600 persons in the Talladega mill can hardly be accepted as scientific evidence for efficacy of the vaccine."[6] Notwithstanding these problems, Dr. Pittman recommended licensure of the vaccine on 10 February 1969, while acknowledging that "clinical data establishing efficacy of the product had not been submitted and that data

---

[4] Pubis, M. Wright, GG. Anaerobic Process for Production of a Gel-adsorbed Anthrax Immunization Antigen. United States Patent Office Record, 28 September 1965, p. 1471.

[5] Philip Coleman, Acting Chief, Investigational Vaccines Activity, letter to Division of Biologics Standards, National Institutes of Health, 25 January 1968.

[6] Ad Hoc Committee letter to Dr. Margaret Pittman, 6 February 1969.

be requested from NCDC (National Communicable Disease Center)."[7] Efficacy data was a prerequisite to licensure by the 1962 Kefauver-Harris Amendments to the Federal FDCA.[8]

On 2 November 1970, the license for the anthrax vaccine was recommended for approval by HEW without any of the required efficacy data.[9] The license was granted on 10 November 1970. In an interesting twist, the efficacy data from the earlier Brachman Study was substituted, submitted, and accepted (yet no documentation of this submission has been uncovered). The Brachman Study is actually referenced on the approved package insert, even though the vaccine used in the Brachman Study differed from the licensed vaccine in *strain, formulation, and production method.* While there are those who will argue (and DoD representatives have before Congress) that the vaccines are sufficiently similar to allow conclusions to be drawn, that is a scientific debate. As a legal matter, it holds no weight. There is absolutely no way *today*, under the existing regulatory-licensing framework, that a company could get a license for a drug from the FDA by substituting a study from some other company's drug, made by a different production method, using a different strain of bacteria. As one former FDA official who worked in the department at that time expressed, "these were the days when we were trying to help the industry."[10]

When the Department of Biologics Standards was transferred under the FDA in 1973, a review began of all previously licensed vaccines that had not been required to show the necessary efficacy data. The anthrax vaccine would not undergo the necessary review for efficacy data until 12 years later, in 1985. During this review, the FDA concluded that "safety of this product is not a major concern, especially *considering its very limited distribution* … "[11]

---

[7] Dr. Margaret Pittman, letter to Dr. Sam Gibson, 10 February 1969.

[8] See Chapter 5.

[9] HEW memorandum from Margaret Pittman to Reference No. file 67-70, 2 November 1970.

[10] Conversation with Mr. Sammie Young, former Director of Biologics Division of the FDA.

[11] 21 C.F.R. 51002, 51008.

The committee also noted that "[a]nthrax vaccine poses no serious special problems other than the fact that its efficacy against *inhalation anthrax* is not well documented."[12] Finally, the panel concluded that "there is sufficient evidence to conclude that anthrax vaccine is safe and effective under the *limited circumstances* for which this vaccine is employed."[13]

During the AVIP rollout, the DoD publicly long claimed that "the vaccine has 'an impressive safety record'" and that "it has been widely used for thirty years," but neither of those statements can be squared with the 1985 review, which resulted in a proposed rule that was never acted upon.[14] The 1985 review noted that "[i]mmunization with this vaccine is indicated *only for certain occupational groups with risk of uncontrollable or unavoidable exposure to the organism. It is recommended for individuals who come in contact with imported animal hides, furs, wool, hair (especially goat hair), bristles, and bone meal, as well as laboratory workers involved in ongoing studies on the organism.*"[15] The license was granted in 1970, but the vaccine was not widely distributed nor widely used, given the narrow slice of the population involved in animal hide handling. In fact, in November 1971, the Division of Biologics Standards of the National Institutes of Health, noting an apparent increase in reports of adverse reactions after individuals received booster shots, published guidance on the vaccine's shot regimen.

> The Division considered it advisable to reevaluate the need for annual boosters and possibly the amount of the booster dose … Although the record is unclear as to whether or not the Division requested the manufacturer

---

[12] Id.

[13] Id.

[14] DoD Press Briefing, 5 December 1997. Available at http://www.defenselink.mil/news, then follow links to 1997 archives.

[15] 21 C.F.R. 51002, 51008.

> to conduct a reevaluation, no such reevaluation has been done to date.[16]

Part of the problem may stem from the vaccine's shot regimen, which consists of the first three shots given within two weeks of each other, and then annual boosters for a total of six shots to complete the series.

The DoD's media campaign, rising to over $70 million dollars spent for a website and other educational information for the troops, includes literature that says the anthrax vaccine "has been safely and routinely administered in the United States to veterinarians, laboratory workers, and livestock handlers for more than 25 years."[17] An April 2000 Congressional House report noted, however, that "testimony at the March 24 hearing indicated between 100 and 300 civilians may receive the vaccine each year. Since approval, and prior to the AVIP, fewer than 68,000 doses had been distributed apart from stocks used in Operation Desert Storm."[18] Shortly after the vaccine was licensed, the mills began closing as the garment industry changed. The risk of exposure and infection from anthrax spores by the general public disappeared. The vaccine's use became limited to experiments on laboratory animals, the researchers conducting the experiments, and the staff at the manufacturing plant. Proof of this is that from its licensing until 1988, when the DoD sought to increase the production lines for it, only 68,000 doses of the vaccine had been produced by MDPH, and MDPH had never made a lot of more than 7,500 doses at one time. If vaccination consists of six shots plus annual boosters, the number of possible persons inoculated is so small as to not even be statistically significant for long-term safety studies. The 1985 panel

---

[16] GAO Report T-NSIAD-00-48, Testimony of Dr. Kwai-Cheung Chan, Director, Special Studies and Evaluations, National Security and International Affairs Division.

[17] 21 C.F.R. 51002, 51008.

[18] April 2000 Shays' report, citing prepared statement of Dr. Kathryn Zoon, Director, FDA Center for Biologics Evaluation and Research, NSVAIR anthrax hearing (II), p. 52-53.

noted that "[t]he vaccine manufactured by the MDPH has not been employed in a controlled field trial."[19]

Finally, there was never any effort to track long-term health effects from those who received the vaccine. There was no database maintained or other central records kept to track an individual's long-term reactions to the vaccine. The Institute of Medicine conducted a review of all available literature and concluded that "[t]here is a paucity of published peer-reviewed literature on the safety of the anthrax vaccine."[20] It also noted that "[t]here have been no studies of the anthrax vaccine in which the long-term health outcomes have been systematically evaluated with active surveillance."[21] At no time in the history of the anthrax vaccine did there exist, or has there existed, support for the DoD's claims of "an impressive safety record." In truth, the DoD's claims are particularly hollow and appear to be part of a campaign of disinformation. As a Congressional Committee noted in April 2000, "[p]reposterously low adverse report rates generated by DoD point to a program far more concerned with public relations than effective force protection or the practice of medicine."

The vaccine's licensed product insert expresses an expected systemic adverse reaction rate of 0.2%. In May 1999, the DoD reported a total of 123 Vaccine Adverse Events Report System (VAERS) filings with the FDA, but included only 65 of those in the calculation of an adverse reaction rate of 0.007% of 890,888 vaccinations given to that date. This means one of two things: either the vaccine is safer than the product label indicates by a factor of 100, or the data is being underreported. Under pressure to conduct at least *some* studies, the DoD has done so and those studies have suggested much higher adverse reaction rates than

---

[19] 21 C.F.R. 51002, 51008.

[20] "An Assessment of the Safety of the Anthrax Vaccine", A Letter Report, Committee on Health Effects Associated with Exposures During the Gulf War, Institute of Medicine, 30 March 2000.

[21] Id.

the PR claims. In a study at Tripler Army Hospital, Hawaii, the data showed that 2.2% of men missed one or more shifts of duty after the first shot, 2.0% after the second, and 0.9% after the third. For women, the numbers were higher, consistent with other studies conducted. Women in the Tripler study indicated rates of 5.5%, 5.0%, and 3.9% for the first, second, and third shots, respectively.[22] A study on soldiers in Korea on systemic reactions also revealed significantly higher adverse reaction rates. Men and women were surveyed regarding symptoms of fever, malaise, and chills. In each of these categories, the numbers reflect results that are in some cases 1,000 times higher than what DoD has testified to before Congress or stated in press releases. The Korea study's numbers for men and women after the first shot are:

Fever 0.9 % men, 2.8% women;
Malaise 6.0% men, 15.6% women;
Chills 1.5% men, 5.5% women.

Second-shot systemic reaction rates are similar or higher.[23] What is disturbing about these numbers is not the adverse report rates themselves; the most disturbing thing is that DoD had similar numbers from a survey taken of soldiers inoculated from 1977-1996 at Fort Detrick, Maryland.[24] This means that the DoD has had similar adverse reaction rates the whole time it has claimed publicly that the vaccine has

[22] GAO Report T00-48, Table 3.

[23] GAO Report T00-48, Table 2.

[24] See GAO Report T-NSIAD-99-226, 21 July 1999. Table below shows the results of Ft. Detrick study.

DOSE NUMBER	MALES (# OF DOSES)	FEMALES (# OF DOSES)
1st	3.75% (1,013)	3.86% (259)
2nd	3.06% (979)	7.29% (247)
3rd	1.71% (938)	5.06% (237)
4th and later	3.40% (5,062)	7.06% (747)

the "preposterously low" rates that they have been reporting—completely provable lies.

The problems with the anthrax vaccine are not mere quibbling, but rather raise significant questions about how this vaccine is made, its component parts, and the actual lots that are currently sitting on the shelf at the manufacturer's facility, ready to be shipped or already shipped to the DoD for use on service members.[25]

---

[25] I would remiss if I did not give credit to the research conducted by Major Russ Dingle, USAFR, whose knowledge about the anthrax vaccine manufacturing process is encyclopedic in its breadth and depth. Any errors are entirely mine.

CHAPTER 10
THE VACCINE FAILS

The manufacturing process for Anthrax Vaccine is not validated.[1]

The anthrax vaccine's manufacturer has had an interesting ownership history, beginning in 1968 as the MDPH, a public entity that manufactured the earliest vaccine through 1997, when it spun off its "biologics" division into a for-profit entity, the Michigan Biologic Products Institute (MBPI), BioPort, Inc. quickly bought MBPI in 1998. While management and ownership structure changed, one thing has remained remarkably consistent: how badly the vaccine has been manufactured from when it first began being inspected. BioPort/MBPI/MDPH has continued to violate the regulations governing the manufacture of the vaccine and CGMP for as long as it has records of inspections. The regulations regarding the manufacture of biologic products is fairly tedious, but the underlying philosophy can best be summarized by the quote above: The manufacturing process for the anthrax vaccine is not validated.

Because AVA is a biologic product designed for human consumption, it is controlled by very stringent requirements. A GAO report pointed this out and explained the necessity for it:

[1] FDA Form 483 Inspectional Observations, 4-20 February 1998.

> The inspection process for ensuring vaccine safety is more stringent and complex than for chemical drug because vaccines have three distinguishing features. First, either they have no clearly chemically defined composition, or chemical analysis is extremely difficult. Second, proper evaluation of vaccines generally requires measuring their effects in animals. Finally, quality cannot be guaranteed from final tests on random samples but only from a combination of in-process tests, end-product tests, and *strict controls of the entire manufacturing process.*[2]

Biologic products are regulated by the PHSA and the Federal FDCA; 42 U.S. Code §262 describes the regulation of biologic products according to the PHS Act. Chapter 9 of Title 21 of the U.S. Code contains the FDCA.

The FDCA provides the following definition of an adulterated drug:

> A drug shall be deemed to adulterated (a)(1) (A) if it has been prepared, packed, or held under insanitary conditions whereby it may have been contaminated with filth, or whereby it may have been rendered injurious to health; *or* (B) if it is a drug and the methods used in, or the facilities or controls for, its manufacture, processing, packing, or holding do not conform to or are not operated or administered in conformity with current good manufacturing practice to assure that such drug meets the requirements of this chapter as to safety and has the identity and strength, and meets the quality and purity

[2] GAO Report T-NSIAD-00-48, 12 October 1999.

> characteristics, which it purports or is represented to possess.[3]

Thus, in sum, a drug is adulterated if it is either (a) made under "insanitary conditions" or, (b) if the manufacturer does not comport with Current Good Manufacturing Practices (CGMPs). The Code of Federal Regulations, specifically 21 C.F.R. §600 and following, sets forth the Current Good Manufacturing Practices for Biologic products. 21 C.F.R. §601.12 reads in part:

> (a) General. As provided by this section, an applicant shall inform Food and Drug Administration (FDA) about each change in the product, production process, quality controls, equipment, facilities, responsible personnel, or labeling, established in the approved license. Before distributing a product made using a change, an applicant shall demonstrate through appropriate validation and/or other clinical and/or non-clinical laboratory studies, the lack of adverse effect of the change on the identity, strength, quality, purity, or potency of the product as they may relate to the safety or effectiveness of the product.
>
> (b) Changes requiring supplemental submission and approval *prior to distribution of the product made using the change* (major changes). (1) A supplement shall be submitted for any change in the product, production process, quality controls, equipment, facilities, or responsible personnel that has a

[3] 21 U.S.C. §351, 2000, emphasis added.

> substantial potential to have an adverse effect on the identity, strength, quality, purity, or potency of the product as they may relate to the safety and effectiveness of the product. (2) These changes include but are not limited to: (i) Changes in the qualitative or quantitative formulation or other specifications as provided in the approved application or in the regulations; (vi) Changes which may affect product sterility assurance, such as changes in product or component sterilization method(s), or an addition, deletion, or substitution of steps in an aseptic processing operation.

Until a 1988 contract with the DoD, the production of AVA was infrequent, a batch being produced every three to four years, with the largest being 7,500 doses. MDPH had one production line for AVA that they alternately used for other vaccine products. The 1988 contract with DoD called for a drastic increase in the amount of production of the anthrax vaccine: 300,000 doses over a five-year period. The only possible way to meet the requirements of the DoD contract was to increase the production facility itself. One production line would simply not meet the demands of that new contract.

The first production line, the only one licensed by the FDA, was built around a 100-liter sintered glass-lined fermenter, where the anthrax bacteria was cultured and grown. In 1990, two new stainless-steel fermenters were added to grow the bacteria. In 1991, the original licensed glass-lined fermenter was removed and two more new stainless-steel fermenters were added, bringing the number of production lines to four.

None of the new fermenters were approved by the FDA prior to being installed and beginning to produce the anthrax vaccine. This was not news to anyone; MDPH was aware of the need for prior FDA approval. Documents show that Dr. Robert Myers, the Responsible

Head of MDPH, was well-briefed in the FDA requirements for amending the ELA. Dr. Myers notified the CBER in June 1990 that BioPort would replace the approved fermenter and chill tank on or about 15 August 1990 with a new fermenter. A July 9, 1990 Conversation Record by FDA employee Rebecca Devine to Dr. Myers indicates that he was informed that this would be considered a major change and should be submitted in the form of an ELA amendment. In December 1990, an FDA official also communicated to Dr. Myers that the new equipment was considered a "major change" to the facility's ELA.[4]

MDPH applied for the necessary amendment to the ELA in December 1990 for the first two new fermenters installed in that same year.[5] This ELA amendment request indicates, however, that the renovation had already taken place. Additionally, the two production lines added in 1990 consisted of *stainless steel* fermenters, *stainless steel* chill tanks, and low-protein-binding nylon membrane filters, while the production line in the original ELA consisted of *glass-lined* fermenters, a *glass-lined* chill tank, and *sintered-glass* filters. The 1990 ELA amendment request, while indicating that stainless steel equipment was being used, failed to identify this as a change in equipment type for the additional production lines. As a result, the FDA was unaware of the substantial likelihood of the amendment request to have an adverse effect on the "identity, strength, quality, purity, or potency of the product as they may relate to the safety and effectiveness of the product." Finally, the FDA did not approve these fermenters until 1993.[6] No amendment was ever sought for the subsequent two stainless steel fermenters, nor was there ever an amendment made to the Product License Amendment for this change in how the cultured bacteria was being grown.

---

4 Conversation record memo from Rebecca Devine to Dr. Myers, 9 July 1990.

5 MDPH letter to CBER seeking to amend establishment license for new equipment, 6 December 1990.

6 CBER letter to MDPH granting approval of new equipment, 27 July 1993.

More troubling is that a July 1990 Trip Report to the Michigan facility by a member of the U.S. Army Medical Research and Development Command (USAMRD) indicates that at least one 100-liter fermenter had been added to the AVA production line and that a recently delivered 100-liter fermenter could be diverted from production of another vaccine to the AVA production line. A September 1990 Trip Report to the Michigan facility discusses the necessity and the ability to put the recently acquired additional fermenter into AVA production. Also discussed is the total number of fermenters that the facility could hold, i.e., three additional fermenters for a total of four fermenters producing AVA. This Trip Report also indicates that FDA must approve the change in fermenter types from glass-lined to stainless steel and that FDA approval would require developing the definitive data that the product from the stainless steel fermenters is the same as from the glass-lined fermenters.

It also bears noting that none of the production lines produced individual lots of the vaccine. After 1990, while the old (licensed) line was running alongside the two new stainless steel lines, each production line's output was stored as a sub-lot and then combined for shipment to form what was labeled as the "final anthrax vaccine" lot (FAV-001, FAV-002, etc.). The stainless steel sub-lots supposedly produced a more potent vaccine. As a result, MDPH delivered at least one dose of AVA to DoD that was produced after the major manufacturing change had occurred and before the ELA amendment was approved.

As if all of the above-listed unapproved changes were not enough, MDPH changed the type of filter used in the manufacturing process. This filter is the only part of the manufacturing process that purifies the vaccine. There were no amendments sought to either the ELA or the PLA. This means that all of the anthrax vaccine produced from these lines was and is, by definition, adulterated. Every dose delivered since the 1990 manufacturing change has occurred without an ELA amendment for the change in filter type. Lest this appear to be scientific or legal quibbling, when the FDA conducted inspections through 1995, this specific filter would fail inspection.

The FDA inspectors conducted numerous inspections of the anthrax production facility over some seven or eight years. During this time, the inspectors would cite repeated and serious problems with the manufacturing process. Below is a list of some of the major findings.

1988[7]

"There is no written procedure for assessing stability characteristics of final biological products."

"No direct physical accountability for packaged undated anthrax vaccine which was stored alongside of packaged and dated vaccine with the same lot number. *906 vials of unfinished vaccine were distributed freely in three cardboard boxes with unknown number of vials in each carton.* Removal of vials as needed was not indicated."

1990[8]

"Anthrax prod. fac. was observed to be in a state of general disrepair in that there was: (A) Paint peeling from the walls (B) Exposed light fixtures (C) Cracked ceiling (D) Exposed raceways (E) Dirt & filth & dust on overhead pipes (F) Cluttered work space."

"Anthrax prod. records are inconsistent in that procedures used to formulate Lot #21 are different from those used to formulate Lots #25, 26 & 27 in that media

[7] FDA Form 483 Inspectional Observations, 26-27 April 1988.

[8] MDPH letter to CBER responding to FDA inspectional observations made on 12-13 September 1990, 10 October 1990.

is autoclaved for sterilization for Lot #21 and filtered for sterilization for Lots #25, 26 & 27."

1992[9]

"Changes in the manufacturing methods for [...] were not submitted as amendments to the product license application prior to releasing the material for distribution ... "

"No SOP [standard operating procedure] exists to describe procedures for handling potentially infectious material ... "

1993[10]

"There are insufficient personnel to assure compliance with current GMP regulations, e.g., failure to report changes in manufacturing, failure to maintain calibration records adequately, failure to adequately validate equipment used in the formulation or testing of product."

1994[11]

"There are insufficient personnel to assure compliance with current GMP regulations, e.g., failure to maintain calibration records adequately, failure to maintain environmental controls adequately in that production area temperatures were above 80°F, and failure to submit changes to CBER."

---

[9] FDA Form 483 Inspectional Observations, 29-31 July 1992.

[10] FDA Form 483 Inspectional Observations, 4-7 May 1993.

[11] FDA Form 483 Inspectional Observations, 31 May-3 June 1994.

"There is no annual review of production batch records [anthrax]."

"Raw material [anthrax vaccine materials] stored in an unapproved warehouse, building [redacted] i.e., no ELA [establishment license application] supplement has been submitted for this area."

1995[12]

"the company did not inform FDA of the procedural and equipment change during the production of … "

"facilities and equipment were not adequate."

"SOPs did not exist for many procedures."

"SOPs were incomplete or incorrect."

"SOPs were not adhered to."

"Frequent contamination during vaccine manufacturing was documented but not investigated."

Finally, on 22 June 1995, the CBER Inspection Task Force recommended the issuance of a Warning Letter to MDPH. Another Warning Letter was issued to MDPH on 31 August 1995. Subsequent inspections found that the warning had no effect on the quality of the product being produced.

---

12 FDA Form 483 Inspectional Observations, 23 April-5 May 1995.vv

1996[13]

"The firm had not completed cleaning validation studies for routine cleaning procedures on multi-use equipment."

"Validation studies to demonstrate microbial retention and compatibility have not been conducted for sterilizing filters … "

"There was condensate dripping onto open [redacted] tanks … "

"There was no procedure for clean-up of live rabies virus spills … "

The anthrax production facility was not inspected because "it comes under military inspection."[14]

In 1997, after some 10 years of continuous violations of CGMPs, CBER issued a "Notice of Intent to Revoke" the license of MBPI.[15] The Army responded by sending in a team to assist the manufacturer develop a "strategic compliance plan." In January 1998, anticipating another inspection by the FDA, MBPI decided to "voluntarily" shut down its production.[16] An FDA inspection in February returned a report which concluded:

"The manufacturing process for Anthrax Vaccine is not validated."

---

[13] FDA Form 483 Inspectional Observations, 18-27 November 1996.

[14] Summary of Findings Report, 14 January 1997.

[15] CBER NOIR letter to MBPI, 11 March 1997.

[16] FDA Form 483 Inspectional Observations, 4-20 February 1998.

The report also noted that "[t]here are no written procedures, including specifications, for the examination, rejection, and disposition of Anthrax and Rabies." And, finally, what should have been reported seven years earlier: "Prior to August 1997, the [redacted] filters used for harvest of Anthrax vaccine were neither validated nor integrity tested. This filter is the only sterile filtration step in the Anthrax manufacturing process." An inspector "questioned W. White, D. Slabbekoorn, and T. Wilsey regarding the filters used prior to this validation. Each reported that the filters used prior to the introduction of the [redacted] filters had not been integrity validated nor were they routinely integrity tested." The filters were approved in August 1997; however, a February 1998 inspection revealed that the validation process used to gain the approval was not valid. Incredibly, the validation for the filters was not done using the anthrax vaccine. "Validation of microbial retention by the [redacted] filters used for harvest of Anthrax vaccine was performed only with [redacted] media, which is used in tetanus production. Studies were not performed using Anthrax product or media." This means that there had been no test done to determine if the filters would even work to filter out the targeted impurities in the anthrax vaccine, but instead had been done on the tetanus vaccine.

Another finding was that "[t]he firm does not trend multiple contaminations with microorganisms in sub-lots." As a result of this February inspection, MBPI "voluntarily" quarantined 11 lots of AVA. The failure of FDA to recall the quarantined vaccine and order it destroyed resulted in some of it being shipped to the Canadian military and being used on their service members.[17] The list of violations, unfortunately, does not end here. Another inspection took place in October 1998, finding:[18]

---

[17] Rees, Ann. "Their Dangerous Dose", *The Province* [Vancouver, Canada], 25 June 2000.

[18] FDA Form 483 Inspectional Observations, 19-23 October 1998.

> "Stability testing has not always been performed in accordance with stability protocols, for example … "
>
> "CBER has not been notified in accordance with Error and Accident reporting of the following […] On 6/30/98, the firm installed a new reaction tank mixer on Tank [redacted]. There is no data documenting that the new mixer is equivalent to the old mixer, including mixing profiles. In addition, CBER has not been notified of this change."

Yet again, in 1999, the FDA found that "[t]he manufacturing process for Anthrax Vaccine Adsorbed is not validated."[19]

Thirty observations were noted. The inspection report ends with this comment: "The observations noted in this FDA-483 are not an exhaustive listing of objectionable conditions. Under the law, your firm is responsible for conducting internal self-audits to identify and correct any and all violations of the GMP regulation." What is unique about these findings is not that they are out of the past trend-line of the manufacturer, but these were found at the new facility! The old facility had been razed in 1998 and a new one built in an extraordinary windfall from the U.S. taxpayers approved by the DoD, which will be discussed in some detail later. Despite all of this, in 2000:[20]

> "The design and construction […] do not assure sterility of products filled … "

[19] FDA Form 483 Inspectional Observations, 25-23 November 1999.

[20] FDA Form 483 Inspectional Observations, 10-26 October 2000.

> "The following product lots failed initial sterility testing for release or for stability testing [...] Investigations into these initial sterility failures are incomplete ... "
>
> "Investigations are incomplete, inaccurate, or not conducted."
>
> "There is no assurance equipment is operating as designed."

In addition to these violations in its manufacture, there were also significant problems in what happened to the vaccine after it was made. A product can be adulterated even after it is manufactured correctly (which didn't happen in this case) if it is "prepared, *packed, or held* under insanitary conditions." The regulations regarding processing also apply to packing and holding. Thus, "[t]he failure to comply with any regulation set forth in this part and in parts 211 through 226 of this chapter in the manufacture, processing, packing, or holding of a drug shall render such drug to be adulterated under section 501(a)(2)(B) of the act and such drug, as well as the person who is responsible for the failure to comply, shall be subject to regulatory action."[21]

Biologic products also have expiration dates as described in Part 600 of 21 C.F.R. Modifications to the expiration dates "shall be made only upon written approval, in the form of a supplement [amendment] of the product license, issued by the Director of the Center for Biologics Evaluation and Research." Expiration dates are also regulated under the CGMP. The reason for this is that biologic products by their very nature may break down chemically over time. In order to "assure that a drug product meets applicable standards of identity, strength, quality, and

[21] 21 C.F.R. 210(b).

purity at the time of use, it shall bear an expiration date determined by appropriate stability testing described in §211.166", which states in part:

> There shall be a written stability testing program designed to assess the stability characteristics of drug products. The results of such stability testing shall be used in determining appropriate storage conditions and expirations dates.

In 1997, MBPI relabeled 1.5 million doses of AVA. That is, MBPI took vials of AVA that were already labeled with an expiration date and soaked the labels off. They then relabeled the vials with new expiration dates. These 1.5 million doses of AVA are adulterated for that reason alone. Also, at the time of the relabeling, MBPI had no approved stability testing program, as observed in the February 1998 FDA inspection. They also had no approved procedures for removing and relabeling filled vials of vaccine. In other words, there was no certified process to guarantee that the originally labeled vials were the same ones when relabeled; that is to say, MBPI could not assure that the vials would be re-identified correctly, e.g., FAV008 or FAV009, etc. Hopefully, whoever soaked the labels off got the right number back on the right bottle.

MBPI also "re-dated" bulk vaccine that had expired without justification or approved procedures. These doses are also legally and scientifically "adulterated." Both of these practices, re-labeling and re-dating, require a supplement to the product license IAW 21 C.F.R. §610.53(d). No supplement was sought or approved at the time of these events. Current good manufacturing practice regulations require compliance with these parts of the C.F.R. Non-compliance renders the drug adulterated.

There is no other way to express the violations of FDA regulations by the manufacturer of the anthrax vaccine as anything other than laughably abhorrent. Two things make it worse: First, the FDA's failure to police a manufacturer who is wantonly violating regulations designed to protect the health of U.S. citizens, and second, the DoD's actions in light of these continued violations, of which it had full knowledge. The public actions of both of these agencies are almost too incredible to believe in light of what both knew was going on at the production facility, but they happened. Now that we've considered the manufacturer's actions, I turn first to the DoD's actions and then to the FDA's.

CHAPTER 11
UNITED STATES VERSUS STONEWALL

"Are you ready?"

Justin and I collected our paperwork. I had defended Marines and sailors facing a lot more time or charged with much more serious crimes, yet I was more nervous than I had ever been before walking into court.

"Hope so," I muttered. I did not have my usual confidence. It wasn't because I didn't believe I would give a good presentation, or that the law and facts weren't on my side—which is the norm in criminal defense. It was because I knew that it wouldn't matter. I had reached the inevitable conclusion that no matter what I did, the judge was not going to find the order to take the anthrax vaccine unlawful or, even a lower standard, allow us to overcome the government's presumption of lawfulness and get in front of a jury. It simply wasn't going to happen.

I turned to Jason Stonewall, who sat in the chair, hands folded in his lap. He had a slight, beatific smile on his face. Stonewall had four-plus years of college and was a bright young man; he also had a sterling reputation as a machine-gunner. He believed in the Marine Corps, in its officers, and in its legal system.

"Are you ready, Lance Corporal Stonewall?"

"Yes, sir!" He stood up. Whenever Stonewall spoke, he reminded me of Cuba Gooding, Jr. He looked a bit like the actor except that Stonewall was broader in the face and chest. His voice even had the same raspy quality. I once told him this and he laughed.

"Captain S," Stonewall began, "if anybody was ever ready for this argument, it's you."

I wanted to say thank you, but I just smiled in return, the pinched kind, the one I knew I used to avoid having to lie or say anything inadequate. Lance Corporal Stonewall also believed in us—in Justin and me—completely, and that was what disturbed me the most. I felt like an actor in a badly written play.

"Let's go."

We headed to the courtroom.

Once there, we took our seats, me on the inside, closest to the opposing counsel and the judge, Justin at the far end of the table, with Stonewall in between us. Just yesterday we had sat here with our expert witness, Dr. Michael Cohen, on the stand, explaining the microbiology of the anthrax vaccine in detail. While his testimony helped, it hadn't won the day, which we knew anyway. Mike Cohen wasn't an *anthrax* expert. In fact, when he first walked into my office, I pegged him as something else entirely. He had a briefcase and an inquisitive manner and he had read about my court case involving Petty Officer Ponder.

Reporter, I had thought, except something was a bit … eccentric about him. After a bit of conversation, I finally figured out he was a scientist and felt guilty. I could easily have been Mike Cohen had it not been for choices earlier in my life. I once wanted to be a research scientist and had spent the summer between my junior and senior years of high school studying astronomy at the University of Georgia under the Director of the Astronomy and Physics Department. Later, I submitted a paper based upon that research to the annual Westinghouse Science Talent Search. I was fortunate to be among the top Forty papers in the nation and invited to Washington, D.C. to compete with 39 other students for some serious scholarship money. I learned two things at that week-long competition: first, that there were some incredibly smart high school scientists out there; second, I was not cut out to be one of them.

Mike Cohen reminded me of some of those students: incredibly intelligent, knowledgeable about his chosen subject matter, but not necessarily able to communicate it outside the circle of academia to the layperson. Mike had come through when the court refused all of our experts from the states to come testify. A biology professor at the University of Maryland, he had his Ph.D. in microbiology and had offered his help in Petty Officer Ponder's case because of his belief that the anthrax vaccine was not properly made, nor safe, nor based upon scientifically valid data. He had Marines in his biology class who had adverse reactions from the vaccine and as a scientist, he had to investigate. I was grateful for his help, but he was just another actor in the U.S. military's comedy of errors.

"All rise," Captain Kolomjec intoned as the Judge came in.

After getting through the preliminaries, Judge Stone got down to business.

"Okay. Let's talk about who should begin first. It is, after all, the government's motion *in limine*, but the defense has the burden of rebutting a presumption in the government's favor. I think we could probably cut to the chase and let the defense go first, given that presumption, unless either party objects."

There were no objections. Major Stone turned to me. "Sir, you have the floor."

I stood up and moved out away from our table and out into the well, the middle of the courtroom.

"Thank you, sir. First, I would like to point out where we are and where we are going. The government has a presumption in its favor, a rebuttable presumption, which is not impossible to overcome. The defense need only put on enough evidence to overcome that presumption in order for the accused, Lance Corporal Stonewall," I turned and gestured to Stonewall, who looked studious with his glasses on, "to get his day in court."

"What's the quantum?" he asked. "I mean, clearly you can rebut, but what is the quantum of evidence required?"

Thankfully, I had looked into this. My law school civil and criminal procedure professor had prepared me well.

"Sir, the case law isn't clear that it's a preponderance, but it would certainly seem contrary to notions of fairness if it were beyond a reasonable doubt. Having analyzed this—"

"Well, is it just some evidence? A scintilla, as it were?"

"Sir, it is the defense's opinion that procedurally this is like a motion for summary judgment in the civilian legal system. The government has essentially asked you to find that there are no genuine issues of material fact with respect to the lawfulness of the order and that the accused therefore has no right to get into court at all, sir. Thus, we find ourselves procedurally, in a similar situation to a motion for summary judgment."

I waited for the judge's reaction. "In reverse, you mean." He had caught right on. That was what I liked most about Judge Eric Stone.

"Exactly, sir—in reverse. Therefore, if the accused can show there is or are genuine issues of material fact, then the case should be allowed to go forward. Support for that, sir, comes from the case of *Unger versus Ziemniak*, which we think is à propos of our current circumstances." I paused a moment to see if he was following, and as I gathered myself for the crux of this first part, Justin quietly slipped a copy of the Unger case onto the podium for me. *Thank you*, I mouthed silently, then turned to pick it up from the lectern behind me.

"In *Unger*, sir, a female Navy Lieutenant refused a mandatory urinalysis test. Appellate case law by then had made clear the validity of the order to submit to a urinalysis in the military. There was no question about the validity of that order. Such orders had already been challenged on Fourth Amendment and a number of other grounds and failed.

"Lieutenant Unger specifically challenged the validity of the provision in the military's urinalysis program—in the written order—that required direct observation of the act of urinating into the cup. She filed a motion that the order was unlawful as a matter of law. The trial judge ruled against her and she took an extraordinary writ, an appeal of the judge's decision, all the way to the Court of Appeals for the Armed Forces."

Judge Stone was leaning forward, squinting, and appeared genuinely interested … so I hoped.

"Interestingly, sir, CAAF decided against Lieutenant Unger on the lawfulness of the order. The Court said, as we would all expect, that the order was lawful. *However*, the Court did not dismiss her claim. Instead the Court found, essentially, that there still existed 'genuine issues of fact' about the circumstances under which she would be required to take the test that a jury might find violated her statutory and Constitutional rights. The Court pointed out, for example, that while direct observation might be lawful, if the direct observation were required by a male, that it might be an 'unreasonable' seizure under the Fourth Amendment. Or, if the order in question had a procedure or was being conducted such that the observer was required to watch from within 18 inches, their face, um, right there, as it were—" I held up my hands as if I were a Hollywood director framing a shot, "—then the Court noted that a factfinder might conclude that was unreasonable."

I had gotten through that entire exposition with no disagreements, no argument from the Bench, which could mean one of two things—either he agreed or he didn't care.

"This is exactly where we find ourselves today, sir. The defense has, under four prongs I will address in a moment, put forth sufficient evidence to show that there exist genuine issues of material fact about the lawfulness of the order. Like Lieutenant Unger, the process under which the shot is given could be viewed by a finder of fact as unlawful because of matters that the defense has submitted. This does not mean that we will win at trial. It might be that a jury decides, after hearing the defense evidence, that it still was lawful and therefore we lose. But for the purposes of this motion and whether you should find that as a matter of law the order was lawful, there exist genuine issues of material fact about the lawfulness. I would like to turn to those matters now."

Still no disagreement, so I plowed on.

"First of all, sir, we turn to 10 U.S.C., section 1107."

I was warmed up now and somewhere inside me, I still believed that a military judge, this military judge, might do the right thing. Justin put the statute in front of me and sat back down.

"Sir, there is no straight-faced argument that the anthrax vaccine is not an investigational new drug or a drug unapproved for its applied use. Those are the words of the statute. If it is either an IND or a drug unapproved for its applied use, then there is a real question about the lawfulness of the order to take the shot. You have, sir—the defense has given you in previous submissions—the 1996 application by the manufacturer of the drug that requests an amendment to the existing license to get an indication for aerosolized anthrax. This is presumptive—conclusive evidence, I would say—that the drug is an IND."

I paused and Justin slid the affidavit of Mr. Sammie Young onto the podium, another gift from Lou Michels and several other persons who were involved in fighting this back in the states. Sammie Young had been Deputy Director of the FDA during the time that AVA had been licensed and the procedures for licensing a vaccine had been developed. He simply couldn't believe that the FDA had given the DoD a pass on the whole issue.

"The idea being," the judge supplied, "why would the manufacturer put it in an IND status if you yourself, if the manufacturer, didn't think it was an IND?"

"Exactly, sir. Also, it's an IND because, as you can see from the affidavit of Mr. Sammie Young, former Deputy Director of the FDA, that once a company submits an IND, the drug becomes an IND thirty days after the submission when used for the purposes listed in the IND.

Thus, one of the listed reasons for the IND is an aerosolized indication. If it is being used for an aerosolized indication, it's an IND. Period."

"Okay," the judge held up his hand, "suppose I agree with you—"

"Yes, sir." Suddenly this seemed to be going too well and I was wary. I had never had a time, in any real or mock proceeding where a judge began with "suppose I agree … " or "suppose I grant your point … " that ended particularly well.

"—that it's an investigational new drug in accordance with 1107. I mean, you can put on, it appears, a lot of evidence on that and it may in fact, be the case. What I'm really interested in is why should this accused be able to, in law, use 1107 in a military court-martial?"

After that question, there was a strange moment of complete Zen-like clarity, where I saw exactly where this was all leading, but my mind simply refused to acknowledge it. I had only had two of those moments of *satori*, of seeing into the heart of things, in my life. The first was as a troubled teenager, not long after I had run away from home.

The second was the only other time in my life in which I could recall a moment, a specific, measurable instant, where my mind simply refused to accept what I could see was about to happen: That other time, I was in a helicopter hovering at 150 feet when the second engine quit. We started to lose turns on our rotor head and we were falling out of the sky.

Now, in the courtroom, I felt connected across time to those other moments, then my mind walled it off.

The judge must have caught that something was wrong. "I don't mean to cut you off, but—"

"No … No, sir."

"Your evidence in support of the argument you have just made is extensive, and it is before me to consider. And I'm telling you that I understand the logic of your argument. But I'm interested in why *this* accused should be able to raise *that* federal law in this court-martial in the absence of a direct statutory conferral of rights."

"Yes, sir, then I'm more than happy to move on to save the court's time." But that was a lie; I was not more than happy. Nothing could have been further from the truth. I knew that this case was over. I should have responded the way I immediately wanted to:

Because it's a fucking federal law, you honor. You mean we get to ignore federal law we don't like in courts-martial now? I can't point out the LAW in a military court, that's what you're saying?

I had been reading some Constitutional law and an idea I hadn't thought of before popped into my head.

"I would point out, sir, that when we're talking about substantive rights, it is the history of our country that rights are not stated in the affirmative, as in 'you have a right to X', but rather are listed as limitations upon the acts of others, particularly the government. For example, the Fourth Amendment doesn't say you have a right to privacy, but rather says that you have a right to be *free* from unreasonable searches and seizures. The Bill of Rights, sir, is almost entirely comprised of limitations on government, not as positive statements of rights." My thoughts started to coalesce. "But let's move on to the more concrete, to 1107."

"Okay." He paused and wrote something down.

"First of all, the DoD has always held the position, and still does today, that 'soldiers are citizens first and have the same Constitutional rights as other citizens—'"

"But that's a non-lawyer speaking about ethics."

"True, sir, but the rule—the law—since Nuremberg has been that informed consent is a prerequisite to experimenting on human subjects. And that was adopted into federal law, sir, at 50 U.S.C. section 1520a. It prohibits military medical experimentation."

"But it's not your position that the force protection argument by the government is somehow a cover for an experiment?"

"Sir, the motives may be well-intentioned—"

"—but you're saying it could be an experiment de facto or something?"

"No, sir, I am saying it is an experiment. By definition. When you are giving someone a vaccine and you have parts of it that are, by Dr. Cohen's testimony and the DoD's own words 'not well-defined', you don't know what's going to happen. You have a hypothesis that this should provide some protection, but you don't know that. You might have a hypothesis that it doesn't cause long-term reactions, but you don't know that because we know there have been no long-term studies. And we also know this: We know that there is a lot of research out there in the peer-reviewed literature that suggests a connection to Gulf War Illness, that the vaccine causes bad things to happen to the human body, like the reaction to the amount of aluminum in the vaccine that Dr. Cohen talked about, or the high antigen load that he discussed and its possible adverse effect on the immune system.

"So, it is an experiment, sir, and unfortunately, the results aren't in yet. And two-point-four million service members are going to be the guinea pigs."

I should have left the point there, but I couldn't.

"We tend, sir, to put ourselves above this—we say Nuremberg was passed because of the Nazis, and we tend to forget that many of their experiments were non-lethal and some of them produced important knowledge for medicine today. But the harm is not just what was done, not just the experiment, it was that informed consent was not obtained. That itself is the harm."

The judge's face told me all I needed to know. He thought I was loony. We had had this same argument in Ponder's case since he was the same judge for all three anthrax refusal cases. His view was that the Nuremberg Code applied to Nazis, not "good guys" in the U.S. military. I decided to move on.

"Now, sir, why does 1107 apply?"

"Well, not necessarily why." he answered. "Let's assume that Congress wanted consent to be derived in this class of drugs."

"Yes, sir."

"And that does seem reasonable. I'm with you that Congress wanted to have an informed consent procedure in place."

"It's an individual right, sir. It doesn't belong to the Secretary of Defense."

He held up his hand. "Why should this court not assume that they were putting constraints on the Secretary of Defense? Why should I assume that they weren't—I mean, what is the intended mechanism of enforcement? It's silent on it. You're asking this court to believe—or to infer—that the mechanism to enforce or uphold this right—is to judicially confer rights upon the accused. That is, recognizing the matter on paper and allowing a defendant to use this law to defend himself against such an inoculation."

I was confused. To this day I still am.

"To read it otherwise, sir," I answered, "is to put a strained interpretation on it. Because what else can be done? What else can this person do when they are told to take a drug that is clearly investigational or experimental? If it is interpreted to mean that it confers nothing to service members, the SecDef could order them injected with anything—arsenic—as long as he thinks it's a good force protection measure. What do they do in the meantime? Go to jail while they wait for Congress to hold the SecDef in contempt of Congress?"

There were a lot better, more eloquent arguments. As I sit here today, I can think of several. But I was spent. I could hear my own incredulity. I could not believe that the judge was saying that if a military order that violates a federal law, even if you can *prove* it violates federal law, unless that law says specifically that the law is meant or allowed to be used in courts-martial, he simply wouldn't look at it.

I felt like a drowning man who knows he is too far from shore to make it, but swims on anyway because of the organism's instinct for survival. I argued on, but it was fruitless. We took a recess. Back in my office, I fell into my chair.

"Dale, I think that was one of the best arguments I've seen."

Justin patted me on the back. I appreciated the compliments, but I had a feeling he was trying to prop me up.

"Thanks, man." Lance Corporal Stonewall sat watching me. I couldn't look him in the eyes.

"Lance Corporal Stonewall, can you give us a minute? I want to discuss some other stuff with Captain Constantine." Stonewall replied yes, stood up, came to attention, and then stepped out. When he was gone, I swore.

"I just couldn't sit here with him looking at me, knowing that we're going in the tank."

Justin didn't say anything for a minute. "Think he's going to rule against us?"

"It's a bet. I had a talk with him and Kolomjec in his office, might have been regarding Ponder's case, but I kept arguing with him about this conferral of rights crap that he says you need. I threw out the hypothetical in our brief, that what if a Lance Corporal is a driver and the General orders him to speed, to do fifty-five in a school zone and the driver refuses and then he's later court-martialed. Under Stone's theory, the Lance Coolie can't plead the speed limit as a defense to the lawfulness of the order; it doesn't confer any rights! The state legislature never intended it to be used as a defense in a court-martial! Fuck.

"Then he started lecturing me about *paradigms* and how the military is different than the civilian world. 'It's a different *paradigm*, he said.' Fuck! Fuck."

I was rambling and Justin knew me well enough to let me blow off some steam. "Well, what do we do now?" he asked. A pragmatic question.

"Let me think." I rubbed my forehead. "Well, he'll announce his findings and then we'll probably take pleas. Then, maybe, we'll set a date for the court next week or something. Once he rules, I don't think he's going to give us a lot of time before the court. What's today, the twenty-fifth?"

I no longer could keep track of days. I wasn't sleeping much at all, and when I did sleep it was usually because I had dozed off at the desk in my base housing quarters, with my office in a section of the living room where my wife would find me in front of the computer if she happened to get up in the middle of the night.

Justin looked at his watch. "Twenty-six July."

"Okay. Well, let's get back into court." I stood up.

"Dale?" I looked back at Justin and raised my eyebrows. "We gave it our best shot, man. You … we couldn't have done any more than we did."

I nodded my head, but it didn't make me feel any better. I walked out the door feeling like a man on his way to his execution.

"The defense contends that the order to submit to anthrax vaccination violates a Presidential Executive Order and Federal and International Laws and is therefore an illegal order, so the accused could lawfully refuse to obey. As the court sees it, there are four issues presented. We'll discuss them in order."

I sat watching as Major Stone read from a sheet he had prepared. He hadn't written it in the recess since our last session, so I knew that he had been drafting it before I had finished my argument. He'd already decided before oral argument and I'd done nothing to change his mind. I already knew the outcome.

"The first one: Does Executive Order 13139 confer legal rights upon the accused enforceable at courts-martial?" Just the way he framed the question bothered me. The question wasn't who got what conferred, it was whether the order was lawful or not. That question had been lost a long time ago and it wasn't going to get answered in this courtroom.

"Answer: No. The Executive Order in question is a policy decision of the President taken in his capacity as Commander-in-Chief of the Armed Forces. Also, violations of an Executive Order are not judicially enforceable unless the Constitution or Federal Law otherwise requires enforcement.

"Two: Does 10 U.S.C. 1107 confer legal rights upon the accused enforceable at courts-martial? No. 10 U.S.C. 1107 imposes obligations on the Secretary of Defense to obtain the informed consent of service members in the event that the Secretary desires to employ an investigational new drug or to use a drug in a manner inconsistent with its FDA-approved usage. The text of the law does not directly state that the Secretary's obligations are also legal rights of service members enforceable at courts-martial, nor does the statute provide a fair basis for conferral of rights by implication because the statute does not employ wording typically associated with such a legislative conferral of rights. Other federal statutes, in particular criminal statutes, expressly provide for the conferral of rights upon service members. Given that Congress has in the past specifically provided for the rights of service members in other statutes and could have done so in 10 U.S.C. 1107, it would be judicial speculation to presume that Congress would desire to do so in this case. In fact, it may well be that Congress does not desire to grant individual rights to two million or so service members, but rather chose to make one officer, the Secretary of Defense, accountable for obtaining the informed consent of service members."

I looked down and noticed I was scribbling notes. Habit. None of it made any sense.

"Finally, along the same lines, any inquiry as to whether or not the Secretary of Defense, a civilian political appointee, has complied with 10 U.S.C. 1107 is a non-justiciable political issue between Congress and the Secretary; that is, it is beyond the reach of decision by military courts-martial."

There it was. I had known that was coming. There was no way he was going to rule that the Secretary of Defense had violated the law, no matter how clear it was.

"Issue three: Does the Nuremberg Code as codified at 50 U.S.C. 1520(a) confer rights on the accused enforceable at courts-martial?" Now this was the real coup. The Nuremberg Code, despite its clear language, did not apply to one class of persons: second-class citizens, known as U.S. service members.

"Answer of this court: No. 50 U.S.C. 1520(a) prevents experimentation on service members without their informed consent. The defense claims that the anthrax vaccination program is essentially a large-scale medical experiment and, therefore, 50 U.S.C. 1520(a) applies. More specifically, the defense argues that because there have been no long-term studies of the effects of the anthrax vaccination, the DoD inoculation program is a de facto medical experiment. This court declines to adopt that view.

"The DoD vaccination program on its face appears to be a reasonable and time-tested force protection measure. That is, inoculation against disease designed to counter a real-world threat of biological attack." I looked over at Lance Corporal Stonewall. He looked back at me and gently put his hand on my arm, grimacing a little, but other than that, no reaction. It was all I could do not to cry. Some lawyers would say that I had become too personally involved in my case, something I had thought about a lot in my brief time as a defense attorney. My reply would be "So what?"

"Four: Is an order for a servicemember to submit to the anthrax vaccination so inherently unsafe and dangerous in light of its proper justification as to make it arbitrary or capricious and, therefore, illegal? Answer: No. The defense has provided no evidence of any death or serious bodily injury that has resulted from administration of the anthrax vaccine to over one-point-seven million service members. The government, on the other hand, has presented evidence that anthrax is one-hundred-percent fatal if inhaled, that several actual military adversaries presently have the capability to attack U.S. Armed Forces with aerosolized anthrax, and that animal modeling studies suggest that inoculation may provide a significant measure of protection against aerosolized anthrax attack."

I had heard a Navy doctor explain that he read the DoD website, but we hadn't been allowed to bring in an expert to show the falsity of those statements and conclusions.

"In sum, then, I find the order to submit to the anthrax inoculation was a legal order as a matter of law and will so instruct the members if that is the forum selected in this case. Accordingly then, based on the reasoning above, as for the two defense requests for experts in this case, those requests are denied."

The cart had come before the horse. We were denied experts to rebut the government's doctor and that had led to a ruling that our requests were denied. The ol' *Catch-22*.

"Does the defense have any other motions to present?"

I stood up slowly. "No, sir."

At that point, I finally believed what Lou Michels, our helpful Reserve Air Force attorney and partner in a big-time law firm, had said to me on the phone one day: No military judge was going to find the order to take the anthrax vaccine illegal. It wouldn't matter how twisted the reasoning it took to get there.

"Then this court is in recess."

CHAPTER 12
THE DOD "EVOLVES" ON THE AVA

MARY PENDERGAST (FDA): As I indicated to you, it was not the type or quantity of information we would have hoped for.

SHAYS (R-CT): That's an understatement.

PENDERGAST: It—it was. We don't disagree with you. This was war. This was the first time, and it didn't work particularly well. We are in full agreement with you on that.

SHAYS: This isn't the first time the military has conducted themselves this way. And as long as they know the FDA's going to be a paper tiger with the military, they will continue to do this. They will continue to basically say, bug off. And [...] as far as I'm concerned, that's what they've said, and that's what you've accepted [...]

... And so we're going to pursue this with the FDA, because in my judgment, the FDA allowed the military to do what they have to do in time of war, to have gotten a waiver from informed consent. They should have required that the troops technically, not just in spirit, be

> notified. And they should have made sure that it was being enforced [...] and [it's] an outrage that it was not kept and data was not kept.
>
> And the FDA has not, in fact, really overseen this ... And frankly, if you had said to me, we really blew it, just like the military, I could accept it. But you're defending it, so now we're going to pursue it.

In hearings on the Nixon impeachment, Senator Howard Baker (R-TN) asked the now famous question: "What did the President know and when did he know it?"[1] This same question is equally applicable to both FDA and DoD officials regarding the anthrax vaccine program. There has been a startling lack of candor and double-speak from both of these government agencies. While some of this could be attributed to normal bureaucrat-ese inside the Beltway, the level to which it has risen with this particular program goes so far beyond the "norm" as to be risible—and impute far darker motives to those involved.

In 1985 (ironically), at the same time that the FDA's panel was preparing its review on the anthrax vaccine, the Army had conducted its own review and sent out a Request for Proposals (RFP) for a contract to develop a new anthrax vaccine. The purpose of the RFP was to solicit manufacturers for their willingness to enter into a contract to create a new anthrax vaccine and the stated justification for fielding such a vaccine was that "[t]here is an operational requirement to develop a safe and effective product which will protect U.S. troops against exposure from virulent strains of Bacillus anthracis." This would seem to be a fairly straightforward proposition, but it immediately raises the question: Why would the Army need a new vaccine, in light of the existing AVA? The Army RFP explains it quite simply:

---

[1] Congressional Impeachment hearings on Pres. Richard Nixon.

> *There is no vaccine in current use which will safely and effectively protect military personnel against exposure to this hazardous bacterial agent.*[2]

In light of later DoD statements already examined and the ongoing program, it seems rather incredible that the Army announced in 1985, when there was only one existing license for anthrax vaccine (as there has been since AVA was developed), that *no vaccine in current use was* ***safe*** *or was* ***effective***—the two fundamental legal requirements for licensure by the FDA—safety and efficacy.

The RFP goes on to point out the AVA specifically, noting that there is "a licensed vaccine against anthrax, which appears to afford some protection from the disease [...] [but] [t]he vaccine is [...] highly reactogenic, requires multiple boosters to maintain immunity, and may not be protective against all strains of the anthrax bacillus."[3] Contrast this with statements by Dr. Kathryn Zoon of the CBER, who claimed in Congressional testimony that "to our knowledge [...] the vaccine that we are using protects against all known natural strains of anthrax."[4] What is absolutely revealing about this statement is that Dr. Zoon, a member of the FDA, the agency that is supposed to regulate biologics, refers to the vaccine that "*we* are using" Dr. Zoon is a senior government official in the division that is supposed to regulate the safety of vaccines and monitor compliance with Current Good Manufacturing Practices. In this same hearing, Dr. Zoon dismissed the Notice of Intent to Revoke (NOIR) letter given to MBPI as if it were a minor matter. When asked directly "what the most serious problems are with the manufacturing of the vaccine and whether the manufacturer is taking steps to remedy those

---

[2] Request for Proposals (RFP) No. DAMD 17-85-R-0078, US Army Medical Research Acquisition Activity, Fort Detrick, Frederick, MD, 16 May 1985.

[3] Id.

[4] Congressional Hearings on the Anthrax Vaccination Program, 12 October 1999, NSVAIR (II), testimony of Dr. Kathryn Zoon, cited in H. Rep. 106-556, footnote 22, "DoD AVIP: Unproven Force Protection."

problems", Dr. Zoon replies that " … the manufacturer has had a notice of an intent to revoke. There were GMP deficiencies, and the manufacturer is currently engaged in remedying those deficiencies."[5] This is from a person whose agency found continuous and repeated CGMP violations such that the process by which the vaccine is made "is not validated", had issued a NOIR letter that led to a "voluntary" shutdown of the entire facility just 20 months prior, had found that they were not notified that "[o]n 6/30/98, the firm installed a new reaction tank mixer on Tank [redacted]", and finally, who, one month later in November 1999, would find again that "[t]he manufacturing process for Anthrax Vaccine Adsorbed is not validated."[6] And yet, in 1985, well before Dr. Zoon's appearance, the DoD was openly on a path to find a new anthrax vaccine. It makes her comment with "we" in it seem rather Freudian.

In 1989, the DoD actually defended the position that the (then) current vaccines were not good enough for mass troop inoculation. A DoD letter to Senator John Glenn of the Senate Committee on Government Affairs from Assistant Secretary of Defense Robert Barker proffered that "[c]urrent vaccines, *particularly the anthrax vaccine*, do not readily lend themselves to use in mass troop immunization for a variety of reasons: the requirement in many cases for multiple immunizations to accomplish protective immunity, a higher than desirable rate of reactogenicity, and, in some cases, lack of strong enough efficacy against infection by the aerosol route of exposure."[7] This can be contrasted with Dr. Sue Bailey's claims in 1999 that "[t]he vaccine […] is effective and has an incredibly safe record. The evidence of vaccine effectiveness

---

[5] Id.

[6] FDA Form 483 Inspectional Observations, 25-23 November 1999.

[7] Letter from former Assistant Secretary of Defense Robert B. Barker to former U.S. Sen. John Glenn, chairman of the Senate Governmental Affairs Committee, 24 Aug 1989, transcript of Senate Hearing 101-744. The letter and quotes from Barker to Glenn are on page 474 and 480.

against aerosol exposure to anthrax is very persuasive."[8] Dr. Bailey was the Assistant Secretary of Defense for Health Affairs. She also offered that "[w]e have a vaccine that can protect our troops from this deadly weapon. It would be irresponsible for us to deploy our servicemen and women without using this *safe and efficacious vaccine*."[9] Evidently, the same vaccine, which in the intervening 10 years had failed almost every conceivable FDA inspection for sterility and purity and potency and quality, had managed to transform itself in the eyes of the DoD from being "highly reactogenic" in 1985 and again in 1989 and lacking in "effectiveness against aerosol exposure" to being an essential force protection measure against anthrax. The only comparable reports of such a remarkable transformation to liquid involves water, wine, and a Jewish carpenter.

In March 1990, two Army doctors, Col. Takafuji of the Army Surgeon General office and Col. Philip K. Russell of Fort Detrick, Maryland, describe the anthrax vaccine as a "limited use vaccine [...] *unlicensed experimental vaccine*."[10] This is interesting because in the same year that two prominent Army doctors were calling the anthrax vaccine "unlicensed" and "experimental", the DoD was arguing to the FDA that it didn't need a Rule 50.23(d) waiver for anthrax—or any other drugs, actually, regardless of their status. This medical admission, however, appears to have been an aberration in the DoD's medical community, or at least in its messaging. The more consistent opinion, from senior Army physicians was actually that the vaccine was *unlicensed* and *potentially hazardous*. In 1994, Major General Ronal Blanck, later the Army's Surgeon General, testified before the Senate Armed Services Committee about the anthrax vaccine as a possible cause of Gulf War Illness.

---

[8] Congressional Hearings on the Anthrax Vaccination Program, 12 October 1999, NSVAIR (II), testimony of Dr. Sue Bailey, cited in H. Rep. 106-556, footnote 22, "DoD AVIP: Unproven Force Protection."

[9] Id.

[10] Infectious Disease Clinics of North America, 3/90, p. 156.

> Although anthrax vaccine had been considered approved prior to the Persian Gulf War, it was rarely used. Therefore, its safety, particularly when given to thousands of soldiers in conjunction with other vaccines, is not well established. Anthrax vaccine should continue to be considered as a potential cause for undiagnosed illnesses in Persian Gulf military personnel because many of the support troops received anthrax vaccine, and because the DoD believes that the incidence of undiagnosed illnesses in support troops may be higher than that in combat troops.[11]

This position was reiterated by Colonel Arthur Friedlander, the Army's Chief anthrax vaccine researcher, in a chapter in a medical textbook, *Vaccines*, stating that the anthrax vaccine was "unsatisfactory for several reasons."[12] Among these reasons were the high adverse reactions and the unknown "degree of purity" of the vaccine. The Senate Committee on Veterans' Affairs, after hearing Major General Blanck's testimony and many others, found in its 1994 report that "the vaccine's effectiveness against inhaled anthrax is unknown. Unfortunately, when anthrax is used as a biological weapon, it is likely to be aerosolized and thus inhaled. Therefore, the efficacy of the vaccine against biological warfare is unknown [...]. *The vaccine should therefore be considered investigational when used as a protection against biological warfare.*"[13]

By 1995, the DoD had, it appears, two plans in place to gain licensure for the anthrax vaccine as a pretreatment for a biological warfare attack.

---

[11] MajGen Ronald Blanck, Commanding General, Walter Reed Army Hospital, to Committee staff, 414 Russell Senate Office Bldg., Washington, D.C., 4 February 1994, from Senate Report 103-97, 8 December 1994, page 35.

[12] *Plotkin's Vaccines*, ed. Stanley A. Plotkin, Walter A. Orenstein, Kathryn M. Edwards. See chapter by Dr. Arthur Friedlander on anthrax.

[13] Senate Veterans Affairs Committee staff report 103-97, 414 Russell Senate Office Bldg., Washington, D.C., 4 February 1994, from Senate Report 103-97, 8 December 1994, Note 61-63.

The U.S. Army Medical Research Institute of Infectious Diseases (USAMRIID) had "developed a new recombinant protective antigen vaccine against anthrax. This vaccine was successfully tested in experiments using animals but has not been tested on humans."[14] USAMRIID officials stated that the testing on this new vaccine "would take about three years, and FDA approval of the manufacturing of the vaccine could take years longer."[15] Either this dissuaded the DoD from pursuing this approach or the DoD had a concurrent plan to approach MDPH to see what kind of arrangement could be made with respect to the existing vaccine. In light of the previous DoD articles, responses, letters and statements, it appears that the length of time to bring an updated, recombinant vaccine through the FDA approval process was unacceptable and the project was abandoned.[16] A House Committee attributed the DoD's abandonment of the new generation vaccine to the time it would take to complete FDA approval, perhaps 6 to 8 years.[17] In 1999, the "DoD consider[ed] further development of this [new] vaccine candidate an unfunded requirement."[18] One has to wonder if this new vaccine's status had anything to do with fear of undermining the new anthrax program that was announced in 1997. The GAO and Congress both criticized the DoD for focusing "almost exclusively on the older, FDA-approved vaccine, to the exclusion of development work on newer, recombinant vaccine formulations."[19] Whatever the reasons,[20] in 1995,

---

[14] GAO T-NSIAD-99-226, 21 July 1999, p. 10.

[15] Id.

[16] Ironically, had this approach been taken, by 2002 we would have had a new-generation anthrax vaccine, presumably more effective and less reactogenic than the current vaccine, but more importantly, one actually licensed for its intended use. The quick fix did not turn out that way. A Congressional committee reached the same conclusion in 2000. See House Committee on Government Reform, 106 H. Rpt. 556.v

[17] H. Rep. 106-556, p. 32.

[18] GAO report 99-226 p. 10

[19] H. Rep. 106-556.

[20] I do offer some hypotheses and supporting evidence for them as to why the DoD changed courses in later chapters. It is for the reader to decide if that evidence is compelling enough to support those assertions.

the DoD shifted its focus from developing a newer, better vaccine to amending the license for the existing vaccine.

In September 1995, the DoD contracted with Science Applications International Corporation (SAIC) to develop a plan to obtain FDA approval for use of the existing anthrax vaccine as a pretreatment for aerosol exposure to anthrax in a biological warfare environment. SAIC conducted an analysis and presented a plan to the Army that explained that there would be a significant informed consent obstacle to implementing this change in order to meet the regulatory requirements of the FDA and CBER. Dr. Anna Johnson-Winegar (U.S. Army) explained the legal status of the vaccine to Dr. Robert Myers (MDPH) in quite simple terms:

"This vaccine is not licensed for aerosol exposure expected in a biological warfare environment."[21]

Here is incontrovertible evidence that the DoD was intimately aware of the legal status of the anthrax vaccine at least two years before the anthrax program was commenced. While this is damning, it is only so because of the subsequent DoD actions. At the time, however, it appeared that DoD was preparing to comply with the regulatory requirements for obtaining a change to the existing license in order to get an indication for use against inhalational (aerosol) anthrax exposure expected in the BW environment.

In October 1995, the Joint Program Office for Biological Defense (JPOBD) held a meeting to develop a plan for obtaining the necessary FDA approval for amending the existing AVA license. The minutes from that meeting indicate that the Army knew it had two big problems in obtaining FDA approval of a new licensed indication for inhalation anthrax. First, the efficacy tests used to license the vaccine were for a different vaccine, the Merck vaccine used by the Brachman study rather

---

[21] SAIC Corporation plan, 29 September 1995, enclosure to memorandum from Dr. Anna Johnson-Winegar (US Army) to Dr. Robert Myers (MDPH), US Army Medical Research and Material Command, Fort Detrick, Frederick, MD, 5 October 1995.

than the MDPH vaccine. Second, there was no scientific data (the necessary two "well-controlled human studies") to support this change by FDA.[22] A meeting was held on 20 October 1995, to discuss the process for modifying the MDPH anthrax vaccine license for several purposes: to indicate a reduced number of injections, to include a different route of administration (intramuscular as opposed to subcutaneous), and to expand the indication to include protection against aerosol challenge of spores. Col. Arthur Friedlander said that "the original series of six doses was established in the 1950s for an anthrax vaccine similar to but not identical with the MDPH vaccine."[23] The minutes also noted what had been commented on by the 1985 FDA panel review of the AVA: "Studies of vaccine (not MDPH product) effectiveness in humans working in tanneries showed protection against cutaneous disease, but there was insufficient data to demonstrate protection against inhalation disease."[24]

This meeting also portended the beginning of the public relations campaign for the anthrax vaccine. Prior to that, however, Brigadier General Busby, the Joint Program Manager for Biological Defense, stated that "the DoD's position is 'soldiers are citizens first' and whatever studies are formulated, they have to be done with this concept in mind. Soldiers have the same Constitutional rights as other citizens." These comments may have been addressing one of the SAIC briefing slides at that meeting. The slide is entitled "Volunteer Considerations" and is a comparison of two groups for use in any studies to amend the license for the vaccine. It depicts two rows: on one side is "At-Risk Forces" and on the other is "Normal Volunteers." There are bulleted points on either

---

[22] LTC David Danley, "Minutes of the Meeting on Changing the Food and Drug Administration License for the Michigan Department of Public Health (MDPH) Anthrax Vaccine to Meet Military Requirements", held on 20 October 1995 meeting; Joint Program Office for Biological Defense memorandum, 13 November 1995.

[23] Id.

[24] Id.

side, indicating pros and cons of using the two groups. The At-Risk Forces have in their favor, it would appear, that using them would serve "Dual Purpose[s]"—"Immunized Force" and "Study Needs." However, on the down side, At-Risk forces have "Informed consent complications," which include record-keeping and "assignment issues," probably referring to the frequent rotation of service members. "Normal Volunteers" have the problem of availability, but once you have them, there is better "access for study needs and record-keeping." They also come with a "cost" and using them "doesn't support immediate readiness needs." Finally, the last point against using soldiers points out the DoD's concerns with public relations from the beginning: "Soldier 'guinea pigs' criticism."[25]

Whether BGen Busby had his mind changed on soldiers' rights by the brief or not, he made an odd pronouncement at a meeting on the license amendment for the vaccine. According to the minutes, he "addressed the need to make the case that anthrax is currently the principal biological warfare threat. By protecting against anthrax and other BW threats, the vaccines serve as a deterrent."[26] We do not have transcripts of those meetings and we don't know how exactly he "addressed" this supposed "need," but it is troubling on many levels because it is a sweeping statement justifying the use of vaccines against an invisible, perhaps even non-existent, threat.

A cynical person might reasonably infer that the General is suggesting running a PR campaign on the American people to justify knowingly using an unlicensed vaccine. It is also odd because this is not a meeting of operational planners discussing the terrorist threat to U.S. Forces. These are doctors mostly, discussing how to get a license amendment for

---

[25] Briefing slide from Anthrax Vaccine License Amendment Plan: Information Briefing for Joint Program Manager, DoD Biological Defense, 19 October 1995, p. 18.

[26] LTC David Danley, "Minutes of the Meeting on Changing the Food and Drug Administration License for the Michigan Department of Public Health (MDPH) Anthrax Vaccine to Meet Military Requirements", held on 20 October 1995 meeting; Joint Program Office for Biological Defense memorandum, 13 November 1995.

the anthrax vaccine and suddenly a one-star starts talking about the need to make a case for the vaccine as a BW deterrent. There is no discussion about the intelligence or evidentiary basis for such a conclusion, nor an explanation as to why military *doctors* would need to "make the case." One can imagine the hushed silence or, perhaps worse, the nodding heads, after the General makes that statement. Was this an implication that informed consent was to be side-stepped and patients were to be told that this was a great deterrent to anthrax attack? Was this to begin some media campaign to justify the use of this vaccine off-label? Whatever it was, the idea of soldiers having the same rights as other citizens did not ultimately win out.

In accordance with one of the decision tree slides from the 1995 briefing, the U.S. Army was supposed to help MDPH prepare an Investigational New Drug Application in an effort to amend the license for three reasons: (1) a new route of administration, (2) a reduced shot schedule (from six to three), and (3) to obtain an indication against aerosolized anthrax. This IND application was *pending with the FDA* during all the courts-martials mentioned previously. The importance of this application cannot be overstated. By law, that application becomes effective 30 days after it is submitted for the purposes set forth therein. This means that if someone administers the drug in accordance with the IND submission protocol, by definition and by law it is an investigational use of the drug. That IND was not withdrawn, modified, or otherwise dismissed by the FDA.

If the above wasn't enough to demonstrate conclusively the absurdity of the DoD position, consider this: The clinical protocol for this IND was being conducted at Fort Detrick, Maryland, a U.S. Army base; it was being run by DoD doctors and administrators; and U.S. Army soldiers were the volunteers. Amazingly, in the *coup de grâce*, the soldiers in that study were given information about the anthrax vaccine; they filled out and signed consent forms; and they were given the exact same vaccine that DoD was concurrently compelling regular troops to take under threat of court-martial. The IND application was submitted following an Army, Joint Staff, and OSD staff process in which there was concurrence that it was necessary to obtain FDA approval of a new licensed indication for inhalation anthrax before DoD could start mass anthrax vaccinations.[27]

For whatever reason, this consensus was reversed within a month of William Cohen's confirmation as Secretary of Defense. This followed significant DoD pressure on the FDA, much like in 1990 prior to the Gulf War, to get permission to begin use of the anthrax vaccine for inhalation anthrax without obtaining a new licensed indication or completing the scientific investigation proposed by the Army in the IND application.[28] There were phone calls made, including one by Admiral Ed Martin, a U.S. Navy doctor, and the Deputy Assistant Secretary of Defense for Health Affairs, looking for a new *interpretation* of the anthrax vaccine license, one different than the DoD's long-standing position that the vaccine was not licensed for inhalational anthrax.

Now (in 1997) the DoD wanted the FDA to say that the anthrax vaccine was licensed for such a use. On 4 March 1997, four days after the retirement of long-time FDA commissioner Dr. David Kessler, the man who had negotiated and required DoD to get a Rule 23(d) waiver on the verge of the Gulf War, Dr. Stephen Joseph, the Assistant Secretary of Defense for Health Affairs, wrote to the acting FDA commissioner and stated that the "DoD has long interpreted the scope of the license to include inhalation exposure, including that which would occur in a biological warfare context."[29] Given what was already on the record by DoD officials, that statement cannot be spun any other way than as a bald-faced lie. In addition, Dr. Joseph asked "whether FDA has any

---

[27] Id.

[28] Dr. Stephen C. Joseph, DoD ASD/Health Affairs, letter to FDA Lead Deputy Commissioner Michael Friedman, 4 March 1997.

[29] Id.

objection to our interpretation of the scope of the licensure for the anthrax vaccine." If Joseph's assertion regarding the DoD's position on the anthrax vaccine was correct and this belief was "long-standing", then why would the DoD need to join in a clinical protocol and get an indication against aerosolized anthrax? Why did they even need to address that indication with the manufacturers? And why would the holder of the license, the maker of the vaccine, who presumably knows something about its own licenses and products, ask for an amendment to get the vaccine indicated for inhalational anthrax? The answer is quite simple and mandated by the Federal FDCA: It is because the AVA was never licensed for use against an aerosolized biological warfare attack.

On 13 March 1997, acting FDA commissioner Dr. David Friedman abandoned the FDA's regulatory role. He offered that "[w]hile there is a paucity of data regarding the effectiveness of Anthrax Vaccine for prevention of inhalation anthrax, the current package insert *does not preclude* this use [...] Therefore, I believe your interpretation is *not inconsistent* with the current label."[30] Notice that Friedman has now completely turned the law and FDA regulations—and the English language—completely on its head. The DoD now had the green light it wanted and needed to go forward claiming that the vaccine was "FDA approved" for inhalational anthrax ...

Almost.

There are two problems with these types of back-door inter-office memos. First, they circumvent the entire regulatory process. One person does not simply wave a magic wand and make a vaccine or drug licensed. Fortunately, someone must have foreseen these kinds of abuses. That is why the FDA has its own regulations regarding what constitutes a binding agency opinion. The FDA, apparently cognizant of the fact that outside entities might place undue reliance on the private informal opinion of FDA staff, drafted strict requirements for what it refers to as

---

[30] Id.

"advisory opinions" that might bind or commit the agency. 21 C.F.R. §10.85(k) specifically states:

> a statement made or advice provided by an FDA employee constitutes an advisory opinion only if it is issued in writing under this Section. A statement or advice given by an FDA employee orally, or given in writing but not under this Section or §10.90 is an informal communication that represents the best judgment of that employee at that time but does not constitute an advisory opinion, does not necessarily represent the formal position of the FDA, and does not bind or otherwise obligate or commit the agency to the views expressed.[31]

This letter, while consistently relied upon by the DoD as "proof" that the AVA was not an IND, was not issued under either of the required C.F.R. sections. Accordingly, this letter is merely an "informal communication" that has absolutely no legal effect. As such, this letter cannot modify the clearly defined legal status of the AVA that results from filing of the IND application by MBPI. This was such a bizarre situation because the company that makes the drug did not seek the FDA's opinion on the vaccine's status; a *third-party* user did. This is like Dow Chemical having an IND application for a drug pending before the FDA and then the American Medical Association stepping in to ask the FDA to announce that the drug is actually *not* an IND, but licensed for the exact purpose for which the drug's own manufacturer is running a clinical testing protocol.

The second reason that the letter is of no legal effect is that the Supreme Court had recently decided a similar case, *Christensen, et al v.*

[31] The informal and nonbinding nature of such "advice" is also made clear in the IND regulations themselves. 21 C.F.R. §312.41(c). Moreover, it is noted that the communication did not even involve the IND applicant, BioPort, Inc.

*Harris Countr*y, *et al*.[32] The Supreme Court specifically found that agency "personal opinion" letters are not entitled to deference by the Court, but only to "respect"—and then only to the extent that the letter's interpretations are persuasive.[33] In this case, in light of the FDA regulations, Dr. Friedman's letter is completely illogical because it rewrites the entire FDA regulatory scheme. His letter states that the DoD's interpretation is "not inconsistent" with the approved labeling. This is nonsensical because drugs are designed, tested, and licensed for a specific purpose, not licensed for what's on their label *and* anything *not inconsistent with* that label. How could such be the case with the requirements for showing efficacy through two well-controlled human studies? In short, Dr. Friedman's letter was worth little more than the combined total of the ink and paper with which it was written. Indeed, there could be no other result, given the fact that the letter is totally at odds with the IND application language of the manufacturer. It makes absolutely no sense to believe that an FDA official writing in his personal capacity can single-handedly invalidate the regulatory scheme adopted by the FDA to prevent the licensing and interstate movement of Investigational New Drugs at the request of some third party.

What is truly mind-boggling about Dr. Friedman's response is that just one week later, on 20 March 1997, CBER, the sub-agency of the FDA responsible for monitoring and inspecting the vaccine's manufacturer, would issue the Notice of Intent to Revoke (NOIR) letter. To emphasize the recurring problems FDA had found at the manufacturer's plant, the FDA letter stated:

> While these deviations were documented in the most recent inspection, we note that significant deviations have been documented during previous FDA inspections of

[32] 120 S. Ct. 1655, 2000 U.S. LEXIS 3003, 1 May 2000.

[33] *Christensen*, 2000 U.S. LEXIS 3003 at 19-20.c

> May 4 through May 7, 1993; May 31 through June 3, 1994; and April 24 through May 5, 1995. The seriousness of these deficiencies was emphasized to you in a letter dated December 22, 1993, and a Warning Letter dated August 31, 1995.[34]

So, at the exact moment that the DoD is seeking and getting back-door approval from the head of the FDA for the AVA, the manufacturer is about to have its entire manufacturing process invalidated and threatened with having its license to manufacture the vaccine pulled by the results of FDA inspections.

In an interview with the Canadian newspaper *The Province*, Mark Elengold, the Deputy Director for Operations at CBER, explained the significance of a NOIR letter. " … In the three years I have been in this job, I have done it about three times," said Elengold. "It is a very serious tool. We view it […] to be equivalent to an injunction […] where we get a court to order compliance."[35] While the legal effect of Dr. Friedman's letter is nil, it does make for great public relations and that's exactly how the DoD would use the letter in seeking to win the PR battle that was about to begin. A number of interesting initiatives, press briefings, and press releases began not long after Dr. Joseph's letter and Dr. Friedman's response in March 1997.

In retrospect, an overall pattern starts to emerge. There were several fronts on which the Secretary of Defense and the DoD tried to outdistance criticism of the program. The first claim was that the vaccine was "licensed." This category had several sub-claims, such as long-term safety, use on veterinarians, and proven effectiveness of the AVA. The problem with these statements is, of course, their lack of completeness and/or their outright falsity. Some of these statements were well beyond

---

[34] FDA letter to MBPI, 20 February 1997.

[35] Rees, Ann. "Their Dangerous Dose." *Vancouver Province*. 25 June 2000.

being just "spin." As another example, at a background briefing on 15 December 1997, two senior defense officials laid out the upcoming (AVIP), noting that it was still six months away. The reporters asked some questions.

> **Q:** The availability of the vaccine at this point, if you wanted to do a large program tomorrow, is there a stockpile of this vaccine available?
>
> **A:** There's a stockpile right now of seven million shots, which is about 1.2 TED—troop equivalent doses—of six shots, if you will. So there's a large stockpile.
>
> **A:** But that's the stockpile ... We're redoing the testing on it just to be absolutely certain before we go out. There's been a great attention to safety in this.
>
> **Q:** You found no impurities in the stockpile ...
>
> **A:** No.

This answer came six months after the process for manufacture had been invalidated by CBER.

The second area in pushing the vaccine harkens back to Brigadier General Busby's statements at the meeting about the license amendment plan. There he talked about the need to "make the case" that anthrax was the number one biological threat. This was fairly easy to accomplish as anthrax is a real biological threat and it plays upon a very real fear. Making it even easier was the constant references to the Aum Shinrikyo cult's sarin gas attack on the Tokyo subway and the U.S. members of the U.N. inspection teams being forbidden from participating in Iraqi weapons inspections by Saddam Hussein. DoD briefers never missed an opportunity to point to the possibility of a terrorist attack on U.S. soil or to exaggerate the lethality of anthrax.[36]

This is not to say that it is not lethal, but DoD briefers constantly called it "100% lethal," which is a bizarrely hyperbolic claim. What does "100% lethal" even mean? Does that mean everyone who breathes in even a molecule of anthrax spores? The answer to that is unequivocally "No." What amount constitutes a lethal dose then? One briefer referred to 10,000 spores, while other DoD information refers to the LD_{50} as the number in thousands of spores that constitutes a lethal dose. The SecDef himself participated in this fear-mongering with his then-famous quote during a live TV appearance, while holding a five-pound bag of sugar, that if "this was anthrax, it could wipe out half the population of Washington, D.C."[37] One expert later called that "one of the most irresponsible statements ever made by a politician."[38] Additionally, Secretary of Defense Cohen gave several speeches about the proliferation of these weapons, exaggerating the number of countries capable of manufacturing and delivering such weapons. In three different speeches, Cohen put the number(s) at 30, 25, and finally 10.[39]

The final area of this media campaign consisted of a fallback position, which consisted of a series of statements that can be summarized as, "What else are we supposed to do?", the old "if it saves even one life" rhetorical play. A number of high-ranking DoD officials made statements to the effect that they would be "derelict" if they didn't give this vaccine in light of the threat or that they were "morally obligated" to vaccinate soldiers, or that "it's the best response" or "it's the only response" that

---

[36] See, e.g., DoD Press Briefing, 15 December 1997.

[37] SecDef William Cohen on *This Week with Cokie Roberts*, November 1997.

[38] Richter, Paul. "Experts Assess Risk of 'New Terrorism' Threat," *Los Angeles Times*. 7 February 2000.

[39] Garamone, Jim, AFPS. "Combating Weapons of Mass Destruction," https://archive.defense.gov/news/newsarticle.aspx?id=40944, 30 April 1997, last accessed 14 July 2020; William S. Cohen, "Preparing for a Grave New World", *Washington Post*, Op Ed., 26 July 1999; William S. Cohen, "Force Protection is My Priority", *Army Times*, 31 July 2000.

we have. These statements frequently relied upon the record of the individual making the statement as a testimonial to the vaccine's necessity. The problem with this is that it ignores three things. First, it ignores the law requiring informed consent. Second, it ignores the lack of efficacy for the claims. In other words, there had been no studies, and ethically, there can never be studies to prove the effectiveness of the vaccine against aerosolized anthrax. Even the animal studies, while promising, indicate a less than stellar performance against certain strains of the anthrax bacillus.[40] Finally, it ignores the validity and viability of other treatments.

There existed at the time a highly effective, fully licensed antibiotic that could be very successful if taken right after anthrax exposure. Since this is the military's method of response to a number of chemical agents, why was it impossible to use these already licensed antibiotics in the event of an anthrax attack?[41] An illustration of the DoD's refusal to consider other treatments occurred at the 15 December press briefing when a reporter asked about other treatments against anthrax. The briefer's answer:

> With regard to those medical countermeasures, antibiotics. They're effective in sustaining service members until antibodies are built. Provides immediate protection, but it has to be sustained over a period of time, until the antibodies are developed. There are limited minor side effects with the dosage required of the antibiotics. Antiserum is a very fast reacting, immediately protection capability, but again, it's limited, and it has to

---

[40] See GAO Report T-NSIAD-99-148, footnote 4, 5.

[41] I address possible/likely reasons that the DoD insisted on this particular vaccine over all other possibilities in later chapters and will let the reader decide.

> be re-administered to sustain protection. It's expensive and the same minor side effects are associated with it.
>
> Vaccines are the way to go. It takes time to develop the immunity, but the immunity lasts for a long time. Limited, minor side effects. I think the rate of those folks that we've vaccinated over the last five years associated with their jobs—either lab workers, workers in industry in the private sector, special operations forces, there's been about a 96-97 percent rate of no reaction at all, and those that did have had limited topical reactions, minor swelling or redness, things like that.
>
> It's extremely difficult to circumvent a vaccine. This would ward against genetic engineering of other strains. Once that vaccine's in, it takes a major effort for an unfriendly nation to try to develop another type of anthrax strain that we would have to dissect, if you will, figure out what it was and then rework our vaccine. But it is very effective. It provides the protection we need over the long haul.

He acknowledges the immediate nature of antibiotics and the long time necessary to develop immunity for vaccines, but offers that "vaccines are the way to go." Additionally, probably most surprising, are the briefer's references to the "minor reactions" (with a negative implication—"you've still got those minor reactions") and the incredible claim of "96-97 percent *no reaction at all*" with the AVA, something that has never been true of the AVA, and that it "would ward against genetic engineering" of other strains, another fact that is used by critics of the program. Either the briefer was unaware of BioPort's problems, the DoD's own studies on the highly reactogenic nature of the AVA, badly informed, or he was straight-up lying. With the DoD and this program, it is difficult to know which it is.

The DoD's media campaign was fairly extensive, involving many briefings with the press in each of the above areas. For example, on 16 April 1997, two senior defense officials gave a briefing on the DoD's role in helping to train and "enhance the capability of federal, state, and local emergency response agencies to prevent and respond to domestic terrorist incidents involving weapons of mass destruction."[42] On 25 April 1997, a notice was sent to the press that the Marine Corps' Chemical Biological Incident Response Force (CBIRF) would "demonstrate its ability to effect consequence management following the simulated detonation of a chemical-biological terrorist device" in the Washington, D.C. area on 30 April 1997. On 28 April 1997, Secretary of Defense Cohen gave a speech at the University of Georgia, speaking at a conference on terrorism, and told listeners that a rogue state attack using chemical-biological weapons was "not only plausible, it's really quite real."[43] In fact, he told his audience that "about 30 countries now possess mature chemical and biological weapons programs with 12 having advanced missile capabilities."[44] Secretary Cohen emphasized a comprehensive response that included active and passive measures against such attacks.

By November 1997, when U.S. members of the U.N. inspection teams were not allowed by Saddam Hussein to participate in weapons inspections, anthrax and chemical-biological warfare (CBW) and weapons of mass destruction (WMD) were being talked about as imminent. There was a 14 November 1997, briefing by a senior defense official on Iraq's CBW capability.[45] On related fronts, General Ronald Blanck, the Army's Surgeon General, and Vice Admiral Dennis Blair, on 6 November 1997,

---

[42] DoD Background Briefing, 6 April 1997.

[43] Garamone, Jim, AFPS. "Combating Weapons of Mass Destruction," https://archive.defense.gov/news/newsarticle.aspx?id=40944, 30 April 1997, last accessed 14 July 2020.

[44] Id.

[45] Garamone, Jim, AFPS. "Combating Weapons of Mass Destruction," https://archive.defense.gov/news/newsarticle.aspx?id=40944, 30 April 1997, last accessed 14 July 2020.

were briefing the press on the DoD's supposedly improved ability to track vaccines and medical health of service members.[46] This would of course be a crucial part of any DoD vaccine program because of its historically atrocious record, as previously documented *supra* during both the Persian Gulf War and Bosnia and highlighted in Congressional investigations.[47] There was no pushback against General Blanck's or Admiral Blair's assertions by the press, Congress, veterans' advocacy groups, or the American public.

46 DoD News Briefing, 6 November 1997.

47 DoD News Briefing, 6 November 1997.

CHAPTER 13
DEFENSE DELAY

In despair, I sent out the judge's ruling in Corporal Stonewall's case to a list of people the same night the judge issued it. Now what would I do? Major Tom "Buzz" Rempfer, USAFR, was an Air Force Academy graduate, former F-16 pilot, then A-10 pilot, and flew for one of the major airlines in his day job; He was the poster boy image of an Air Force pilot. He also had been appointed by his Reserve Squadron Commander to a "Tiger Team" to investigate some of the "rumors" that were going around about the Anthrax Vaccine. His team's investigation would get him thrown out of his unit and publicly branded a coward by his CO. Tom and Major Russ Dingle, another member of the Tiger Team, were on the leading edge of the anthrax program's problems. The "rumors" about which their CO was concerned began with the first Reserve squadron, based in Dover, Delaware, to receive the vaccine. Most of the Reserve Air Force pilots who got the vaccine were also airline pilots in their day jobs. Thus, when some pilots started having adverse reactions, it meant they also lost their flight status in their civilian jobs because they were medically grounded. Colonel John Richardson, USAFR, was involved early on, as were Major Sonnie Bates's attorneys, Lou Michels and Bruce Smith.

Someone in that group mentioned the name of an attorney in California who was filing an extraordinary writ in an anthrax refusal case. The writ asked the intermediate appellate court, the Navy-Marine Corps Court of Criminal Appeals (NMCCA), to find that the judge had erred by ruling that the order to take the vaccine was not just lawful, but *unquestionably* lawful. California was seventeen hours behind Okinawa.

I looked at my watch. I was on the phone at 12:30 a.m. my time, 9:30 a.m. Pacific Standard Time.

On 9 August 2000, I made the same arguments I had made in Jason Stonewall's case in David Ponder's case. It was even more surreal because the judge had already ruled in Jason's case and we both knew it. I tried my best to pretend that we both didn't already know the outcome, but what was the point? It was the same judge. What were the odds he was going to arrive at a different conclusion in Ponder's case? I gave it my best effort, but most of my energy was being spent working on the extraordinary writ appealing the judge's rulings on our motions in Corporal Stonewall's case.

I pounded the table, addressed his four findings specifically, probably even stepped over the line in calling his logic "ridiculous" that one could not plead a federal law in defense at a court-martial. I was heated and I wouldn't have cared if he threw me in jail for contempt. We finished at 3:25 p.m. Wednesday afternoon.

At 4:00 p.m., I was right back in court on Jason Stonewall's case. We set dates for our next session of court, which would be the trial. We would have to listen to Stonewall's legal officer say that he gave the order, it wasn't followed, and then case over. Time was running out on us.

On 18 August 2000, I got tricked, bamboozled, swindled, hornswoggled, whatever name you can use to describe being duped. It really happened sooner, right after our prior session of court, but the trap wasn't sprung until 18 August. I walked right into it.

The prosecutor had asked me a few days after our oral arguments in Ponder's case if we could have a "quick" session of court in order to take the testimony of the officer who had actually given Ponder the order to take the shot. The officer had flown in from the mainland or Korea and *was there any reason we couldn't preserve his testimony now while he was here*? I had just come off of the rifle range a day early and the request seemed fairly benign. After all, it was a Friday afternoon at 1:30. What could happen? The prosecutor had asked me if I would mind letting him proceed with his witness and then he wouldn't oppose a continuance request by defense. It seemed reasonable to me and the collegial thing to do was accommodate the request. On such minor accommodations the courts continue to function and without them, the courts simply would not function at all.

By then, I had already filed my extraordinary writ with the appellate court, which was "extraordinarily" *rough* because of the time constraints, but it was filed with the court. I was also worried, but optimistic by then. NMCCA had issued a stay in the case of Ocean T. Rose, another Marine who had refused the vaccine in California. Rose's case had proceeded a little ahead of our cases, but they were all essentially mirror-image cases. The stay meant the court-martial below was stopped while the accused got a hearing in front of the appellate court on the judge's denial of his motions. I was in steady contact with his counsel about potentially joining our cases for purposes of the stay. I figured the stay would issue within a week, maybe two. *Sure, Chris we'll take the government witness' testimony, continue the case, and then boom! I'll get my stay*. I had even come out of the funk of depression I had been mired in for weeks.

Imagine my surprise when the prosecutor stood up in court and objected to my continuance. When I stared over at him, less than two feet away, my eyes bored into him. He wouldn't look at me and that was probably wise on his part. A lifetime of playing hockey did not make me forget being wronged or improve the gentlemanly disposition I was supposed to display in court. I felt like I had just gotten a proverbial slash on the back of the legs while the ref wasn't looking and I was ready to drop the gloves and punch his teeth down his throat on the spot.

"Sir, an extraordinary writ is currently pending before NMCCA," I began in response to the Judge's question about why I wanted a continuance. "It has been served on that Court. In light of that Court's issuance of a stay in the case of *United States versus Rose*, we believe there are good grounds to request a continuance, especially where there have been no continuances requested by defense up to this point. This would be our first and it's not an undue burden on the government to ask for one. Finally, sir, we are willing to stipulate to the government witness' testimony, or allow that witness to be heard and then have the case continued, or we could even depose the witness. Additionally, sir, you haven't even officially ruled in this case on the record. Normally, the rules for appellate procedure allow the defense twenty days to appeal an adverse ruling."

Judge Stone seemed to think for a moment. "Have you made a forum election in this case?"

I wondered what that had to with anything and I went through my own mental checklist.

"No, sir, we have not," I answered evenly. Already the wheels were turning in my head. I had ridden an emotional rollercoaster in this case, into hopelessness after the judge's ruling on our motions and back out with the Rose stay. I was not going to plummet back down again. Worst of all, I had violated my own rules, and I had given Ponder—and his wife—my solemn word that he would not be going to jail tonight. I should have been tipped off when he told me that the command had him inventory his gear and was acting oddly. I should have put it all together then, but I hadn't.

"I am going to need a moment to reflect upon your proposal and the government's opposition."

The judge sat back, pensive.

"Sir," the prosecutor began, while I fantasized of having a hockey stick in my hands, "the defense has just raised an issue. If you haven't ruled yet, then what are they appealing at this point—"

I was on my feet instantly.

"Let's talk about that for a moment," the judge said. He turned to me. "Did you receive my electronic mail with regards to my anticipated ruling?"

"Yes, sir, and that was the basis for sending the writ up to NMCCA."

The judge sat for a moment longer. "I'll tell you what. What I am going to do is put my ruling on the record in a minute and then we'll take up the matter of what, if anything, we're going to do today. My current inclination is to proceed through arraignment and the taking of the government's evidence and possibly ask you for evidence. Is that fair enough?"

"Yes, sir," I replied warily.

"This court stands in recess."

I started to leave the courtroom, but the judge indicated he would be right back and motioned for us to stay. He exited out his side door. I stared at the prosecutor. He still wouldn't look in my direction.

The judge came right back in and hopped into his chair.

He read through the identical findings he had made in Stonewall's case on the motions. It still made my stomach sink to hear it in open court.

"Now, at this point I'll take the accused's forum election."

I had a bad feeling about this.

"Sir, if we could, we'd like to get a ruling on our request for a continuance before the accused elects his forum." I no longer cared what the judge thought. If he didn't grant our continuance, I was going to tell Ponder to elect a jury with enlisted members as his forum. If the trial counsel was going to lie to me in order to get me into court, I was more than willing to go back on an e-mail I had sent that I anticipated we would elect judge alone as our forum. Fuck 'em both. The gloves were now off.

"Well, you'll have to give me a better reason than that … Or provide me with some law." The judge looked at me and I knew he had every intention of finishing this case today. I had no lawyerly pretense left in me.

"Sir, if this court does not grant a continuance, that means that if the accused elected judge alone as his forum, we could proceed through the entire case today. The government has one witness. In all likelihood, there is no question about whether or not the order was given. It is quite possible then that this case could conclude with an adverse finding against the accused with a writ pending before NMCCA where a stay is likely to issue. Sir, in the Rose case, the writ was served on NMCCA on 4 August and the stay was issued three days later on 7 August. We served our writ on the court on Wednesday afternoon, eastern standard time. That means tonight it will have been two days. I start a contested trial on Monday in another case. What harm is there to the government's case to grant a six-day continuance? If the stay doesn't issue in that time, then we go forward. This is a minuscule request, sir. If the judge denies that continuance request, then the accused will elect enlisted members in anticipation that the stay will be granted. We will need time to get the members' questionnaires, prepare *voir dire*, et cetera. So, quite frankly, we're using the procedure to give us the time we need for a stay to issue. Straight up, that's what we're going to do."

I didn't know if I had just violated a half dozen rules in the code of professional conduct or the JAG Instruction and at that point I didn't care.

The judge paused. He wasn't angry, but he certainly didn't seem too pleased.

"I appreciate your candor, counsel. Nevertheless, I would imagine it's an improper reason. Actually," he paused for a moment, "there is no improper reason. If the accused wishes to be tried by members, that is a perfectly fine selection as far as the court is concerned. I do appreciate your candor. I hate to put the accused in a bind of forcing him to choose trial by members solely to for the purpose of getting delay in the case." He turned to the prosecutor. "Do you have anything?"

"Basically, sir, they're threatening members if they don't get their continuance because their sole purpose of requesting members is for a delay tactic." If I had accomplished little else, I had gotten the prosecutor pissed and that alone made me feel better. "And we believe that to be improper. However, that's within the discretion of the court."

"You know as well as I do that defense may and has every right to select trial by members. Would you like a few moments?"

"Yes, sir, we'd like a brief recess." The prosecutor stormed out of the courtroom. I turned to Ponder, who really looked nervous now, the first time I had seen him visibly shaken in the entire case. It had come home to him; he could be going to trial and likely jail in no time at all. He turned to me.

"I'm not going to the brig tonight am I, sir?" I leaned over and looked at the back of the courtroom, out the door where Captain Kolomjec had gone.

"Not tonight," I whispered back. I said it with a confidence that I didn't really feel. I had never promised a client anything, but overcome by my own confidence and trusting in the prosecutor's promise, I had given Ponder and his wife Jennifer my word that he was not going to the brig that night because there would be no trial.

When Kolomjec returned, the judge allowed us to argue on why a continuance should be granted. I didn't want to have Ponder elect members, but I was willing to try anything at that moment. Ponder's freedom, Stonewall's, PFC Arroyo's—everything hinged on a stay being issued.

After we argued, the judge denied the continuance, despite the judicial mandate that continuances should be granted liberally. Worse yet, because I was starting a contested general court-martial in an officer case on that following Monday, the judge ordered that we would start the trial tomorrow, on a Saturday morning. I noted my objection three times, but we were sunk. If the writ didn't come by the end of the workday east coast time, Ponder would be going to the Brig the next day.

CHAPTER 14

COHEN'S "FOUR POINTS"

In December 1997, the anthrax vaccine manufacturer was shut down and could not manufacture anything related to the AVA. Notwithstanding that hurdle, Secretary of Defense William Cohen announced that before the mandatory program would begin, it would have to meet four prerequisites:

1. Supplemental testing, consistent with Food and Drug Administration standards, to assure sterility, safety, potency and purity of the vaccine;
2. Implementation of a system for fully tracking personnel who receive the anthrax vaccinations;
3. Approval of appropriate operational plans to administer the immunizations and communications plans to inform military personnel of the overall program;
4. Review of health and medical issues of the program by an *independent expert.*[1]

One cannot help but wonder why condition number one would need to be in place if the DoD was confident in the safety and potency of the AVA, as it had started saying publicly. In fact, this appears to have been

[1] My emphasis added.

nothing more than a media campaign to assuage fears because none of these four "prerequisites" were ever met before the program kicked off, which is exactly why the manufacturer had been shut down in the first instance. Each of these factors revealed fundamental flaws with the program from its inception.

With regard to point 1, "supplemental testing" may well have been the worst idea for the DoD could have ever come up with because what it demonstrated, unequivocally, was failure of lot after lot after lot of the vaccine.[2] One of the first findings in CBER's February 1998 inspection was that "there is no validation of the length of time sub-lots are held until they are used in a lot. Sub-lots have been held longer than three years prior to use. There is no stability data to support this hold time."[3] Lest this seem picayune, consider a little more history of one particular sub-lot:

> Sub-lot AV456 was produced [...] in 5/95 [and stored] until 3/97 at which time it was transported to the formulation room [...] with other sub-lots to make FAV039. Here it was discovered that AV456 was contaminated with mold, and it was destroyed.[4]

While some may say that the fact that it was caught is good news, it ignores the other, older sub-lots where mold or other impurities were not caught. One finding (among many like this) is particularly noteworthy:

> Lot FAV023 was filled on 12/13/93 and passed a potency test on 3/29/94. It was submitted for redating

[2] It would take up too much space to detail all of the failed lots, for their various reasons during the 20 February 1998, CBER inspection on the lots of AVA. Some of the more egregious violations are listed. See CBER Inspection report dated 20 February 1998 for a complete listing.

[3] FDA Form 483 Inspectional Observations 4-20 February 1998.

[4] Id.

> on 4/2/97 and was placed in the stability program (zero time) at the same time. It is reported as failing potency on 4/2/97. It was tested again on 8/12/97 and is reported as failing potency. A fourth potency test conducted on 10/6/97 is listed as passing by 0.01. There is no investigation into the original result and justifying the additional testing.[5]

This finding is most disturbing because it indicates a testing regimen that ignores negative test results—twice!—and somehow chooses to validate a subsequent positive after two negatives. How can one know which test result is correct with two failing and two passing results? And how many people would like to line up, roll up their sleeve, and take their shots from *that* particular vial of the vaccine? Stability testing of biological products is crucial because of the possibility for these products to break down over time. Note that this lot was "filled" in 1993. Four years later it passes a test by .01 after having failed twice previously. This particular finding is in no way isolated: Lots FAV 010, 011, 018, 021, 022, 025, 028, 040, 041, 042, 043, and 044 all had at least one failed potency test that was not investigated and then a passing result was somehow chosen over the negative one.

FAV016 has its own uniquely disturbing history.

> Lot FAV016 had 6579 vials rejected due to particulates during post-filling inspection. These particulates were not identified, nor was an investigation conducted. The batch was released.

Someone, somewhere, had unidentified "particulates" injected into them. As a practical aside, one has to wonder how those individuals will

---

[5] Id.

get VA compensation if they have an illness as a result of this contaminated product being injected into them in light of the DoD's positions that there had only been 74 adverse events from the vaccine.

The list of violations goes on and on and includes several different lots being tested and found with such contaminants as "Penicillium species"—a danger to anyone allergic to penicillin; Cladosporium—a fungus that can cause infections leading to "rough skin, black lesions on the hands, and sometimes a brain abscess"; Alternaria—a fungus that can cause dermatitis in humans; Micrococcus—a contaminant that is relatively harmless to humans; Staphylococcus saprophyticus—a significant cause of urinary tract infections; Staphylococcus epidermis—a significant cause of opportunistic infections, usually for those with some skin puncturing, such as needle/IV intrusions, medical appliances, or surgery; and Staphylococcus capitis—another infection-causing bacteria.

Despite all of these findings and more in February 1998, the program was launched on 15 May 1998, with Secretary Cohen claiming, with a straight face, that "all conditions for implementing the anthrax vaccination program for the total force have now been met."[6] There is simply no possible way Secretary Cohen could have said that in good conscience if he was aware of the inspection results in February. And given everything going on around the program, it is impossible to imagine that he didn't know—because the manufacturer "voluntarily" shut down for "renovations" in January 1998. In reality it shut down as a result of the Notice of Intent to Revoke letter by the FDA; otherwise, the February inspection results would have resulted in the facility's license revocation.

The second condition of the program was tracking of immunizations. Two DoD briefers talked extensively on 6 November 1997, about a new program that would be used to track immunizations and of the terrific

---

[6] SecDef memo, 15 May 1998.

job the new system had done in Bosnia.[7] At a March 1998 Senate Armed Services Committee hearing, however, Dr. Randolph Wykoff, the Associate Commissioner for operations at the FDA, and Mark Gebicke of the GAO, pointed out that the Bosnia experience left a lot to be desired, particularly of the tracking of immunizations under an IND protocol for an investigational encephalitis vaccine.[8] One report called the DoD's tracking "an abysmal failure."[9] Lest this seem hyperbole, a letter from the FDA to the Asst. Secretary of Defense for Health Affairs, Edward Martin, dated July 22, 1997, is as damning a piece of evidence as exists about the failures of DoD's compliance with rules when administering drugs and biologics, with a point by point listing of the complete bungling of the program.[10] Once again, the Assistant Secretary of Defense for Health Affairs promised to get better, but also talked about a new procedure for getting relief from the FDA from the requirements of an IND. The FDA associate director maintained that the "FDA firmly believes the IND process, as defined in our rules and regulations, is sufficiently flexible [for DoD's needs]. Additionally, FDA is convinced the DoD has the scientific, clinical, and logistic capability necessary to comply with the requirements of the IND process."[11] Evidently, however, they could not and did not do it in Bosnia. A GAO report issued the same day stressed the importance of being able to track vaccine immunizations in order to ensure "that (1) sufficient supplies of vaccines will be available at the various worldwide immunization sites; (2) vaccines that are older than their 1-year shelf life are destroyed; and (3)

---

[7] Background briefing, 6 November 1997.

[8] Senate Hearing, Committee on Veterans Affairs Holds Hearing on the Nomination of Togo West as Secretary of Veterans Affairs and on U.S. Biologic Vaccines for Gulf War Veterans, 17 March 1998.

[9] Special Report of the Presidential Advisory Committee on Gulf War Illnesses, 1997, p. 9.

[10] This letter is Appendix EE to the Committee on Veteran's Affairs Report 105-39, "Senate Report of the Special Investigation Unit on Gulf War Illnesses, Part I", https://babel.hathitrust.org/cgi/pt?id=pur1.32754068922131&view=1up&seq=3, last accessed 14 July 2020. The letter by itself is available here: https://gulflink.health.mil/library/senate/appx_ee.pdf, last accessed 14 July 2020.

[11] Id.

records of vaccines received, administered, and destroyed are kept to allow for monitoring and tracking."[12] Worse yet, the GAO found that during the "Bosnia deployment in 1997 [...] DoD could not account for more than 3,000 (20 percent) of the total number of doses sent to Bosnia."[13]

Requirement number three was that there would be approved operational plans to communicate to service members about the anthrax vaccine program. Whatever the operational plans were, in May 1999, the Department of the Air Force circulated a memo to its judge advocates, specifically defense counsel, telling them that "a small number of military members have refused to follow their commander's direct order to take the [anthrax] vaccine" and that the cause of their fear in taking the shot is "misinformation obtained from websites set up by special interest groups[.]"[14] This was a frequent refrain of the DoD, in front of Congress and in the press. The memo also points members to the DoD's own website, which was established after the program had begun, in order to "counter" in DoD parlance "internet misinformation." Evidently then, in March 1998, when the program was about to begin, prong number three hadn't been met, either.

It is worth noting that the Army's AVIP Agency existed solely for the *promotion* of the anthrax vaccine. It was budgeted at $74 million over a six-year period (FY99-FY05).[15] No other military medicine program has ever needed to be forced on service members with an orchestrated campaign of this type. William Arkin, a defense writer and former Army intelligence officer observed that " ... this is the Pentagon versus its own service members. It is a depressing window into the breakdown of

---

12 GAO Report T—NSIAD-98-83, 17 March 1998, p. 8.

13 Id.

14 AF memo, 18 May 1999.

15 Charles Cragin, PDASD, Reserve Affairs, testimony, 3 October 2000.c

discipline and basic confidence in the political and military leadership. That has nothing to do with the Web."[16]

Criterion number four probably cost the DoD as much credibility (if one can say it had any to begin with) as number one. It would be comical were it not for the stakes involved. Secretary of Defense Cohen announced that there would be a "review of the health and medical aspects of the program by an independent expert."[17]

Doctor Gerard N. Burrow was the doctor who *allegedly* reviewed the program at the request of Deputy Secretary of Defense Rudy DeLeon. Dr. Burrow concluded that "[t]he anthrax vaccine appears to be safe and offers the best available protection against wild-type anthrax as a biological warfare agent."[18] Unfortunately, Dr. Burrow is a professor of gynecology at Yale University School of Medicine, a specialty that one would not normally associate with some expertise in weaponized anthrax toxins. When that unfortunate snippet from his CV leaked out, Dr. Burrow was subsequently asked by Congress at a 28 April 1999, hearing to testify about his review. He declined to appear. Instead, in a 26 April 1999, letter to Representative Christopher Shays (R-CT), Burrow stated that

> "[t]he Defense Department was looking for some [sic] to review the program in general and make suggestions, and I accepted out of patriotism. I was very clear that I had no expertise in Anthrax and they were very clear they

---

16 Arkin, William. "Bugged by the Net." *Washington Post* online. 27 September 1999. https://www.washingtonpost.com/wp-srv/national/dotmil/arkin092799.htm, last accessed 14 July 2020.

17 AVIP Impl letter, 18 May 1998.

18 Previously at http://www.defenselink.mil/other_info/burrows.html.

> were looking for a general oversight of the vaccination program."[19]

The DoD's claims of misinformation on the internet had a particularly hollow ring in light of its blatant lack of honesty and candor in having something as simple as an independent review conducted. Nothing was ever done about this lie that was foisted off on American service members. No one has ever been taken to task for this laughably blatant fraud perpetrated on U.S. military members and the broader American public.

Thus, in the end, the DoD's four-point plan to reassure the public and service members of the safety of the anthrax program—as a prerequisite to beginning inoculation—was nothing more than a PR campaign that ultimately cost the DoD credibility that it did not have to spare. As the truth came out, and was certainly made available on the internet and elsewhere, the DoD's cries of "misinformation" went unheeded. Service members on active duty and in the reserves began to refuse or leave the service rather than take the anthrax shot.

If the DoD's actions appear incredible, the FDA's inaction is equally baffling. The FDA is charged, under the Administrative Procedures Act, with the duty and authority to regulate, among many other things, the safety of drugs and biologic products. The FDA has had no hesitation in cracking down on manufacturers who do not comply with its regulations or decisions. The cases in the D.C. circuit are legion with the FDA disciplining manufacturers who try to market a drug for a purpose not clearly delineated on the approved labeling or who otherwise fail to comply with IND protocols. For some reason, however, in the case of the AVA, the FDA had an absolutely incestuous relationship with the DoD, a third party who was *not* even the manufacturer! Letters were exchanged between the two agencies regarding non-compliance with

---

[19] Id.

IND protocols after the IND protocol was not properly administered in Bosnia. At the 17 March 1998, hearing, the following colloquy took place on this issue between Senator Rockefeller and Dr. Wykoff, the FDA's associate director for operations:

> **ROCKEFELLER:** ... It's also not clear to me that FDA's shoes are entirely clear or clean on this matter. In fact, some would say lax. I think that FDA and DoD have been exchanging letters about all of this for some months now. And the fact is that seven years after the Gulf War, the situation is still not resolved. If DoD does not adequately answer FDA's questions with respect to these matters and others, what is FDA going to do about it? [...] And why, for example, was it necessary for the Presidential Advisory Commission to address the waived informed consent matter six years after the end of the war? So I put to you what FDA would recommend and would do if DoD does not come in compliance more?
>
> **WYKOFF:** ... We have tried very hard to make sure that they are absolutely clear what our rules and regulations are and what our expectations are. We believe that they understand that. We believe that they have the capability of complying with all of our IND rules and regulations. As to whether they will comply in the next deployment situation, obviously we can't predict that.
>
> **ROCKEFELLER:** And if they don't, is there anything that you can do about it?
>
> **WYKOFF:** Yes, sir. Obviously, there are a range of options that we have. We would have to determine what

the specific concerns are. That drives what our specific actions would be.

ROCKEFELLER: What are some of the options?

WYKOFF: Well, as we interact with any trial sponsor, we learn more about their ability to conduct IND trials, we would be more or less willing to grant waivers or exemptions to particular requirements. We could hold them to more—all of the requirements as outlined in the rules and regulations—based on their performance.[20]

It boggles the mind to think that the first words out of the FDA's mouth are talk of waivers for non-compliance with regulations, particularly in light of DoD's history in this area. There was, and is, a clearly documented squeamishness on the part of the FDA to step in and bring the DoD into compliance. In downright shocking testimony before a House Committee, Dr. Kathryn Zoon of CBER was questioned by Rep. Christopher Shays (R-CT) about the FDA's regulatory responsibility.

ZOON: This is a licensed vaccine. If a physician uses it or DoD uses it, that does not really fall under our jurisdiction.

SHAYS: So it's your statement before us now that if DoD doesn't abide by the protocol, you have no responsibility? That you have set out a requirement? Who

[20] Senate Hearing, Committee on Veterans Affairs Holds Hearing on the Nomination of Togo West as Secretary of Veterans Affairs and on U.S. Biologic Vaccines for Gulf War Veterans, 17 March 1998.

> is responsible then? Who's going to make sure that DoD abides by the protocol, if you don't do it?
>
> **ZOON:** We don't have the authority.
>
> **SHAYS:** I can't believe—I just want to say, Dr. Zoon, I cannot believe that you have just said under oath that you do not have the responsibility to deal with this issue or the authority. You said you don't have the authority.
>
> **ZOON:** I said—yes, that's correct.
>
> **SHAYS:** That is your testimony.
>
> **ZOON:** We don't have the authority.
>
> **SHAYS:** Well then who is going to protect our men and women if you aren't going to do it? Who? Who has the authority?

The tricky part of this testimony is that it is partly correct. The FDA does not regulate end-users of a product, normally. That is, they do not tell a doctor that he cannot use a drug off-label. However, if the end-user *is participating in a clinical protocol*, then the FDA *does regulate* that user. Thus, the DoD's participation in BioPort's IND application in order to get an indication against aerosolized anthrax should make them subject to FDA regulation, just as the DoD was during the Gulf War when applying for a Rule 23(d) waiver. FDA's willingness to accede to DoD's interpretation essentially allowed the DoD to slide. This is an open abdication of the FDA's regulatory role.

FDA officials have repeatedly acceded to DoD doctors' interpretations of the anthrax vaccine label, as well. This is an absurdity. It is particularly appalling in light of the DoD's involvement in the manufacturing process. The DoD fundamentally became a manufacturer, for all intents and purposes, and the FDA looked the other way, hiding behind the fiction that the DoD was an "end-user" when convenient. The DoD was involved from the very beginning in the development of the anthrax vaccine. Additionally, when problems arose with the manufacturer, the DoD sent in its own "inspection" teams to ensure the supply of the vaccine. The DoD had paramount liens on every piece of equipment that the manufacturer had. A GAO report in June 1999 found that

> DoD has made a significant investment in renovating BioPort's biologic facility to meet the military's requirements for anthrax vaccine [...] Since 1988, DoD has provided about $112 million in contracts, including options, to help ensure the viability of the anthrax vaccine biologic facility. As shown in figure 1, DoD's contracts provided monies to (1) produce the vaccine, (2) renovate and expand the production facility, (3) provide various support services, and (4) purchase equipment to enhance production capacity. DoD has also provided contract terms and conditions to help ensure the success of the anthrax vaccine program. For example, under Public Law 85-804, which allows for government indemnification of contractors for unusually hazardous risks, DoD indemnified BioPort against product liability. In addition, DoD agreed to allow the company to sell up to 200,000 doses of anthrax vaccine to others, using government-furnished equipment rent-free, after DoD's requirements are met.[21]

[21] GAO Report GAO T-NSIAD-99-214, 30 June 1999.

Amazingly, this is *chump change* compared to what the Defense Contract Auditing Agency found in 2000! That report led to an Inspector General Investigation.

Notwithstanding numerous audits that found that the company was not financially viable, BioPort requested contract amendments that included $1.28 million in bonuses for senior management that amounted to 109% of the managers' base salary. This was deemed an "unreasonable expenditure" by the DCAA in light of "BioPort's current financial condition."[22] Okay, so someone disapproved, right? Well, sort of, because the manufacturer had almost no real financial incentive to produce an FDA-approved vaccine under its contracts with DoD: The contract paid the manufacturer 90% of the contract price before the FDA inspected the vaccine. Yes, read that again.

Put another way, BioPort only gets paid 10% more for the product being approved by the FDA. At one point, the Department of Justice was looking into criminal charges, as some six to eight million dollars of the money provided to the manufacturer was unaccounted for. Additionally, the fact that the former Chairman of the Joint Chiefs of Staff was a co-owner of the facility, as well as Dr. Robert Myers (formerly of MDPH and MBPI) can hardly escape attention. While both have disavowed any "inside" preferential treatment from the DoD, one must wonder if the decision to award BioPort the contract had anything to do with either's presence as an owner. Finally, e-mails from inside the DoD suggest that the agency actually had its own people "on site." During hearings held by Representative Christopher Shays in May 1999, an e-mail was sent from Brigadier General Eddie Cain, the Director of the Joint Program Office for Biological Defense, to an Army Colonel John V. Wade. In the e-mail Cain warned that "[I]f you think Congressman Shays was critical of the current relationship between FDA & DoD, wait

---

[22] IG Report dated 22 March 2000.

until he finds out that DoD is calling the shots on-sight [sic]."[23] When this e-mail surfaced during the court-martial of Air Force Captain (and medical doctor) John Buck, the FDA had "no comment."

> The FDA has, for whatever reasons, backed down from the DoD to the point that after the warning letters, the NOIR letter, and a failed inspection thereafter, the agency still withheld pulling the manufacturer's license because the DoD interceded on behalf of the company. In a 25 June 2000, interview with the Vancouver newspaper *The Province*, Mark Elengold, the Deputy Director for CBER, explained what happened.
>
> The FDA held off pulling the licence [sic], in part because it would have left the U.S. Department of Defence [sic]—which had just announced that all soldiers were to receive anthrax vaccine—with no domestic source.
>
> "This is a one-source product so we tend to try to work with firms and put additional monitoring steps in to avoid revoking the licence," said Elengold. The prestigious British medical journal *Lancet* reported at the time that "a plea from the Pentagon has prevented an "eleventh-hour" closure of the only U.S. producer of anthrax vaccine," according to an e-mail to DND [DoD?] medical headquarters in February 1998.
>
> Elengold confirmed the Pentagon sat in on a crucial call to the company in which he discussed revoking the licence.[24]

---

[23] Eberhart, Dave. *Stars and Stripes*. May 2001.

[24] Rees, Ann. "Their Dangerous Dose," *Vancouver Province*. 25 June 2000.

Electronic mails that surfaced in and around 2000 show not only did the DoD convince the FDA not to revoke the license, but DoD also attempted to bully both the manufacturer and the GAO at the same time. In one e-mail, a Pentagon official discusses how other agency supervisors were urging the U.S. FDA and the manufacturer of the vaccine to release lots that had been held up for scrutiny by them (the FDA). Again, this is *despite* Secretary Cohen's public insistence on supplemental testing to ensure safety of the vaccine.

On 22 February 1999, Dr. Michael Gilbreath, a civilian Pentagon biological defense employee sent an e-mail to U.S. Army Brig. Gen. Eddie Cain, then Director of the Joint Program Office of Biological Defense (JPOBD). Gilbreath wrote that he had "received information this morning from BioPort that individuals within the DoD contacted them and threatened that DoD would circumvent BioPort and contact the FDA regarding availability of anthrax vaccine lots currently under review at the FDA [...] Any such actions by DoD would be inappropriate."[25]

E-mails also reveal that the Pentagon was having trouble countering the U.S. General Accounting Office's assertion that the vaccine is improperly licensed, and that it has not been proven safe and effective. Cain indicated in one e-mail that then Secretary of Defense William Cohen would be writing to the GAO, whose findings have consistently gone against the Pentagon, to protest "the expertise put on this [vaccine] project" by the watchdog agency.

"If we cannot answer these questions," Cain said in a 3 May e-mail, "we [DoD and the Administration] are in big time trouble. [...] We are digging ourselves a hole that will be too difficult to crawl out of."[26]

---

[25] Williams, Thomas D. "E-mails Suggest Pentagon Pressured FDA On Anthrax Vaccine." *Hartford Courant*, 17 May 2001.

[26] Id.

The FDA also stood by when adulterated vaccine was shipped to the Canadian military and when 59 Marines were given shots from expired lots of the vaccine.[27] The FDA's complicity with the DoD's actions has left service members with no recourse but to either take the shot, be court-martialed for refusing, or leave the service somehow if their commitment allows it. If the service member simply will not take the chance on the vaccine's safety, the penalty for refusing is court-martial with a certain conviction. Military judges simply would not hear that the vaccine is investigational, nor would they even allow service members to present that information to a jury. The FDA's refusal to act leaves the judge with an out: If the FDA thought it was investigational, why wouldn't they just issue an opinion to that effect? Worse yet, some military judges would not wade through the necessary materials in order to understand the FDA regulatory process and what an IND is, or they would find that the Secretary of Defense's actions were, in legal parlance, "non-justiciable" disputes between "co-equal branches of government."

The service member who fights will be convicted and punished. When an Air Force doctor, John Buck, tried to submit evidence that the specific lot that he was to have received, FAV044, was subject to a recall because it was expired, the judge did not allow the evidence to come into court. The only option left for service members was to resign quietly, leave at the end of a service obligation, or fight behind the scenes to ensure that the law is followed. That is what a group of persistent officers had been doing from the word go.

---

[27] Rees, Ann. "Their Dangerous Dose," *Vancouver Province.* 25 June 2000. Also see GAO report T-NSIAD-00-36.

CHAPTER 15
THE STAY

"Well, if they're going to issue the stay at all, now would be a good time!" I'm on the phone to appellate defense in Washington, D.C. I look at my watch. The digital face reads 00:31—10:30 in the morning east coast time. "I mean, if no stay today, by tomorrow night my guy is eating with the big metal spoon, if you know what I mean." I listen. "All right, bye." I hang up. I'm looking at documents, but I'm not really seeing anything—Ponder's record book, letter from his wife, character statements, and I'm trying to imagine how I'm going to defend him tomorrow. I've got one last motion that I'll bring at the close of the government's case, one last grasp that has a sound basis in law, but at this point, it's one the judge will undoubtedly deny. This is a technicality.

From the beginning, I had the sense that they have mischarged the offense, perhaps intentionally. The prosecution has charged it as willful disobedience of a superior commissioned officer. Under the UCMJ, that has a stiffer penalty than the more general charge of violating a lawful general order, such as the order from the Secretary of Defense, to take the anthrax shot. The government has charged it as violating the specific Navy Lieutenant's order, but there is an old case that stands for the proposition that merely repeating a higher order cannot make an orders violation the more egregious willful disobedience of a superior commissioned officer. It is called the "ultimate offense doctrine," but it probably isn't going to work. Nothing else has.

I'm tired. I haven't slept much, I need a shave, and my back is killing me from my tiny desk chair at home and my broken desk chair at work. I need to get Ponder sentencing case together, review my opening statement and closing argument, and make sure all of the documents are in my case file, with necessary copies for each of the jurors …

My head nods and I realize I've drifted off at my desk. I look at my watch and see it's 2:33 a.m. I rub my face and decide to take a walk.

The building is dark and empty except for me and the feisty Okinawan cockroaches. I stroll the dark corridors, my sneakers making a light tread on the tile. I stretch my arms over my head as I walk to the entrance. Out the window, the open field beside our building is dark. I can barely see the slope that I know rises up to a road that runs next to the next set of office buildings and the barracks.

I hear the phone in the clerk's office ring, but there's nothing particularly unusual about that at this hour because of the time difference; people frequently fax documents from the States during our nighttime in Okinawa. The fax ticks away, a counterpoint to the flying bugs banging into the glass on the door and the light just outside of it. Tick-tick-tick. In seven hours, Ponder is going to be facing a jury, and likely going to jail. Unless that fax …

I walk hurriedly to the defense clerk's office and go to the fax machine behind it. Letter-sized sheets are spitting out, face down. I grab one and flip it over to see if it has anything to do with me. The cover sheet is from the Washington Navy Yard. I grab the whole stack while more keep sliding out.

My eyes flick over the words.

"YEAHHHHHHHHHHH!!!!!" I let out a guttural yell that echoes throughout the empty building. "Can you feel that, huh?! Baby, can ya?!" It's my best Ace Ventura, hips thrusting, fist pumping. I want to cry with relief. We beat the clock by seven hours. I've kept my promise to Ponder and his wife, to Stonewall, and Arroyo. We have a stay from the Navy Marine Corps Court of Criminal Appeals. No one's going to jail tomorrow.

I take my time packing up and make a few copies of the stay. Before I leave, somewhere near 3:00 a.m., I take a ten-penny nail and hammer the stay to the prosecution's office door. I don't do it right through the middle, however, because I'm still a Marine officer and someone might bitch to the CO about a nail in the door. I only hammer the nail just deeply enough to look like someone was careless. I also place the nail an inch or two above the center of the sheet, close enough to the top that it doesn't look like it was intentionally in the middle, but far enough down that someone will have to either rip the paper in half to get it off or pry out the nail. It's an asshole move, to be certain, but I know it might be all the satisfaction I'm going to get in the long run, so I indulge myself. It's the little "fuck you"s that matter in life. It won't be the last laugh, but it's enough to make me smile as I walk to my car for the drive back to Kadena Air Base officer housing and my wife and four daughters.

CHAPTER 16
GUARD PILOTS QUIT

While many factors can influence an individual's decision to leave the military, surveyed Guard and Reserve pilots and aircrew members cited the anthrax immunization as a key reason for leaving or otherwise changing their military status. Since September 1998, an estimated 25 percent of the pilots and aircrew members of the Guard and Reserve in this population transferred to another unit (primarily in a non-flying position), left the military, or moved to inactive status. While several reasons influenced their decision, when asked to rank the one most important factor, the anthrax immunization was the highest, followed by other employment opportunities, and family reasons. Further, about one in five (18 percent) left before qualifying for military retirement benefits. Additionally, 18 percent of those still participating in or assigned to a unit reported their intentions to leave within the next 6 months. These individuals also ranked the anthrax immunization as the most important factor for their decision to leave, followed by unit workload and family reasons. Each of these groups—those who have left and those who plan to do so—had accumulated an average of more than 3,000 flight

> hours, which symbolizes a seasoned and experienced workforce.[1]

The impact of the anthrax program on the Armed Services was substantial. DoD representatives continued to assert that the impact was negligible and that the refusals and courts-martial were only a misinformed minority. This is because the Armed Forces have to answer to Congress for recruiting goals and retention and how money is being spent. Even if the DoD doesn't have to answer to service members, it does have to answer to Congress for end-strength and staffing. If the anthrax vaccine program was a significant cause of members leaving the service, Congress could quash the program on those grounds alone. Thus, when asking the DoD about the AVIP's effect on retention and recruiting, the answer was always "minimal."[2] Both anecdotal and empirical evidence, however, show exactly the opposite. Service members left both active duty and reserve forces because of the anthrax vaccine program. Those who had no other alternative were refusing the vaccine outright and suffering the consequences.

Unfortunately, the DoD did not want to know how bad the statistics were and as of October 2000, they still were not tracking refusal numbers or reasons people left the service. When the GAO recommended that exit surveys include a question about whether or not the anthrax vaccine was a factor in their decision to leave, the DoD objected to the question as being "leading" and that it would result in survey bias.[3] In the study conducted on National Guard and Reserve aircrew, the GAO found significant numbers of people who cited the anthrax vaccine as the number one reason for either transferring to a new unit or for leaving the

---

1 GAO 01-92T p. 6.

2 Statement of MajGen Paul Weaver, USAFR (see background brief).

3 GAO T-NSIAD-00-36 p. 37.

Guard or Reserve.[4]As the GAO noted, "[t]hese components [Reserve and Guard forces] provide essential support to critical defense operations on a worldwide basis. They provide strategic and tactical airlift, aerial refueling, aeromedical evacuation, and augment DoD's overall fighter force."[5]Not noted in these reports, but important to understand, is that most Reserve and Guard aircrew are made up of former active duty service members. While it is not definitive, neither is it a stretch to opine that the views of this particular segment of Guard and Reserve society is closely reflective of the views of their brethren on active duty. The survey, conducted from May to September 2000, reveals two disturbing trends:

First, pilots and aircrew left or transferred in significant numbers because of the anthrax vaccine to the tune of one out of every four. Of the remaining members, another 18% (about one out of five) indicated that they were leaving within the next 6 months and they listed the anthrax vaccine as the number one reason. This means that if a unit started with some baseline number of aircrew, it initially lost 25% citing the AVIP as the number one reason. Therefore, the unit is (setting aside new acquisitions for the moment) at 75% of its prior strength. At the same time, 20% of the remainder will leave within six months. That cuts the unit down to 65% of original strength. The most disturbing aspect of this trend is that new acquisitions will not return the unit to its former functioning. The members leaving had an average experience level of 3,000 flight hours, a fairly significant experience level new acquisitions would not have.[6]

---

4 GAO 01-92T.

5 Id., p. 1.

6 In the Marine Corps, for example, someone with 3,000 flight hours would most likely be a Major returning to a squadron for a second tour or already into a second tour.

Second, adverse reactions were being massively underreported. The GAO survey of 1,253 Guard and Reserve aircrew found that of the 42% who had received one or more shots,

> 86 percent reported experiencing side effects or adverse reactions. About 60 percent indicated that they had not discussed any side effect to the anthrax vaccine with military health care personnel or their supervisors—some (49 percent) citing as their reasons fear of losing their flight status, adverse effects on their military or civilian careers, and ridicule. Seventy-one percent reported that they were unaware of the Food and Drug Administration's Vaccine Adverse Events Reporting System. Slightly less than 6 percent of those who had a reaction reported to this system.[7] Here is proof that the VAERS system, upon which the DoD bases its 0.007% adverse reaction rate, is only being reported by 6% of those having adverse reactions. Perhaps it would be better to say that adverse reaction reports are being underreported by a factor of just under 20 (approximately 17). These numbers, as well as the anecdotal evidence, seem to correspond more closely to the AVA package insert's serious adverse reaction rate of 0.2%.

One related outcome of the study points to the most serious flaw and consequence of the AVIP: the loss of trust in military leadership. There is perhaps nothing more tenuous, and yet necessary and essential, to a military organization than the trust that flows from those being led to their leaders. Unfortunately, in an effort to quash dissent, senior military leaders adopted a leadership style that was characteristic of the Soviet

---

[7] GAO 01-92T p .5-6.

bloc armed forces we stood against for some 50 years—leadership by fear and threat of punishment. In the long run it did not work for those countries and our country is even more ill-suited for that style because of the free-flow of information within the United States. Quite simply, whenever a senior officer makes some factual assertion or claim about the AVA, or the anthrax program, or the manufacturer, or the threat of anthrax, it is a short trip to the library, internet, or other source of information for a soldier to check the veracity of that statement.

The results of the GAO survey showed that while "[m]ost Guard and Reserve pilots and aircrew members support immunization programs in general [...] relatively few appear to support the anthrax program or future immunization programs for other biological warfare agents."[8] If the correlation between Reservists and active duty members is valid, service members appeared to recognize what the DoD was not willing to discuss publicly: Using vaccines against diseases like the public at large is entirely acceptable, but using vaccines as pretreatments for chemical-biological warfare is a different matter entirely and people are understandably hesitant to allow their bodies to become the future battleground, particularly with the DoD calling the shots. The hard data validates this conclusion.

> Almost three out of four (74 percent) of the pilots and aircrew members of the Guard and Reserve believe that immunizations in general are moderately to very effective, and 60 percent believe that immunizations are moderately to very safe. On the other hand, 65 percent, or two out of three service members, reported little or no support for the anthrax immunization.[9]

---

[8] GAO 0192T p. 4.

[9] Id., p. 4.

This statistic is interesting also because it shows that the DoD's extensive education campaign was entirely ineffective. The reason for this is, unfortunately, because as more facts were uncovered, it became increasingly clear that the program evolved from telling less than the whole truth to "spin" to (in many cases) outright fabrication. There is nothing more damaging to the trust from subordinates to seniors than for subordinates to believe that their senior leaders have lied and are continuing to lie to them. In fact, several Reserve officers filed a complaint against two senior military officers involved in the anthrax program from the very beginning.

One of the charges in the Inspector General (IG) complaint alleges that Colonel Arthur Friedlander, an Army doctor, lied under oath at a Canadian court-martial. A Canadian soldier was being court-martialed for refusing to take the anthrax vaccine, the same one produced by BioPort. The prosecution in that case called Dr. Friedlander as one of its witnesses. On cross-examination, Dr. Friedlander was questioned regarding his knowledge of the 1996 IND license amendment submitted by MDPH, along with the DoD.

> **Q:** If I'm going to suggest to you, sir, that the drug was licensed for cutaneous anthrax only and that there has been a subsequent amendment for coverage for inhalation anthrax, would you agree with me or disagree with me?
>
> **COL FRIEDLANDER:** *I'm not aware of that …*
>
> [Later]
>
> **Q:** In particular, the fifth paragraph, it says that the office, and this is referring to the Joint Program Office for Biological Defense, quote: "managed and funded efforts

leading to the submission of a Biologic Licensure Application amendment to the FDA," including data to support its proposal "to license the vaccine to provide protection against aerosol exposure to anthrax." Is that something you're familiar with, sir, or would you disagree with that statement?

A: *I'm not sure the details of this.* I do know that there were questions that were raised, since there are no direct studies in humans with this vaccine, and that a statement was made by the FDA that the use of the vaccine in the Gulf War against the threat of aerosol use of spores was not inconsistent with the product license [...].

Q: If I was to suggest to you, sir, that we've heard evidence that the vaccine was licensed for cutaneous anthrax and that there was an application placing the drug into IND status with the FDA for three reasons: one, is to change for inhalational anthrax; two, was to change the route of administration; and, three, to change the scheduling of the drugs, would you agree with that or do you know?

A: I know that there have been studies dealing with trying to reduce the number of doses and to look at the route of administration.

Q: So are you saying, sir, that you're not familiar with what I've said, or you disagree with it?

A: *No, no. I don't know that—I'd have to look back at the documents that you're referring to.*

> **Q:** Okay. So you're not saying the drug is not in an IND status for those three variations?
>
> **A:** *You know, I'm not clear what you're saying in terms of—I mean, I'm not quite clear what that means, in other words. There are studies that have been done, that I'm involved with, looking at reducing the number of doses and changing the route of administration.*[10]

Here, Colonel Friedlander repeatedly denies having knowledge about the license amendment for the anthrax vaccine or the vaccine's investigational status. This is impossible because Colonel Friedlander was personally involved on three occasions in DoD meetings, during which *he specifically briefed* the three reasons for the IND application, including an FDA license amendment to add an indication for inhalation anthrax. For example, at the 20 October 1995, meeting of the JPOBD Colonel Friedlander presented a briefing "covering three topics: (1) evidence for a reduction in the number of doses of anthrax vaccine, (2) evidence for vaccine efficacy against an aerosol challenge, and (3) progress towards an in vitro correlate of immunity."[11] At this same meeting, Dr. Friedlander acknowledged that "there was insufficient data to demonstrate protection against inhalation disease."[12]

At another meeting on 9 February 1996, which was a follow-up to the October meeting, Colonel Friedlander presented another briefing titled "Research Plan to Support Reduction in Dosage of Licensed Anthrax

---

[10] Canadian court-martial trial transcript, Judge G.L. Brais, 30 March 2000, Office of the Chief Military Judge, Canadian Forces.

[11] David Danley, LTC. "Minutes of the Meeting on Changing the Food and Drug Administration License for the Michigan Department of Public Health (MDPH) Anthrax Vaccine to Meet Military Requirements," held on 20 October 1995 meeting; Joint Program Office for Biological Defense memorandum, 13 November 1995.vvvv

[12] Id.

Vaccine (AVA) and Indication for Aerosol Exposure."[13] The meeting minutes reveal that Friedlander discussed the need for the study to show a correlation between animal and human immune response to the vaccine—a recognition that the anthrax vaccine had never demonstrated efficacy for inhalation anthrax in humans.[14] This shows an intimate knowledge on Colonel Friedlander's part about the FDA's requirements for human studies to prove efficacy of the vaccine.

Finally, on 10 November 1997, Colonel Friedlander presented another briefing to DoD and contractor representatives entitled "Supplement to AVA License." This was 14 months after the submission of the IND application by the manufacturer, which was submitted in September 1996. The briefing slides clearly show the three changes sought (including an indication for inhalation anthrax) and that Colonel Friedlander was responsible for the pre-clinical portions of these studies intended to obtain FDA approval for these changes.[15] There are only two possible conclusions to be reached when re-reading Colonel Friedlander's denials at the Canadian court, and neither is particularly favorable. In the best light, he completely forgot everything he knew about the anthrax program and his participation in it. In the worst light, he intentionally lied under oath. In either case, these types of inconsistent statements by senior military officers involved with the program break down the trust between service members and their leaders. This is not the only instance of this happening.

There was a separate complaint filed by 74 Guard and Reserve officers surrounding statements made by Major General Paul Weaver

---

[13] David Danley, LTC. "Minutes of the Meeting on Changing the Food and Drug Administration License for the Michigan Department of Public Health (MDPH) Anthrax Vaccine to Meet Military Requirements," held on 20 October 1995 meeting; Joint Program Office for Biological Defense memorandum, 13 November 1995.

[14] Id.

[15] David Danley, LTC. "Minutes of the Meeting on Changing the Food and Drug Administration License for the Michigan Department of Public Health (MDPH) Anthrax Vaccine to Meet Military Requirements," held on 20 October 1995 meeting; Joint Program Office for Biological Defense memorandum, 13 November 1995.

before Congress. The complaint cited testimony before the House Government Reform Committee's Subcommittee on National Security, Veterans Affairs and International Relations. At a 29 September 1999, hearing in front of the House, Weaver stated:

> "So, when I hear all of these other figures about these mass resignations [due to members refusing the anthrax vaccine], and what not, they're just not there. There are challenges with explaining, with discussing, as they all are, with the members of their unit, on the anthrax issue. But when it really gets down to it, we've had 10,700 people inoculated for anthrax in the Air National Guard, with one known refusal."[16]

The problem with this testimony is that months before his statement to that Committee, Weaver had been made aware of the resignations of pilots from both the Connecticut Air National Guard and Wisconsin Air National Guard. In the case of the Connecticut pilots, a memo was forwarded to Weaver about the Connecticut resignations. Additionally, both the Wisconsin and Connecticut resignations received widespread media coverage, including the Connecticut resignations being referenced by former Pentagon spokesperson Kenneth Bacon on 21 January 1999. While ultimately the DoD IG did not punish Major General Weaver, it did find that his statement "lacked the necessary element of 'straightforwardness,' and so was inconsistent with guidelines for honesty as set forth by the Joint Ethics Regulations (JER)."[17] Major General Weaver later qualified what he meant by a refusal, which he defined as a person who had a commitment to the Air National Guard and could thus

---

[16] House Government Reform Committee's Subcommittee on National Security, Veterans' Affairs and International Relations. 29 September 1999.

[17] Eberhart, Dave. *Stars and Stripes*. 11 May 2001, quoting from March IG Report.

be subject to disciplinary action, as opposed to someone who could simply resign because their status allowed them to. There were some e-mails by staff members prior to the General's testimony that confirm that this definition was being contemplated, but it is clear no such qualifiers were made in the broad statement made to Congress—only one "refusal", period.

The sum total of these kinds of parsings, misrepresentations, or lies, is a disintegration in the trust between those being led and those who are supposed to be doing the leading. When 74 officers are filing a complaint because of a General officer's misstatements before Congress, there is a serious problem. The DoD's refusal to acknowledge in sworn testimony before Congress that such a problem even exists, rather than making it go away, only exacerbates the problem and further erodes trust in senior leaders. The final example of this is the most disturbing because at best, it illustrates a severe disconnect between senior military leaders and those they lead and have led (i.e., veterans) and at worst, it is a case of an intentional cover-up of experimentation on service members.

In testimony to the Senate Armed Services Committee on 13 April 2000, then-Army Surgeon General Lieutenant General Ronald Blanck misrepresented the purpose of the Investigational New Drug application prepared by the Army for the manufacturer. The Senator who queried LTG Blanck was unfamiliar with the Food, Drug, and Cosmetic Act and accepted LTG Blanck's testimony without question. This question goes directly to the heart of the legal status of the vaccine and the General either lied or was grossly misinformed. It is difficult to believe that the United States Army Surgeon General was not "in the know" about the DoD's plan to amend MBPI (and then BioPort's) license.

> **SEN. ROBERTS:** General Blanck, the annual Congressionally mandated chemical and biological defense program report to Congress submitted on March 15, 2000, states: "The Department submitted data to the

> FDA last year to license the vaccine to provide protection against aerosol exposure to anthrax." My question is why is the Department seeking a license for the vaccine when the license for the anthrax vaccine has existed since 1970?
>
> **GEN. BLANCK:** It is really for the facility, not for the vaccine per se.
>
> **SEN. ROBERTS:** Oh, I see, okay. All right. That clears that up.

There is a big difference between seeking a license change for a new facility and getting a new indication for the vaccine itself. In light of e-mails later discovered regarding DoD's people "on site" and the supplemental testing conducted by the DoD, even in a light most favorable to the General, if he wasn't lying, then he was either completely misinformed by his subordinates about what was going on (which isn't reassuring in any way) or he completely misunderstood the FDA regulatory process, which doesn't speak well for his knowledge as the Surgeon General. Furthermore, in 1994, General Blanck, when he was the Commanding General of Walter Reed Army Medical Center, briefed a Congressional committee that

> Therefore, its [AVA's] safety, particularly when given to thousands of soldiers in conjunction with other vaccines, is not well established. *Anthrax vaccine should continue to be considered as a potential cause for undiagnosed illnesses in Persian Gulf military personnel because many of the support troops received anthrax vaccine, and because the DoD believes that the incidence of*

> *undiagnosed illnesses in support troops may be higher than that in combat troops.*[18]

Just a few years prior, General Blanck asserts that the DoD believes that the AVA should be considered a cause of Gulf War Illness. Yet after his promotion to Surgeon General of the Army and the launch of the AVIP, he tried to disavow these statements. It would be understandable if General Blanck's change in position were due to some scientific evidence that proves that the AVA is not a potential cause of Gulf War Illness. Unfortunately, the evidence continued to mount that the AVA was a possible source of Gulf War Illness. The DoD consistently opposed any study that showed a link between vaccines or other medicines that were given to soldiers and Gulf War Illness. The evidence supporting this would eventually become conclusive and the VA would acknowledge pyridostigmine bromide pills as causal of Gulf War Illness for VA benefit purposes.

The problem with the dissembling and misstatements by senior military leaders isn't just the loss of trust from the junior service members. When all of the dissembling continually concerns the anthrax vaccine, it only serves to make people more suspicious of the program. The DoD repeatedly complained that it was "internet misinformation" undermining the program, but the real culprit was the DoD's own misinformation that served to erode all faith in this program. This pattern of deception was most evident when the issue of the anthrax vaccine and Gulf War Illness came up. The DoD showed just how far it would go to protect the AVA.

---

[18] Senate Report 103-97, note 143.

CHAPTER 17
SCIENCE INTERVENES & PROJECT BADGER

A study was conducted on 8,195 British Gulf Wcar-era veterans. The British, serving alongside American forces, gave their servicemen untested vaccines as well. There were two important findings from the study:

- The Gulf War cohort reported symptoms and disorders significantly more frequently than those in the Bosnia Era cohorts, which were similar [...] Gulf War veterans were more likely than the Bosnia cohort to have substantial fatigue, symptoms of post-traumatic stress, and psychological distress, and were twice as likely to reach the CDC case definition [of Gulf War Illness]. [...] Vaccination against biological warfare and multiple routine vaccinations were associated with all outcomes.[1]

- Service in the Gulf War was associated with various health problems over and above those associated with deployment to an unfamiliar hostile environment.

[1] Unwin, Catherine, et.al., "Health of UK servicemen who served in Persian Gulf War," *The Lancet*, 16 January 1999, p. 169.

> Since associations of ill health with adverse events and exposures were found in all cohorts, however, they may not be unique and causally implicated in the Gulf War-related illness. A specific mechanism may link vaccination against biological warfare agents and later ill health, but the risks of illness must be considered against the protection of servicemen.[2]

The state of Kansas Commission of Veterans Affairs funded a study of 2,030 Kansas Gulf War-era veterans. Despite over $150 million spent on Gulf War Illness research, DoD has never conducted a comparable study on US service members. The Kansas study concluded:

Gulf War Illness [...] occurred in 34% of Persian Gulf War (PGW) veterans, 12% of non-PGW veterans who reported receiving vaccines during the war, and 4% of non-PGW veterans who did not receive vaccines [...] Among PGW veterans who served away from battlefield areas, Gulf War illness was least prevalent among those who departed the region prior to the war (9%) and most prevalent among those who departed in June or July of 1991 (41%). Observed patterns suggest that excess morbidity among Gulf War veterans is associated with characteristics of their wartime service, and that vaccines used during the war may be a contributing factor.[3]

Britain and Canada also conducted studies and found a possible link to vaccines given to their veterans. One of the most interesting studies is one by France that found no Gulf War Illness at all among its veterans. In September 2000, France's Defense Minister Alain Richard created an independent commission to look into the health of the French military

---

[2] Id.

[3] Steele, Lea. "Prevalence and Patterns of Gulf War Illness in Kansas Veterans: Association of Symptoms with Characteristics of Person, Place, and Time of Military Service." *American Journal of Epidemiology*, Vol. 152, No. 10. 15 November 2000. p. 992-1002. https://academic.oup.com/aje/article/152/10/992/55709, last accessed 14 July 2020.

service members who participated in the Gulf War.[4] Interestingly, a French medical corps spokesman, said that

> "France's belief that allied troops were victims of their own protective measures were based on a long series of meetings with U.S. medical experts [...] 'About 100,000 of the 600,000 Americans who served in the Gulf complain of ailments that have tentatively been lumped under the Gulf War syndrome heading. No one has yet come to definitive conclusions but we note that of 25,000 Frenchmen who served in the Gulf, only 180 have ailments whose origin could be in question. The only really major difference between the two groups is vaccinations,' he said."[5]

These studies received little to no attention in the U.S., and in some cases, were immediately disclaimed by the DoD. There was also a considerable amount of anecdotal evidence regarding adverse reactions to the anthrax vaccine. Perhaps the DoD was right in one respect: The advent of e-mail allows large numbers of people to communicate around the world quickly. It is an ideal tool for service members, who are deployed the world over, to communicate with friends quickly regardless of time zones or presence at the receiving end. I personally received dozens of e-mails from different people detailing adverse health effects from the anthrax vaccine. One e-mail contained a list of at least a hundred names with phone numbers and/or addresses, as well as the particular adverse effect.

---

[4] Weber, Wim. "France Investigates Gulf War Syndrome." *The Lancet.* 18 November 2000, p. 1747. https://www.thelancet.com/journals/lancet/article/PIIS0140-6736(05)71948-6/fulltext, last accessed 14 July 2020.

[5] Nicolson, Garth L., et al. "French to Check Liaison Officers for Gulf Syndrome." *Journal of Chronic Fatigue Syndrome.* 2003; 11(1): 135-154. https://www.tandfonline.com/doi/abs/10.1300/J092v11n01_04, last accessed 14 July 2020.

Finally, the most compelling study conducted on Gulf War Illness, and perhaps revealing the worst about the DoD, is a study conducted at Tulane University and the controversy it started. Originally, a 1999 *Vanity Fair* article stated that DoD had used an experimental anthrax vaccine on troops going to the Gulf War. This article explained that the vaccine was experimental because it contained a substance known as squalene. Squalene is an experimental adjuvant, which is a substance added to a vaccine in order to increase the body's immune response to the vaccine itself. Squalene is produced naturally by the body in very minute quantities but it is not licensed by the FDA for injection into human beings. Squalene not only boosts the immune system's response, it also decreases the time necessary for the body to develop immunity to the vaccine. The *Vanity Fair* article posited that there was squalene in the anthrax vaccine given to service members during the Gulf War.

> Questions about vaccine adjuvant formulations were raised to DoD in June 1994. At that time, an immunologist from the private sector notified the Defense Science Board that some symptoms being reported by Gulf War-era veterans were very similar to those of her patients with autoimmune diseases. These patients had a range of symptoms affecting more than one of the body systems and the immunologist believed they were associated with exposure to vaccine adjuvant formulations. In October 1995, DoD, before a meeting of the Presidential Advisory Commission on Gulf War illnesses, dismissed this hypothesis on the grounds that it had administered only vaccines with aluminum salts as adjuvants. In November 1996 and again in 1997, the immunologist notified DoD, based on independent research, that she had found antibodies to squalene in the blood of a few sick veterans who had served in the military during the Gulf War. However, DoD has not responded to

> these findings. According to the researcher, she continues to be willing to discuss the research with DoD.[6]

The Tulane scientists had developed a test, called an assay, for detecting the presence of squalene antibodies in the bloodstream. Some Gulf War veterans who were found to have squalene antibodies in their blood early on approached Congressman Jack Metcalf (R-WA). In 1997, Representative Metcalf asked the GAO to conduct an inquiry into the possibility that squalene was in vaccines given to service members. This study by the GAO took three years to complete and the timing of its release in March 1999 could not have been worse for the DoD. The report found a "pattern of deception" by the DoD with regards to the use of squalene adjuvants.[7]

At an initial meeting with DoD officials, GAO notes show that the DoD claimed that they "had not performed or sponsored any research on synthetic or natural squalene or squalene until after the Gulf War."[8] The GAO investigators, however, found articles and databases that indicated there had been squalene studies before the Gulf War. The investigators confronted DoD officials with some of these public records and some of the DoD officials began to admit that they had conducted five human trials involving squalene and that a sixth was planned. Furthermore, the GAO investigators found that the DoD "had conducted numerous animal studies, particularly to develop a modern vaccine for anthrax. In fact, in most cases they only admitted to conducting research after we had discovered it in public records. On three occasions, people attending a meeting did not report their own research on squalene adjuvants."[9]

---

6 GAO Report 99-5, March 1999, p. 2.

7 Background working documents, GAO Report 99-5, DI-23.

8 Background working documents, GAO Report 99-5, DI-2.

9 Background working documents, GAO Report 99-5, DI-23.

The GAO investigators also met with various officials, including the DoD's Director of AIDS research during the Gulf War, members of the FDA, who all pointed to Colonel (Dr.) Carl Alving as the person who "was most interested in developing own adjuvants at WRAIR [Walter Reed Army Institute of Research]."[10] During meetings with DoD officials, Dr. Alving was never present nor mentioned, despite NIH and FDA officials calling him the top DoD researcher on vaccine issues. When finally interviewed by GAO investigators, Dr. Alving initially denied any participation in vaccine adjuvants. When pressed, he recalled that he had been called by someone at United States Army Medical Research Institute of Infectious Diseases "who asked if he could develop a new, more potent anthrax vaccine on a crash basis to use in Operation Desert Shield. He worked on it and thought he could do it, but no one ever called him back. He wouldn't say who called … or why he just didn't return the call."[11]

Interviews with Dr. Anna Johnson-Winegar revealed a Tri-Service Task Force operation called Project Badger. Winegar mentioned that Dr. Alving was the DoD's in-house adjuvant expert. She also mentioned that "[s]ome in the group were willing to jump out and use everything. (She refused to say who.)"[12]

The GAO then interviewed General Blanck, Army Surgeon General, who disclosed that the DoD had very little botulism toxoid vaccine and so "we contracted with Porton to make them." Porton refers to Porton Down, a British vaccine manufacturer. According to General Blanck, "we got it, but didn't use it."[13] General Blanck also pointed the GAO investigators to a Peter Collis, who headed oversight for Project Badger and vaccine efforts. Peter Collis refused to talk to the GAO. First, he cited the classified nature

---

[10] Background working documents, GAO Report 99-5, DI-23.

[11] Background working documents, GAO Report 99-5, DI-23.v

[12] Background working documents, GAO Report 99-5, DI-9.

[13] Background working documents, GAO Report 99-5, DI-8.

of the research, which was a non-issue for the GAO. He then said he couldn't look at some matters as a civilian without a clearance (GAO offered to get him a temporary clearance). Mr. Collis then called to say he didn't know much, even though notes from Badger showed him at the center of all Badger discussions and running the briefings.[14]

By September 1998, the GAO investigators were discussing the Tulane study's assay for determining the presence of squalene antibodies. DoD officials acknowledged that they could develop their own assay inexpensively and test Gulf War veterans, which would either refute or corroborate the Tulane results. They refused to do so, even after urging by the GAO. The DoD, in an effort to try to put the issue to rest, contracted to have lots of the anthrax vaccine tested by Stanford Research Institute International. The tests did not find any squalene in the AVA. This gave the DoD what appeared to be unimpeachable proof that no squalene-laced vaccine was given to Gulf War veterans. The Tulane study was still very compelling, however, because of the extremely high percentage of Gulf War veterans with Gulf War Syndrome who had squalene antibodies in their system, including those who didn't deploy to the Gulf but received vaccines. These persons all suffered some form of autoimmune disorder. This is also in keeping with laboratory studies on animals given squalene formulations. These animals had an increased incidence of autoimmune disorders.

After the GAO report's release in March 1999, the DoD began a concerted effort to discredit both the report and the Tulane research. The GAO encouraged the DoD to participate in the Tulane study by testing Gulf War veterans in its own studies using the Tulane assay or developing its own to validate the Tulane assay. The DoD's response was that even though "they [DoD] could develop an assay … for detecting antibodies to squalene … [and] it would not be expensive to develop [and] … test it on a sample of Gulf War-era veterans that are sick" they

[14] Background working documents, GAO Report 99-5, DI-23.

refused to do so.[15] The DoD medical people recited a litany of reasons why they would not and should not participate in such research.

> They [DoD scientists] believed that since DoD did not use adjuvants with squalene, DoD does not need to develop such an assay or to screen the veterans for the antibodies. Second, squalene is a substance that occurs naturally in the human body, and they doubted that an assay could be developed to differentiate antibodies to natural and manufactured squalene. Third, they noted that squalene is also found in numerous topical creams that some soldiers could have used. Finally, DoD officials do not believe that funding squalene antibodies in veterans would prove that the antibodies caused Gulf War illnesses.[16]

Here is promising scientific research that shows a strong link between Gulf War Syndrome and a potential cause, yet rather than at least encourage or aid the research, which one would think DoD would do if it were truly concerned about finding a cause and perhaps treatment for Gulf War veterans' illnesses, DoD responded by circling the wagons and denying that such a link could exist and then offered that "topical creams" used by soldiers could be the source of the squalene. The DoD responded to the report by asking that it be definitively entitled "GULF WAR ILLNESSES: Gulf War Veterans Did Not Receive Vaccine Adjuvant Formulations Containing Squalene."[17] Additionally, the DoD asserted that "in view of the GAO's conclusion that Gulf War-era veterans did not receive vaccine adjuvant formulations containing squalene, the GAO proposal to test Gulf War veterans for the presence

---

[15] Background working documents, GAO Report 99-5, p. 8.

[16] Id.

[17] Background working documents, GAO Report 99-5, p. 22.

of squalene antibodies seems scientifically and fiscally irresponsible."[18] The GAO responded in its report:

> DoD misstated our finding on whether Gulf War-era veterans may have received vaccine adjuvant formulations containing squalene. We did not conclude that Gulf War-era veterans were not given adjuvant formulations containing squalene. Rather, we cannot say definitively whether or not Gulf War-era veterans were given these formulations. We have modified the report text to make this point clear.[19]

Now the DoD was caught "misstating" the GAO's conclusions and asking the GAO to change the title of its report on the squalene issue.

At the same time, the DoD began an attack on the Tulane research. On 24 May 1999, Dr. Carl Alving called Dr. Robert Garry, a respected scientist who was working on the Tulane study. Dr. Alving expressed a "purely scientific" interest in Dr. Garry's research and asked for a copy of the in-progress work. Dr. Garry agreed to fax a copy, asking Dr. Alving not to circulate it as it was preliminary only. The final report differed significantly from the in-progress work. Dr. Alving not only circulated it, but subjected it to a scathing review and placed that review on the DoD's website prior to the paper's final publication. The review included an accusation that the Tulane researchers had an "anti-military agenda," though there was little evidence to support this. In fact, the DoD claimed on its website that the Tulane "conclusions derived from the test have no scientific basis."[20] Dr. Garry later stated that this preemptive strike by the DoD might well hinder the chances for the

---

18 Id.

19 Id.

20 Letter from Rep. Jack Metcalf to Secretary of Defense William Cohen dated 25 February 2000, quoting from the DoD's anthrax website in February 2000.v

research getting published in a peer reviewed journal. At the same time, the DoD repeatedly denounced the Tulane results by claiming that the paper had not been published in a peer-reviewed journal.

Notwithstanding these attempts to prevent the paper's publication, the Tulane study was published in February 2000 in a peer-reviewed journal. Despite the DoD's refusals, Congress finally required the DoD to participate in a squalene study as part of the Defense Appropriations bill for Fiscal Year 2000. The DoD claimed that "the FDA verified that none of the vaccines used during the Gulf War contained squalene as an adjuvant." The FDA was queried by Representative Metcalf and responded in a much more qualified manner, stating that "neither the licensed vaccines known to be used in the Gulf War, nor the one investigational product known to have been used, contained squalene as an adjuvant in the formulations on file with FDA."

On 3 October 2000, while I sat coolly with Ponder and his wife Jenn in the Rayburn Building waiting for his chance to testify before Congress, Representative Jack Metcalf read from a report his staff had prepared, including the shocker (or perhaps not) that re-testing of the lots revealed trace amounts of squalene in the AVA. The original tests had been sensitive to detecting squalene in parts per million. The supplemental testing detected squalene in parts per billion, 1,000 times more sensitive. An independent vaccinologist from Baylor University, however, offered that even in those amounts the presence of the adjuvant could boost immune response.

The DoD then took a new position. At this point, the DoD claimed that "amounts were so minute as to be insignificant." Additionally, the FDA came in to disclaim what its own scientists had found. What is interesting about the DoD position is that it still doesn't explain the presence of squalene in the vaccine. It is one thing to point out that the body produces squalene naturally and that the amounts are small. The DoD and the manufacturer have still not come forward to state that squalene is naturally produced in the vaccine by either the bacillus anthracis or some other aspect of the manufacturing process. Until that explanation happened, and it didn't, in addition to all of the other failed inspections and contaminated lots, the anthrax vaccine should have been considered adulterated, containing an experimental adjuvant. More startling is that on the same day that Ponder testified before Congress, a press conference was held where DoD spokesman Ken Bacon answered questions about squalene in the anthrax vaccine.

> **QUESTION:** And just to be clear, and I know that this has come up many times before over the years, but squalene also is not present in vaccines used during the Gulf War, before the Gulf War, after the Gulf War and to this day; is that correct?
>
> **BACON:** I have been told—I'm not an expert on vaccines and certainly not on squalene, but I've been told that squalene has not been in vaccines for—or certainly in the anthrax vaccine for a considerable period of time.

According to this statement by DoD's own spokesman, the AVA did have squalene in it at some point, but not "for a considerable period of time."

The history of this DoD research seems incredibly coincidental. Between 1988 and 1998, DoD sponsored 101 clinical trials on vaccines under IND protocols; this means tests involving human subjects. None of these human studies involved an anthrax vaccine, although five studies involved squalene and two occurred before the Gulf War. More questionable were several experiments on animals, using vaccines with adjuvant formulations containing squalene, for a wide range of diseases, including anthrax, toxic shock, and malaria. The anthrax vaccine experiments with adjuvant formulations containing squalene began in

1987, and some of the results were presented at conferences and published in several medical journals. The GAO noted that

> DoD's animal studies are of interest for two reasons. First, because tests on animals are generally performed before human trials, they represent the first step of vaccine research and provide a more complete picture about the state of research on adjuvant formulations with squalene before the Gulf War. Second, since vaccines against biological warfare cannot be tested for efficacy in humans, animal research is considered essential by researchers.[21]

In light of all of this compelling research and evidence, the question becomes why? Why would the DoD not want to find out the cause of Gulf War Illness? Even if it were the anthrax vaccine, wouldn't the health of veterans be more important than one vaccine? The answer to that question involves a mix of politics, personal agendas, and, of course, money. Unfortunately, it also reveals something about the leadership of the U.S. Armed Forces.

---

[21] GAO Report, 99-5, p. 5.v

CHAPTER 18

THE WALKING WOUNDED

One year ago today, I was stationed in Dhahran, Saudi Arabia. I received my fourth anthrax vaccine. That's when my problems began. Until that point, I weighed 175 pounds, 5"9', excellent physical condition. That night, I had a raging fever and my physical condition continued to deteriorate over the next couple of weeks. During that time, I lost facial hair, my testicles shrank to the size of a peanut—the right one that I could find. I had rapid weight gain, mainly in the form of subcutaneous fat, suffered mood swings, had severe groin pain, and I lost muscular strength. I went from a normal workout bench press of 280 pounds to less than 100, and that was in the space of less than two weeks [...]

As I got ready to leave Saudi Arabia in May, I visited with a new flight surgeon. He reviewed my records and he noted the strong link between a shot on one day and being ill the next. He also directed that I put in a VAERS report at an Air Force medical company co-located on that same compound. I wrote up the report, I walked over and an Air Force—a senior Air Force doctor came out and blocked the report. He scrawled across the back of the page that he did not think they were related, that I needed to see a urologist, and if the urologist concurred then he'd go ahead and file the report. Had he asked, or

> had he looked at my records, he'd see that I'd been under medical care, specialist care, for over six months.[1]

"Sir, they're saying that they're not going to let me come there to testify." Ponder's voice echoed over the phone. I waited to answer.

"Listen, don't worry. Jen's calling Beth Clay on the staff of the House Government Reform Committee. I'll get hold of someone there. Believe me, your command isn't going to take on a Congressional committee." Ponder had been invited to testify before the House Committee on Government Reform. He was calling from Okinawa.

"I hope not, sir." Although we had gotten the stay, Ponder was still worried that he would be left in Okinawa. This was because members of his command had told him that he would be left in Okinawa until the stay dissolved and/or the case was resolved, even though his unit was preparing to return from its seven-month deployment in the first week of October 2000.

Coincidentally, in the first week of October 2000, the House Committee on Government Reform was holding another hearing on the anthrax vaccine program. The Committee had already issued an extraordinarily condemning report in April 2000, after some eight or nine hearings. Specifically, the report was critical of DoD's media campaign against members who refused to accept the vaccine and it called for a moratorium on the entire program. In an interesting comment on the state of military-civil affairs, Marine Major General Randall West, a Cobra pilot of some repute and point man for the AVIP, immediately held a press conference rebutting the Committee's report. It was surprising, and disturbing, to hear a senior military officer criticizing a committee of Congress because of its disagreement with a DoD program.

---

[1] Testimony of Major Jon Irelan, US Army, before the House Government Reform Committee, 5 October 2000.

"Don't worry, David. We'll get you here." I said it with more conviction than I felt. I was in my house in Quantico, Virginia. I had to leave Okinawa early because of medical needs for one of my daughters. The Marine Corps had been fairly accommodating in sending me to Quantico to be near appropriate medical care, but it meant I had been removed from defense. I was now a prosecutor, while retaining my anthrax cases that were subject to the stay.

"It's hard not to, sir."

"We'll get you here." If Ponder's command didn't send him, I wasn't sure what I would do. Ponder's wife, Jennifer, was very active in lobbying for Ponder with Congressional members. I hoped she would be able to put some pressure on a representative who would in turn put the heat on Ponder's command. I was already way over my head. An appellate stay was above my paygrade as a Captain, but General Officers giving press rebuttals to Congressional reports was way, way out of my depth.

When I was detailed Ponder's case in Okinawa, my first thought was to deal it out quickly and move on. As I learned more about 10 U.S.C. §1107, I was shocked, but excited, as a defense attorney. I never really focused on, nor was it particularly fruitful for me to argue in court about the safety of the anthrax vaccine. I myself was skeptical of people reporting adverse reactions. Sitting in the Rayburn Building on 5 October 2000, in a chair right behind Ponder, I had a change of heart. I watched and listened to human tragedies. One woman, the wife of BioPort worker Richard Dunn, explained how her husband died from a systemic reaction to the vaccine. The coroner for Ionia County, Michigan, announced that Richard Dunn had inflammation throughout his body as a reaction to the vaccine. Mr. Dunn had taken his eleventh shot of the anthrax vaccine in May. He died on 13 July 2000. Richard Dunn was required to take the same shots as service members, as well as annual boosters, because he cared for some of the animals at BioPort.

Immediately after the coroner's statement, BioPort issued a general denial, including a claim that they had never heard anything about such reactions at the plant. This statement was hard to square with the testimony of Mr. Dunn's wife, who claimed that BioPort actually called several times to see how Richard Dunn was doing and called doctors for him. Either way, her testimony and the coroner's finding were significant for me because it offered some legal hope for Ponder, Stonewall, and Arroyo.

Part of the basis for the judge's ruling in our cases was that we had been unable to show any serious adverse reaction to the vaccine that would justify someone refusing the shot. As I listened to some of the stories of people on the panel, I realized that there were some seriously injured people. One young man, who had begun to have lesions that looked like burn marks all over his body immediately after he received a shot, testified about how he had lost his vision and continued to have medical problems. Incredibly, his father had served in the Army also in Vietnam and had cancer from the defoliant Agent Orange. An Army Major, John Irelan, detailed how Air Force doctors had refused to connect his illness with anthrax and blocked his filing of a VAERS form.

This refusal of military doctors to even acknowledge adverse reactions was a common theme that I heard repeated by many service members. It was disturbing because it allowed Major General West, in the panel that followed ours, to claim that "of all the people that were here today, there was only one person that has a medical diagnosis that directly links it to vaccine."[2] In other words, if military doctors do not diagnose it as anthrax related, then it's not anthrax related, and therefore there really aren't that many adverse reactions. Even responding to the coroner's report finding a systemic reaction to the vaccine General West claimed that "[t]here are other medical experts who believe it [the death] was not [AVIP

2 Testimony of MajGen Randy West, USMC, before the House Government Reform Committee, 5 October 2000.

connected]."[3] It became clear to me the military wanted it to be a battle of experts and the DoD could always trot out its own medical personnel and how could anyone gainsay them, given the classified nature of DoD vaccine research? And who would dare to question a doctor's impartiality or medical opinion, even though they were essentially under orders and saying what their employer wanted them to say?

This is yet another sordid aspect of the anthrax program—the compromise of military medical professionals in service to a corrupt and illegal DoD vaccine program. Report after Congressional report and inquiry after Congressional inquiry reveal that military personnel were not told required information about vaccines or medications, and worse yet, told only that they had to take it. Congressional and GAO reports detail this repeatedly, from the Gulf War's use of investigational drugs to failed recordkeeping attempts in Bosnia with the encephalitis vaccine. The anthrax vaccine was no different, in large part because the DoD, from the program's inception, made it a "commander's program."[4] This oft-repeated phrase transformed the medical officer from an independent expert bound by his profession's ethical rules to provide medical care to service members into a Commander's staff officer responsible solely for ensuring that the "commander's program" is carried out, with such trivial consideration as laws or medical ethics thrown in the garbage. Medical officers were given nothing more than talking points around the AVIP, entirely from DoD briefing slides and a DoD website. When I cross-examined the Group Surgeon for Third Force Service Support Group, he acknowledged this was explicitly the case, all while still defending the program.

During the government's direct examination, the doctor made broad, sweeping pronouncements about the AVA's effectiveness against aerosolized anthrax. When I questioned him about the manufacturer's

---

[3] Id.

[4] "Department of Defense Anthrax Vaccine Immunization Program AVIP: Unproven Force Protection," Report of the House Comm. On Govt Reform. 3 April 2000. p. 3.

IND application filed in 1996, he was unaware of it. His answer was that there "may be some political ramifications why they filed that. I don't know."[5] I questioned him about the rhesus monkey studies using the AVA and his knowledge of them.

Q: [...] have you read the actual results of the study?

A: I haven't read the actual study.

Q: Well how do you know then that it is what you said it is? What is your testimony based upon?

A: Based upon the briefing sheets that I get. I also looked at the DoD anthrax website which is information that *we* have—

What was interesting to me about the exchange wasn't just his ignorance about the most basic aspects of the vaccine or the program, but was that people refusing the vaccine, who are still patients like any other patient, were now "they" and the doctor and the DoD were "we."

This is what happens to those who refuse. Even doctors, who should appreciate more than anyone patient fears about taking shots, had become zealots in defense of the anthrax program. In no other medical treatment regimen do we find doctors in lockstep with a military commander about the nature of a medication or treatment. The DoD and military leaders were not providing briefing slides or medical information about hepatitis B, for example, or Japanese encephalitis. In those cases, the commander relied upon the expert advice of the doctor to advise the commander of the need for a particular treatment or medical intervention. Somehow with the AVA, however, the entire

[5] Testimony of Cdr Gregory Chin, USN, in *U.S. v. Stonewall*, record at p. 81.

process was reversed. The histrionic portrayal of the biological warfare threat was such that commanders were now in the position of advising doctors about the necessity of treatments and, more importantly, about the history, background, and safety of such treatments. Had the doctor at Stonewall's trial looked in a basic microbiology textbook, he would have found that among 36 vaccines, the anthrax vaccine was the only one listed under the category "special immunization and experimentation."[6]

Unfortunately, military doctors, non-warriors in a warrior culture, found in biological warfare a chance to be in a position heretofore unheard of for military doctors, as a kind of "biological warfare intelligence officer," using their medical expertise to advise commanders about the "threat" from disease via biological attack. In the past, the threat from disease was no different for the military than it was for the civilian population and the military doctor's role was much like a civilian doctor's: treat people for illness and injury, using preventative medicine to the extent possible. In the Gulf War and post-Gulf War, doctors became special advisors, responsible for ensuring that a vaccine—now considered a part of "total force protection"—was administered to the troops, no matter what. Military doctors stepped all too willingly into this role, abandoning professional objectivity in an effort to be "part of the team."[7]

The media bombardment surrounding the anthrax threat allowed doctors to convince themselves of the necessity for their involvement. If it is psychologically understandable, it is still professionally inexcusable. Doctors have an ethical duty to their patients outside of their job as

---

[6] *Principles and Practice of Infectious Diseases*, 4th ed., p. 2770 (1995).

[7] This phenomenon is by no means limited to doctors. I have noticed many other non-combatant staff advisors guilty of doing the same thing, abandoning professional doctrines in an effort to please commanders and "get the job done." Lawyers who serve as Staff Judge Advocates are known for this, frequently acting as if they are the personal attorney of the Commander. I have sat in classes given by senior judge advocates, more than one, who have stated that "the challenge is not just to tell the Commander what the law is, but to find a way to allow him to do what he wants, to fit that within the law." I call that spin. Better to tell a commander that his actions are unlawful, defend that position if it is honestly held, and suffer the consequences than to prostitute one's legal opinion and engage in some scholarly rationalization to justify going along with the commander.

officers, just as lawyers do to the law. If a commander told his staff judge advocate that he was contemplating murdering innocent civilians, then the lawyer would be obligated not simply to advise the commander not to do it, but to stop him from completing such unlawful action or to turn him in for the violation if he went forward. George Annas, in his excellent article on this subject, addressed this question with respect to military doctors.

> What should physicians in the military do when asked to administer investigational agents without the informed consent of the soldiers? Even if such administration is legal [...] it is unethical and following orders is no excuse for unethical conduct, even in combat. It would seem that the only justification a physician could have for participating in the administration of experimental or investigational agents without consent is that the physician sincerely believes that the agents are therapeutic under combat conditions. This is a difficult position to defend, because war does not change the investigational nature of a drug or vaccine. Such a decision would also be contrary to military regulations, which state that although a serviceperson must accept standard medical treatment, or face court-martial, soldiers have no obligation to accept interventions that are not generally recognized by the medical profession as standard procedures.
>
> A related question is whether the military physician is primarily responsible for the health and well-being of the soldiers under the physician's care (as in civilian life) or must subordinate the medical interests of the soldier-patients to the military mission. Remarkably there is no written policy or standard view on this question in the military. This issue deserves critical attention in peacetime, because it is not susceptible to rational

> thought during wartime. An unequivocal policy upholding traditional patient-centered ethics, although not legally required, seems the most responsible position for U.S. military physicians to take.[8]

Unfortunately, there still was no unequivocal policy by the respective service Surgeons General on the military doctor's role. In the case of the anthrax vaccine program, it is important to realize that we were not at war. The rule regarding informed consent has gone from the Nuremberg Code's absolute position, to Desert Storm's wartime exigency, to the peacetime potentiality of terrorism. This happened with very little scholarly or public debate and notwithstanding the harms suffered by World War II, Korean, Vietnam, and now Gulf War veterans from investigational treatments administered without informed consent. Mr. Annas, who holds a law degree and a Master's in public health from Harvard, testified before the FDA rulemaking committee regarding the Rule 23(d) waiver.

> In December 1995, I was invited to participate in a meeting on Rule 23(d) sponsored by the Presidential Advisory Committee on Gulf War Veterans' Illnesses. During the meeting, DoD representative continually referred to American soldiers as "the kids" and the responsibility of DoD to protect "the kids." I probably waited too long to tell him that I found this offensive, but he apologized for his choice of words. Nonetheless, the words are telling. Rule 23(d) treats American soldiers like kids and applies the basic rules for research on children to them with regard to consent—someone else makes the decision for them because they are seen as too immature to

---

[8] Annas, George J. "Protecting Soldiers from Friendly Fire: The Consent Requirement for Using Investigational Drugs and Vaccines in Combat." *American Journal of Law and Medicine*, Vol. 24, 1 January 1998.

> make it for themselves. For an adult this is always an affront to human dignity and disrespectful of personhood. In this regard, Rule 23(d) is a mistake and an aberration.[9]

This reference to soldiers as "kids" has another, more subtle, persuasive use. While Mr. Annas viewed the use as derogatory with respect to consenting adults, it also conveys to the listener that the speaker is seeking to protect children, and who could possibly argue that protecting children is not a worthy cause? Of course, as Mr. Annas pointed out, military members are hardly children.

Mr. Annas was also troubled by the DoD's insistence that keeping the waiver of Rule 23(d) in place was "consistent with law and ethics." As he notes,

> Soldiers are not pieces of equipment. They have numbers, but they retain their humanity and basic human rights. DoD should have exercised a third kind of courage—the courage to admit its mistake—and asked FDA to rescind Rule 23(d) and removed this pointless blot on our military laws. Instead, when Public Citizen petitioned FDA to revoke the rule in 1996, DoD supported continuing the waiver of consent rule as "fully consistent with law and ethics." In mid-1997, FDA asked for public comments on what should become of the rule. The answer remains simple: it should be rescinded because it violates every code and ethical principle developed since World War II to regulate research with human subjects, and it is unacceptable to permit commanders to turn soldiers into research subjects.[10]

---

[9] Id.

[10] Id.

CHAPTER 19
FIGHTING BEHIND THE SCENES

> Executive Order 13139, which implements 10 U.S.C. §1107, clearly states that the requirements it incorporated from the statute are for internal management only and confer no right enforceable by any party against the United States E.O. 13139, §6(b). Additionally, Secretary of the Navy Instruction 6230.4 of 29 April 1998, which implements the Department's anthrax vaccination implementation program states that the anthrax vaccine is an FDA-licensed product and not an IND requiring informed consent for its administration.[1]

"Someone from the editorial board will be down to get you and bring you up to the board room in a minute." The secretary smiled politely and then went back to answering the telephone, no longer concerned with my presence. I looked around the foyer of the Army Times Publishing Company. It was a large, open-air affair. Just past the circular receptionist's desk there was a staircase leading to the upper floors. Beyond that the ceiling opened up all the way to the top of the building

[1] *Ponder v. Stone*, 56 M.J. 613 (NMCCA, 2000).

and I could see people moving on the upper catwalks, worker bees in the hive. Off to my left was a hallway that disappeared out of view, with an elevator at the beginning where it opened into the foyer. To the right looked like a glass-enclosed company store with the usual assortment of sweatshirts, tee-shirts, and coffee mugs with the company logo on them. *Army Times* published a newspaper dedicated to each service, with the imprint *Marine Corps Times*, *Navy Times*, etc. The papers were widely read and respected in each service. I didn't know how it had happened, but my friends had gotten us a meeting with the editorial board of the parent company.

The door behind me came open and I could feel the cold December air blow in. I played with the zipper on my flight jacket, trying not to fidget. A Marine officer in uniform should not appear nervous. An older gentleman walking by with a long-sleeve tee-shirt with the company logo smiled at me.

"How are you today, Captain?" He was looking at the leather patch with the wings on it on the front of my jacket.

"Fine, sir. Thank you." I flipped my fore and aft cap around in my hand and then looked at my watch. I was 45 minutes late but the receptionist told me when I asked that the meeting had gotten a late start. I hoped my part hadn't come up yet. I started thinking that maybe I should have brought my briefcase in with me. Right then a young black woman appeared from the stairs and looked at me for confirmation.

"Captain Saran?" I nodded. "Come with me, please."

"Thank you," I responded and followed her up the stairs. As we turned for the second flight I saw a familiar face. Colonel John Richardson, United States Air Force Reserve, was coming down the stairs in a light blue power-suit. He smiled and stuck out his hand.

"Great to see you, Dale. Traffic was terrible, huh?"

We shook hands as he reached my step.

"No, just sick as a dog." I tried not to whine but I felt like crap. "I would have stayed home had my boss not made me go in this morning."

My wife and four girls were all sick at home with some kind of stomach virus that had everyone throwing up, including me. I had gotten back from the hospital with my wife the night before at 2:00 a.m. and I still felt weak and achy.

"Well, go on up," he said. "Lou is on right now, then Russ, then you. Are you sure you're still okay doing this? You know you don't have to."

"No, J.R., I'm fine. I just don't care anymore. Lou and I talked about my status and the relevant instructions. This is a freely made decision. Sometimes a man's gotta stand up and be counted." Though he was quite senior to me, I had come to know and think of him by his nickname from our many e-mail chats.

"Okay." He nodded reassuringly. "I'll be up in a minute." J.R. turned and continued down the stairs.

"Great," I answered with more enthusiasm then my body had in it. J.R. turned and continued down the stairs.

It wasn't bravado, nor was it some inflated sense of honor; I felt comfortable talking to John Richardson about such matters as personal honor and integrity. All of the members of our small band had incurred significant professional risks and opprobrium already in order to bring the flaws and illegality of the anthrax program to light. I couldn't very well be a part of their group and not be willing to stick out my neck. They had all done a lot more.

My guide and I reached the top of the stairs, turned left, and I could see a set of large oak wooden doors. As we got closer, I could see a little placard that read "Main Boardroom."

"Here you are," the young lady said and turned away as I reached for the door. I could hear voices. I wanted to make as unobtrusive an entrance as possible so I turned the doorknob slowly and tried to slip in.

I took in the room with a glance. There were two groups of people—ours and theirs. About seven or eight reporters and editors on the far side of a long meeting table, none of whom I knew or recognized. Everyone had a placard identifying them, but I didn't have time to read each one. Behind "them" was a bright light with an umbrella behind it and a photographer taking pictures. On "our" side of the table there were five men—three I knew and two whose identities I deduced from our e-mail correspondence. "Lou" Michels (J.J. Michels, Lieutenant Colonel, USAFR, attorney-at-law, as well as partner at McGuire, Battle, and Woods, whom I had met at Ponder's Congressional testimony) was speaking intently.

"Hey, Dale! Come on in." He waved me in without breaking stride.

"Hey, Lou" I replied and started to take off my coat, heading for the seat on his left, farthest from the door.

"So again," he went on, "the informed consent issue is completely separate from the issue about whether or not the vaccine is safe and effective." As I reached the seat beside him and slid into it, I could feel people on the other side of the table watching me. The photographer started snapping pictures of me.

I am not impressive in uniform, but I had a few "been there" ribbons. I was with the squadron that rescued Air Force Captain Scott O'Grady from inside Bosnia-Herzegovina in 1995. Atop the few ribbons I had was a set of gold Naval Aviator's wings. I could tell the reporters on the other side of the table were curious about where I fit into all of this. Not wanting to appear self-conscious, I swiveled my chair to face Lou as he spoke. I could hear the shutter of the camera clicking. I could only imagine what my boss was going to think if a color photo of me showed up in the next issue of *Marine Corps Times.* I began to wonder if I should have agreed to do this after all. I was just snapping into my new job as a prosecutor and here I was (still) playing defense attorney—to the media, no less, against the entire U.S. military.

I listened attentively, even though I had heard Lou make this argument before Congress and I had made a more detailed version of the same to a judge on several occasions myself. Lou Michels, as a seasoned attorney at a prestigious law firm and a former active duty Air Force officer, is articulate and confident when he speaks, particularly on the legality of the anthrax vaccine. Although I was a Captain and he was a Lieutenant Colonel in the Reserves, I had come to think of Lou, and all the members of our group, as a kind of Robin Hood and His Merry Men. There was J.R., who was the most senior of all, a full-bird Colonel; Tom "Buzz" Rempfer, a Major, Air Force Academy graduate, F-16 and A-10 pilot; Russ Dingle, also a Major and A-10 pilot, and Redmond Handy, another Colonel. Despite the fact that I was by far the junior member of the group, it all felt quite easy and natural. I was conscious of my place in the hierarchy, but certainly not anything like a chain of command. Perhaps it was because more than a few of us were former pilots and pilots have a long history of being somewhat less conscious of rank and more conscious of ability, a byproduct of the nature of aviation.

"It's like Rogaine," Lou continued on, "which has some particular relevance to my own situation," he added parenthetically, looking upward with his eyes toward his own hairline. I noticed for the first time that he had a small patch of thinning hair on the back of his head. "It was originally licensed by the FDA as a blood pressure medication. Now, during some of the trials they determined that it would grow hair on a billiard ball. Notwithstanding the fact that it was already licensed, they had to go back and get a change in the license because of the change in the purpose for which it was going to be used." He paused for that to sink in. He looked around the table at each of the editors and reporters, the shutter of the camera clicked away. "That's the law for getting medications legally approved. It is even more imperative when it involves biologics like vaccines."

Lou went on for a while longer, hitting the high points of his brief and then excusing himself. I knew he had another meeting to attend at his law firm. We had talked on the phone the day before and everyone knew what their role was in this presentation.

Russ Dingle, Major, USAFR, went next. He gave a presentation of how the vaccine was, by the definition in the FDA regulations, an "adulterated product" and thus should not be allowed to be shipped in interstate commerce. I had not heard his presentation and, though we had exchanged a few e-mails over the previous nine months, I had not met Russ before. His knowledge of the company that makes the anthrax vaccine, BioPort, Inc., was unmatched. The reporters asked questions and Russ always had an answer and could cite to the document from which he got it. I was known among my colleagues for being able to pull legal case cites out of my ass on demand, but Russ made me envious.

I had read all of the FDA inspection reports, but he obviously had access to information that I had never even guessed at. John Richardson had told me that he and Russ had been going through 26 boxes of information that they had gotten access to from the House Committee on Government Reform. Russ appeared to have memorized all 26 boxes. When he started describing how BioPort's predecessor in interest, Michigan Biologic Products Institute had added two fermenters to its production line without FDA approval, then added two more and removed the original fermenter from the production line, I felt like my defense of Ponder and Stonewall had been inadequate.

As I listened to Russ detail the failed inspections—the dripping paint into production vats, contaminated product lots containing other medicines like penicillin in them, and a list of other egregious quality control violations—the anger and frustration of nine months of defending Ponder and Stonewall welled up in me. Even worse, the Navy-Marine Corps Court of Criminal Appeals had denied our writ-appeal of the judge's ruling on our motions. I had until today to submit an appeal of the NMCCA decision to the highest military appellate court, the Court of Appeals for the Armed Forces, one step below the Supreme Court of the United States. My turn was approaching, though, so I tried to focus and make sure I maintained the momentum in our joint presentation. I also knew I had to control my mouth; the Judge Advocate General (JAG) Instruction that controls the conduct of Navy and Marine Corps attorneys had strict limits on what attorneys could say to the press and I still technically had pending cases on this issue.

As a practical matter, most Judge Advocates (myself included) avoided the press completely and referred any questions to the Public Affairs Office. I was cognizant of the Code of Professional Responsibility for lawyers that also prohibits using the press to influence the outcome of a court. As I had just moved to Quantico, Virginia, now working as a prosecutor in the Office of the Staff Judge Advocate, I didn't think my new boss, a long-time Colonel, would be particularly enthused to see my name popping up in the *Marine Corps Times* bashing the government's anthrax program.

An Air Force doctor, Captain John Buck in Biloxi, Mississippi, had requested me to be his Individual Military Counsel (IMC) and that request had been denied by my bosses—they had good legal reasons, but in my heart I had hoped that they would carve an exception and let me do it. It dawned on me that perhaps I had become too personally involved with the anthrax issue and that it might be affecting my judgment as a lawyer, but I had been over that ground both in my own mind and with my clients many times.

"And that's the vaccine that the DoD is making your service members take, under threat of imprisonment," I heard "Buzz"—Tom—saying. Tom, who with Russ, had been thrown out of their Connecticut Guard unit over the Anthrax Vaccine Immunization Program, looked nothing like what I had imagined. He looked young, lean, handsome, the archetype for an Air Force pilot. I had pictured him much older from my conversations over e-mail with him.

"And now," he went on, "Captain Dale Saran, U.S. Marine Corps, will brief you on some of the current anthrax cases and their status. Dale." Tom turned to me and winked.

"Thanks, Buzz," I answered and turned to my section in the briefing book that Richardson and some of the others had put together the previous few days. I looked up at the reporters across from me. I tried to ignore the photographer snapping pictures. I could handle my portion of the brief any number of ways: The cool, dispassionate, quintessential picture of a lawyer was a bit of an act for me, as I am much more direct and blunt naturally, but I was trying to gauge my audience. What would be most convincing to a group of reporters? I could be more intense, somewhat exasperated at the situation my clients found themselves in. I decided against that—the last thing I wanted to do was come across as histrionic. I had thought a lot about this moment and had never been able to arrive at a decision. I decided to just start speaking and see where it took me.

I cannot remember exactly what I said, but at one point I recall answering some questions about the status of our appeal.

"This is nothing new," I blurted out. There was silence from the other side of the table. "I invite any of you to look at the history behind the current version of Title Ten, section 1107." And then I launched into my argument. I could feel myself heating up as I recounted the use of the investigational and experimental drugs on troops prior to and during the Gulf War. I explained how the FDA had struck a deal with the DoD to grant a waiver to allow these drugs to be used on service members without telling them what was being used on them. I recounted the withdrawal of this waiver and the reports of Gulf War Illness. I spoke forcefully, passionately, without consideration for what the ramifications might be to me. I spoke The Truth as I had come to know it in the past year defending my clients.

I took a breath and looked around. Tom Rempfer and my cohorts were looking at me, waiting for more. I gathered myself, the calm after the storm.

"That is exactly why this statute was passed, to prevent these types of things from happening again, to prevent another Gulf War-type illness." There were some questions. I answered them. Eventually Tom or someone else picked up a thread and my turn was done. I had so much more I wanted to say. I wanted them to know The Truth, The Whole Truth, as I had come to know it deep in the marrow in my bones.

I looked at my watch. *Shit!* I thought. I still had to get to Court of Appeals for the Armed Forces in downtown D.C. and turn in Petty Officer Ponder's writ-appeal of the NMCCA decision rejecting our request for extraordinary relief. I had to go.

I listened for a while and slipped out at an appropriate time, saying my goodbyes by touching each man's shoulder briefly as I passed on the way out. I was proud to have been invited to be a part of their panel.

Outside, the snow was beginning to fall more heavily. I started our family minivan and quickly got into the flow of traffic inbound on I-395 for the District. I had a writ-appeal to finish typing on my laptop and I didn't have much time to get it into the Court. With the NMCCA decision, the stay on our court-martial had been lifted. Although Ponder had come home to Mississippi and his wife and son, Stonewall and Arroyo were still in Okinawa, six months after their unit had left and returned to Camp Lejeune, North Carolina, and all three were facing the brig unless I got a higher court to listen to me and overturn the lower appellate court. I looked at my watch again. Suddenly that stay—and the nail in Kolomjec's door on Okinawa—seemed a very hollow victory.

CHAPTER 20

WHY?

As a mandatory, force-wide countermeasure to the real threat of weaponized anthrax on the battlefield, the vaccine effort is unrealistic. It expands and distorts the use of invasive, dated medical technology to address perceived weaknesses in detection technology and external physical protection against biological attack. Born of a post-Gulf war panic over apparent weaknesses in chemical and biological [CB] warfare defenses, the AVIP is an unmanageably broad military undertaking built on a dangerously narrow scientific and medical foundation.

At best, the vaccine provides some measure of protection to most who receive it. Just how much protection is acquired, by whom, for how long, and against what level of challenge are questions DoD answers with an excess of faith but a paucity of science.

Many members of the armed forces do not share that faith. They do not believe merely suggestive evidence of vaccine efficacy outweighs their concerns over the lack of evidence of long-term vaccine safety. Nor do they trust DoD has learned the lessons of past military medical mistakes: atomic testing, Agent Orange, Persian Gulf War drugs, and vaccines. Heavy handed, one-sided informational materials only fuel suspicions the program

> understates adverse reaction risks in order to magnify the relative, admittedly marginal, benefits of the vaccine.
>
> As a military operation, the AVIP rests on weak conceptual and logistical footing. It suffers from poor planning, inflexible execution, and over-extended supply lines. As a health care effort, the AVIP compromises the practice of medicine to achieve military objectives.[1]

Given how flawed the program has been from its inception—and all of the documents involved are public records, most of which were created by the U.S. government itself—the most salient question becomes "Why?" Why would the DoD continue to push such a flawed program when the manufacturer long ago provided sufficient reason to back away from the program and still save face? What I offer here is likely by no means the complete list of answers, but I have tried to compile all of the reasons and justifications of which I am aware because it is my view that all of these, or some combination of these and other reasons not seen, are contributing factors to the totality of what was done. It wasn't some monolithic "conspiracy," but as with most bad ideas in government, the totality is a conjunction of interests and attitudes that "conspire without speaking" to deprive others—specifically military service members and veterans in this case—of their humanity and their rights. I have also attempted here to offer both the DoD's claims and rebuttals in order to place the entire anthrax vaccine program in a larger context that would roughly equate to "motive," the essential (but not logically so) element of a case without which prosecutors will tell you it is awfully hard to "hang your hat," or a conviction, even in a "slam dunk" case.

---

[1] House Report 106-556. "The Department of Defense's Anthrax Vaccine Immunization Program: Unproven Force Protection Measure." 3 April 2000, p. 2.

The reasons that the program was launched (and still survives) reflect a variety of considerations: political, personal, and philosophical. At their best, the motives are noble; at their worst, they're just another instance of massive government corruption gestated by greed and sustained by ego. None of them alone—or even together—provide a justification for beginning or continuing the program, particularly considering that the AVIP violated numerous laws including, most importantly, service members' right to informed consent and to not be guinea pigs in a massive DoD experiment. Before looking in detail at the why, it is important to examine some of the rhetoric used by the DoD in regard to this program. These statements help illustrate the underlying philosophies and motivations of those driving the program at the highest levels of government.

In 1997, at the background briefing announcing the program's launch, two high-ranking DoD officials presented a scenario to reporters, using a map to demonstrate a hypothetical attack on a U.S. military unit:

> Now if the threat released an anthrax cloud through a long line release, aerosol release from an aircraft, upwind of our forces, and it drifted down over them, the fact that anthrax is 99 percent lethal in an aerosol inhalation delivery means the warfighting strength of that corps would be at about 34 percent. Onset of symptoms in 24-72 hours. It's lethal in five days. Pretty significant capability. Again, this is an aerosol release, exposed personnel who are unwarned—we have no detectors. They are unprotected. Because we have no warning they're not in their MOPP suits with their mask on, and they are unvaccinated. Significant degradation to warfighting strength. Tremendous casualties.

The most frightening aspect about this press conference and these statements on behalf of the DoD is not their substance, but rather that that no one, not a single reporter, questioned or challenged these figures or assumptions. If it would be unethical to test human beings against an aerosolized anthrax attack, how does the DoD have these kinds of exact numbers for an aerosolized anthrax attack? Where did they come from?

In truth, each of these assumptions is contradicted by reality. In a 17 March 1998, Congressional committee hearing, Bernard Rostker, the Special Assistant to the Secretary of Defense for Gulf War Illnesses, asserted that the DoD had a vehicle that could detect and sample for some biological agents. He called on an Admiral Cowan to discuss the Biological Integrated Detection System (BIDS) vehicle and how many platoons there were. Here, Admiral Cowan replied that " [...] there are five platoons of the BIDS. Each one of them is seven vehicles, and each one of them covers a pretty substantial area. The CENTCOM [United States Central Command] plan was for two of those platoons. Of the five, one is active duty and the other four are reserve."[2]

It is impossible for high-ranking DoD officials, undoubtedly flag officers from the tone and content of the briefing, to claim in December 1997 that there is *no way* to detect these biological agents ("we have no detectors") and then less than three months later (82 days, to be precise) an Admiral to discuss "five platoons of seven vehicles *each*" that can detect biological agents. In fact, within the original briefing, after saying there were "no detectors," one of the briefers backtracked and started explaining that

> we have *some* capability ... By and large, it is point detection. You find out you have the agent when you are there with your detector. That is in place now, and there's more coming. Enhancements also are being developed

[2] Testimony of Admiral Michael Cowan, Senate Committee hearings, 17 March 1998.

> where we get a standoff capability, so that we not only can see a cloud or an agent in the distance, we have the standoff to be able to detect and identify what it is before it gets to where the troops are, the service members, so they can take protective action, put on their masks that will protect them against those type of agents.[3]

No one called the briefers on this ~~blatant lie~~ inconsistency. Additionally, the claims about the lethality of the anthrax bacteria in aerosolized form are so vastly overblown as to blow right past *hyperbole,* catch and pass *exaggeration,* and come within a nose of *pants-on-fire.*

In 1979, there was an accidental release of anthrax in Sverdlovsk, Russia, from a biological warfare plant. Professor Jeanne Guillemin, Sociology Department, Boston University, in her book about this incident observed that

> Based on experiments with hundreds of monkeys done at Fort Detrick in the 1950s, the U.S. Army standardized a value of eight thousand inhaled spores as the dosage lethal for 50 percent of a human population receiving it, the so-called LD_{50}. But nowhere in Sverdlovsk was the case fatality rate 50 percent. Even at the ceramics factory pipe shop, apparently right on the centerline of the passing spore cloud, only ten of about four hundred and fifty workers fell ill and died, a fatality rate of 2 percent."[4]

Despite this, two flag officers are quoting a fatality rate that leaves only 34% of an entire corps of troops intact. This claim is also being

---

[3] DoD Background Briefing, 15 December 1997.

[4] Guillemin, Jeanne. *Anthrax, The Investigation of a Deadly Outbreak.* University of California Press, Berkeley, CA, 1999, p. 241.

made of a population of hand-picked 18- to 25-year-old healthy young men (for the most part). This also assumes that an enemy aircraft or artillery shell perfectly releases the anthrax spores, undetected by anyone, no one is in their MOPP gear, nor does anyone suspect the release or take any action. Evidently, the unit is also standing still for this release, out in the open, in a desert environment with no trees, no buildings, nor any other obstructions that might prevent them from inhaling the spores. And it's not windy, either. Nor is it raining. And the service members seem to not have the ability to use antibiotics because the DoD has not fielded the one treatment that is truly proven safe and effective: antibiotics.

To compound this fabricated scenario, these same DoD spokespersons go on to proffer the benefits after vaccination:

> Now we've vaccinated. We don't have any better detection, we don't have any better protection, but what we now have is this force, on the ground, vaccinated. You can see, personnel without immunity is a little enclave. What that is is, they are in the proximity of the delivery of the agent and that proximity has caused them to be hit with a dose that overwhelms their immune system even with the vaccine. So if they're very nearby, that is a potential. But the warfighting strength now with this protection is at 95 percent—a vast difference. With enhanced detection leading to protection, we can get that up to 99 percent plus. This is the first big step. Those casualties, again, are because of over-exposure to the attack.

There are several interesting bits of verbal legerdemain in these statements. First, there have never been any efficacy studies done with human beings against an aerosolized anthrax spores (or there would have been no need to modify the license, setting aside the ethics of such an experiment). The GAO has found that the animal correlates do not work very well, nor can they equate to human protection because antibody level does not correlate with immunity in those animal studies. How then does this officer assert that there will be a 95% success rate for vaccinated individuals? Based upon what scientifically validated evidence is this statement made? Furthermore, notice how for purposes of showing how good the vaccine is, the briefer adds that with "enhanced detection" the figure is up to "99 percent plus." Now, why does his original hypothetical posit no enhanced detection? He has changed his original hypothetical in two variables, in prior detection and vaccination. One wonders how the original stationary corps would have fared if they had put on their gas masks with the same enhanced detection that the vaccinated hypothetical got the benefit of. The answer should be 100% as the masks are supposed to be completely effective. Here the General compares apples to bacon, acts as if the differences prove his point, and no one in the audience says a word or asks a single question.

This hyping of the program appears to have been part of a concerted effort. Milton Leitenberg, Senior Fellow at the University of Maryland Center for International and Security Studies, commenting on the Secretary of Defense Cohen's bioterrorism pronouncements, noted that such hype is

> exaggerated and alarmist. They are probably even dangerous and counterproductive, since they virtually solicit and induce precisely what they portray as fearing [...] No agency of the U.S. government has prepared a threat analysis that provides indications that these events are imminent or even likely. Instead, various analysts have provided vulnerability projections and scenarios, which are always easy to concoct in the abstract [...] Either the advice reaching the secretary of defense and other senior

> officials on this subject is extraordinarily poor, or they are intentionally disregarding real-world experience.[5]

All of which brings us to one part of the *why*.

Science journalist Daniel Greenberg offered a possible motive for hyping the threat of a biological terrorist incident. " [... I]t should be noted that there's a whiff of hysteria-fanning and budget opportunism in the scare scenarios of the saviors who have stepped forward against the menace of bioterrorism."[6] Professor Jeanne Guillemin reiterated this theme:

> Cohen has said publicly that a bioterrorism attack is a question of "when," not "if." This is surely one of the most irresponsible statements of our times from a government official ... the American public deserves better than being manipulated by the military-media scare industry. And maybe a future *Frontline* [sic: *Nightline*] will educate us on how that $10 *billion* against terrorism is really getting spent.[7]

As one might have guessed up front, good old-fashioned "filthy lucre" provided billions and billions of reasons for the anthrax program's inception and continued existence. Lots and lots of money was there for the taking—and not just short-term personal interests, either, although various individuals certainly made generational fortunes on the vaccine program. Bio-terrorism provides a virtually unassailable reason to pour taxpayer money into the DoD, which gets more than just a bigger budget

---

5 Lietenberg, Milton. "False Alarm." *Washington Post.* 14 August 1999, p. A15.

6 Greenberg, Daniel S. "The Bioterrorism Panic." *Washington Post,* 16 March 1999, p. A21.

7 Guillemin, Jeanne. "Scare Campaign about Biological Weapons is Itself a Threat." *Boston Globe.* 2 December 1999, p. A27.

for all of the possible treatments and measures surrounding it. As the quotes above show, it provides an entirely new reason for force structure changes, new units to respond to this "new" threat, and what person would question the necessity to defend against these kinds of threats?

In fact, events at the time show that the program received unanimous support: The 1996 Nunn-Lugar-Domenici amendment to the FY1997 Defense bill passed in the Senate by a 96-0 vote.[8] One observer noted these same trends and pointed out the underlying dynamics.

> Several factors inflamed the tenor of the US debate. The problem of terrorism truly began to crystallize for Americans when prominent buildings in New York City and Oklahoma City were bombed, sinking in even further with bombings of US targets in Saudi Arabia and Africa. The backdrop for these events was the revelation of frightening details about the extent of the bioweapons programs in Iraq and the former Soviet Union. Adding to the tinder, international terrorist Osama bin Laden threatened to acquire mass destruction weapons specifically to use against Americans. Other, more political factors, also fanned the debate, such as the vested interests of defense contractors and government offices in larger budgets, not to mention the desire of elected officials to be perceived as "doing something" about the problem.[9]

At the same time that the anthrax program was being launched, two DoD military officials also briefed the press on how the AVIP and DoD

---

[8] Debate Nunn-Lugar-Domenici amendment to the National Defense Authorization Act for Fiscal Year 1997, US Senate. Congressional Record, 26 June 1996, p. S6988, et seq.

[9] Smithson, Amy. "Ataxia: The Chemical and Biological Terrorism Threat and the US Response." The Stimson Center, Report No. 35, October 2000, p. 12.

would fit in with the Nunn-Lugar-Domenici bill. This amendment to the 1997 Defense Authorization Act included a provision that would allow military chemical-biological response teams (from both the Army and the Marine Corps) to aid civilian first responders. At a press briefing on 16 April 1997, two DoD officials explained that

> DoD has a crucial, important, supporting role to the other agencies that are involved, *and for whatever reason, the funding flows through the Department of Defense.* So in many ways, not only do we have the role to support via the expertise that we have, *but it so happens that in the legislation the funding, at least for the initial years here, flows through the Department of Defense.*
>
> *In a broad sense we're looking at 120 cities over three years. We're looking at 27 cities to be assessed in FY97, and training to be initiated in about nine of those 27.*
>
> We're looking at the emergency responder training aspects only of the legislation, and that's in Title 14, subtitle A. There are several paragraphs in that piece of the legislation on the requirement for emergency or first responder training, and that's what we're focusing on here today.[10]

Thus, the anthrax program had an even larger context as part of military aid in civilian incidents of domestic terrorism. This is why the program was a "total force" program, including the Reserves *and* the National Guard. The inclusion of the National Guard received little debate, but it should be striking because such a program is unprecedented. National Guardsmen are part of each state's own sovereign force for state purposes under Title 32, subject to the orders of

[10] DoD Background Briefing, 16 April 1997.

each governor. It is only during a time of declared "national emergency" that these troops may be activated by the President and thus subject to federal control. This is extremely important legally because if a Guardsman is injured by the vaccine, there is a real question about legal remedies. While the federal government enjoys sovereign immunity under *Feres*, the states do not enjoy the same blanket immunity. That is why several states asked their legislators to make the program voluntary; it was how Tom "Buzz" Rempfer had found himself caught in the political world between an active duty commander and the Governor of Connecticut as his State Guard unit was preparing to be activated and their status changed from Title 32 to Title 10. The vaccines were a prerequisite for being called up to Title 10 status and flying sorties in some far-flung locale where the US was enforcing a no-fly zone. If a guardsman could prove in state court that the state issued an unlicensed vaccine that caused irreparable harm, what could the possible damage award by a jury be? And why would pilots flying thousands of feet above the battlefield even need to be protected from the threat of anthrax?

The DoD AVIP was simply one part of a much larger mosaic. Presidential Directive, PDD-63[11] anticipated DoD involvement in a "consequence management" (civil defense) role as noted above. The anthrax vaccine program also reflects the premise that there were/are going to be more of these types of vaccine programs in the future. In fact, the AVIP is/was but the first in a series of vaccines that were/are part of Joint Vision 2010, the DoD's plan for the military of the future, and a part of that plan is the Joint Vaccine Acquisition Program (JVAP), which, as of 2000, had some 20 vaccines in various stages of development, including an AIDS vaccine.[12] The anthrax vaccine was

---

[11] https://fas.org/irp/offdocs/pdd/pdd-63.htm, last accessed 14 July 2020.

[12] See, e.g., "Protecting Our Forces: Improving Vaccine Acquisition and Availability in the U.S. Military," Lemon SM, Thaul S, Fisseha S, et al., editors—preview/overview available here: https://www.ncbi.nlm.nih.gov/books/NBK220954, last accessed 14 July 2020. See also "Report on Biological Warfare Defense Vaccine Research & Development Programs," DoD, July 2001. Available here: https://archive.defense.gov/pubs/ReportonBiologicalWarfareDefenseVaccineRDPrgras-July2001.pdf, last accessed 14 July 2020.

supposed to be the crown jewel of the JVAP, paving the way for future vaccines, including the "possible" mandatory vaccine of civilians. Yes, you read that right—mandatory vaccination of the U.S. population against the possibility of bio-terrorism, including children. Indeed, after 9/11 and the anthrax letter attacks in September 2001, serious academics in and around government were engaged in considering that possibility.[13]

Each of those individual vaccines and the associated program represents uncountable billions of dollars to drug companies making vaccines, such as BioPort. It also provides budget dollars to a military that increasingly needed to justify its size and even existence in the post-Cold War era. This, coupled with the DoD's hype of the threat, has convinced Congressmen that the DoD could be useful in the civil defense role. Both the Marine Corps and the Army now have special Chemical and Biological Response Forces with special equipment and vehicles that are considered "first responders" in the event of a chemical or biological "attack", *Posse Comitatus* be damned (and ignored).[14]

The bioterrorism threat, as a subset of the broader "terrorism" threat, provides a monolithic enemy on which to focus the troops; a surrogate "evil empire" to replace the faded Soviet Union. The language quoted throughout this book by DoD officials bears this out. This threat also unifies the Armed Services because it transforms every servicemember into a potential target, making previously non-combatant occupations essential members in the fight against anthrax. Every service member's body is the new battlefield and DoD believes it has the authority to command that battlespace.

While it may seem hard to believe, it still takes more than just the promise of money to make a program like this continue. Even senior

---

[13] For example, the Department of Health and Human Services contracted Stanford University's Evidence-Based Practice Center to produce a report entitled "Pediatric Anthrax: Implications for Bioterrorism Preparedness," published in 2006. Available for download here: https://www.ncbi.nlm.nih.gov/pmc/articles/PMC4780971, last accessed 14 July 2020.

[14] The Posse Comitatus Act of 1878 forbid the use of the military (U.S. Army) to enforce domestic law in the aftermath of the Civil War.

military officers are unlikely to see any personal checks in their bank accounts as a result of this program, so there has to be something more at play for the DoD to have continued in the face of the evidence against the AVIP. As incredible as it seems, loss of face coupled with bureaucratic intransigence may account for a significant part of DoD officials' unwillingness to back down and admit wrongdoing.

> "It speaks to DoD culture more than anything else," says a congressional staff aide who asked not to be named. "The Pentagon just does not have a corporate culture. Once they decided to go with this program (BioPort), they stuck with it, even though oversight indicated they had built their biodefense program on a foundation of sand, and they had an unreliable producer. *The DoD is simply incapable of admitting a mistake. They genetically just can't back out.*"
>
> The Pentagon and BioPort deny they made a mistake, of course, and they believe their problems will be solved, perhaps next week. Government sources close to the process say as early as Monday, the FDA will approve BioPort's renovated facility, and enable it to resume shipments of the vaccine it has been stockpiling since 1999.[15]

The DoD can be a particularly "linear-thinking" agency when trying to push through pet programs and the AVIP is just one among a long list I could provide of bad ideas that DoD will ever refuse to admit were bad: The list of weapons and equipment procurement failures alone could fill volumes, from the Vietnam-era M-16A1 to the canopy removal system

[15] Rozen, Laura. "The Anthrax Vaccine Scandal." *Salon*. 15 October 2001. https://www.salon.com/2001/10/15/anthrax_vaccine, last accessed 14 July 2020.

(CRS) in my old aircraft (AH-1W) to an entire list of procurements and programs that I will leave to others to round out. This tendency toward organizational arrogance even coupled with the budgetary considerations, however, could not explain the heroic lengths to which the DoD went to prop up a failing company and violate the rights of its service members.

The answer as to "why" in this context is clearly not as simple or straightforward as proponents of the AVIP suggest. It is not, as they have stated, a simple matter of "classic deterrence."[16] It is not, though the DoD continues to beat this drum, because of the "immediate" threat of anthrax. In fact, a GAO report at the time concluded that "the threat of a biological attack by anthrax remained the same as it was 10 years prior to the program's launch."[17] The State Department, with persons in as dangerous (possibly more so) positions as military members, made the same vaccine optional. In fact, a State Department fact sheet at the time stated that

> The Department of State has no information to indicate that there is a likelihood of use of chemical or biological agent release in the immediate future. The Department believes the risk of the use of chemical/biological warfare (CBW) is remote, although it cannot be excluded. There are, of course, no guarantees. Until a threat becomes known, American citizens must make their own decisions with regard to those precautions they might take to avoid injury.[18]

---

16 DoD Background Briefing. 5 August 1999. The Defenselink website no longer appears to carry these, but the entire transcript is available for download here: https://www.hsdl.org/?view&did=1052. Last accessed 14 July 2020.

17 GAO Report 99-148, p. 2.

18 US Department of State, Fact Sheet Chemical-Biological Warfare. The previous link, http://www.travel.state.gov/cbw.html now returns a 404 error, but is also referenced for the same point by other authors with an October 2001 date. The State Department has moved all of these somewhere that I

Like any good scandal from the era, there is also/always the "Clinton angle." Not only was there political pressure to "do something" about biological warfare, but the President himself, Bill Clinton, had a strong personal interest in the issue. According to several sources,

> Clinton became fixated on the emerging germ threat and ways to counter it among civilians, aides said. Influences are said to have included the Iraqi crisis, the Russian claims, the intelligence reports and a novel, *The Cobra Event* (Random House, 1997), about a terrorist attack on New York City with a genetically engineered mix of the smallpox and cold viruses.[19]

> Clinton said he hoped that a major legacy of his Presidency would be to stave off unconventional attacks.[20]

> [...] abandoning the vaccination program could unravel the administration's entire response to biological threats, discrediting a major element of Clinton's self-described legacy.[21]

In addition to the incentives from the DoD, the anthrax program also apparently had political and personal "legacy" considerations concerns of the President. Of course, like any good "Clinton Angle" story, there was

---

currently cannot locate, but the Internet Archive (The WayBack Machine) has what appears to be the referenced page with dates September to November 2001. https://web.archive.org/web/20010912080322/http://www.travel.state.gov/cbw.html. Last accessed 14 July 2020.

19 Broad, William J. and Judith Miller. "Clinton describes terrorism threat for the 21st Century." *New York Times*. 22 January 1999.

20 Broad, William J. and Judith Miller. "Germ defense plan in peril as its flaws are revealed." *New York Times*. 7 August 1998.

21 Bacevich, Andrew J., Ph.D. "Bad Medicine for Biological Terror." *Orbis*. Spring 2000, p. 224.

also the issue of payback for services rendered, which centered around one person: (retired) Admiral William Crowe, USN.

When Democratic governor and Presidential candidate Bill Clinton was running for office against noted World War II veteran and youngest naval aviator George H.W. Bush, the discussion in and around the military was all about Clinton's history of protesting the Vietnam War and how he could possibly command the respect of the Armed Forces. It almost seems quaint by comparison to more recent elections, but there was genuine angst in the officer corps about a Clinton presidency.

The *New York Times* headline on 19 September 1992, was considered a blow to Bush the Elder: "Former Military Chief Plans to Back Clinton." Admiral Crowe was not only well-regarded and a widely recognized name, but he had been Bush I's own Chairman of the Joint Chiefs. At a time when people wondered if Clinton would be able to find a single notable general officer to publicly back his candidacy, Crowe's public support was seen as a serious setback to Bush and a coup for Clinton.

As President Clinton worked through his first term, the now-retired Admiral William Crowe was given the plum post of Ambassador to Great Britain, in which he served from 1994-1997. During his time there, he met and became friends with a gentleman named Fuad el-Hibri, who was an owner and manager in Porton Products, Ltd. *Porton Down* is the location of Great Britain's equivalent to Fort Detrick, Maryland, where the U.S. has its chemical and biological weapons testing and development. Porton Down's Defense of Science and Technology Laboratory (DSTL) has been involved in chemical, biological and other weapons and experiments in the same way the Fort Detrick has because it was set up as such. Indeed, much of the exact same experimentation conducted on U.S. soldiers detailed in this book previously has been mirrored in the UK, right down to the covert administration of LSD to soldiers in the 1950s and 60s and resulting lawsuits. Ironically, unlike the DoD's reliance on the *Feres* doctrine and *sovereign immunity*, the British government actually settled its lawsuits and paid the service members it experimented upon, in one case after a British jury found against the government. During the Gulf War, Great Britain also injected its soldiers with an anthrax vaccine that was manufactured by El-Hibri's company.

By 1996 and 1997, after President Clinton's re-election, the DoD began to ramp up its rhetorical concerns about bioterrorism. There was a move to begin looking for alternative manufacturers to the Michigan state-owned producer of the anthrax vaccine. William Crowe left his ambassadorship in 1997.

A 2005 article in the *Daily Press* explained how Crowe had come to be in such a position.

> Until 1998, the nation's only manufacturing plant for anthrax vaccine was owned and operated by the state of Michigan. The state agency that ran the plant was losing money, so the state put the operation and its license for making the anthrax vaccine up for bid.
>
> Fuad El-Hibri, a 40-year-old German businessman with a Yale University management degree, formed a team of investors to buy the business, which included a $100 million contract with the Pentagon. His bid faced a problem, though: He and his father, Ibrahim El-Hibri, a wealthy international financier from Lebanon, dominated ownership of the company, which they named BioPort.
>
> Both were considered friendly to the United States. Father and son had directed a company involved in Britain's anthrax vaccine program and they had worldwide interests in cell phone networks and other ventures. But the U.S. government was not keen on letting a foreign-owned company control its anthrax vaccine. The only other bidder was also based overseas.
>
> So Fuad El-Hibri played a trump card: A family friend, former Chairman of the Joint Chiefs of Staff Adm.

> William Crowe, was made a director. *Crowe put no money into BioPort but got about 10 percent of the stock, government records show.* El-Hibri says Crowe immediately advised him to apply for U.S. citizenship.
>
> Crowe's advice was good, El-Hibri said. But Crowe's connections were better: He was the military's top officer during the Reagan administration, then endorsed Bill Clinton for president in 1992. Clinton made him U.S. ambassador to the United Kingdom, and while serving there, Crowe was close to the El-Hibri family, congressional testimony shows.[22]

The article goes on to explain in detail what this book—and every public record—has already been shown: MBPI/MDPH/BioPort failed every single FDA inspection it had, yet Congress continued to appropriate funding at DoD's behest, with taxpayers footing the bill to the tune of tens of millions.

---

[22] Evans, Bob. "How a company cashed in on anthrax." *Detroit Free Press.* 7 December 2005. https://www.dailypress.com/news/dp-anth-day4-bioportdec06-story.html, last accessed 14 July 2020.

CHAPTER 21
BACK TO OKINAWA

I was stoic on the ride to the airport. It had nothing to do with emotional control; it was strictly a survival mechanism. While it had taken me some nine years to learn it, keeping my mouth shut was the smartest thing I learned to do when my wife and I fought. We never parted particularly well. All of my time in the Marine Corps, nine-plus years, more than a fair number of departures—not one of them pleasant.

At Dulles, I left without saying more than a brief goodbye. Seething would be an understatement. I was not good at holding my tongue or letting go of an argument. A short temper and a big mouth do not a successful combination make.

I watched our minivan accelerate out into the flow of traffic from Dulles while I stood there. I turned, shouldered my bag, and dragged my carry-on behind me into the airport.

Dulles to Chicago. A two-and-a-half-hour layover. I found an airport barber shop for a haircut. I called home from a pay phone and made up. It seemed trivial now that we were a thousand miles apart.

Chicago to Narita. The flight was cramped, the food tolerable, my circadian rhythms a wreck. As we descended over Tokyo Bay, I looked out my window when the wing dipped down. I watched the fog slide over the chord—the width—of the wing.

A flash and suddenly I was back at flight school, upside down and hanging in the seat straps, the parachute cutting into my collarbone, doing precision aerobatics in the T-34C Turbo-Mentor—a jet-engine propeller-driven aircraft, affectionately known by students as the Tor-Mentor. We were inverted and I was trying to pull through the bottom of a split-S when I caught the condensation on the wing out of the corner of my eye as I tried to pull harder on the stick, but the G-forces worked against me.

The maneuver started at about 8,000 feet with the aircraft straight and level. Flip upside down with an aileron roll, and then pull the stick back into your lap, and keep pulling through until the aircraft is straight and level again, some 1,000 or so feet lower. Except something was wrong. The control forces were incredible, I was wrestling with the stick trying to pull through, and the altimeter was unwinding like a Bugs Bunny cartoon.

"Lieutenant Saran," my on-wing instructor, Lieutenant Tim King, United States Navy, began in his thick Georgia drawl, "why might we be descendin' so fast?" He was laconic even as we plummeted out of the sky, upside down. The way he spoke over the inter-cockpit communication system, or ICS, I could just see him buffing his nails while I searched frantically for the problem. The vertical speed indicator was way too fast and the canopy filled with the sight of the green and brown farmland of Alabama rushing up at us. I looked out the side again and saw the wing flexing and condensation, a wisp, rushed over it.

Then it hit me. I reacted as I spoke.

" … That happens," I began as my hands manipulated the controls while I talked, "when one is dumb enough to have the power still at full throttle, rather than at idle," I finished as I pulled the power control lever to flight idle and our descent immediately slowed and the forces on the stick became bearable. We scooped out at 5,000 feet, much lower than we should have, but in plenty of time. I felt the sweat roll down my face. I was an idiot.

"A cheap lesson," King said to no one. "You'll never make that mistake again, will you." It was an observation, not a question. I just shook my head from side to side; I knew he could see my head from where he sat from behind me.

I looked out again and my eyes came back to the present, the moisture dancing on the wing, the lights of Tokyo and the bay beyond it. The pilot said something in Japanese and I put my tray table up. I stretched as much as I could in a coach window seat.

Because of typical military travel booking problems, I had to take a train from Narita Airport in Tokyo to Haneda Airport some thirty miles away, on the other side of Tokyo Bay. I had about two hours to get there by train. It would be close. One of the airports, I couldn't remember which came first, had been built as a modern upgrade to supplement the other, older airport and alleviate congestion, not unlike Chicago's or Washington, D.C.'s airports. Of course, like those two cities, all the two airports did was eventually make more traffic. Now instead of one very crowded airport, Tokyo had two very crowded airports.

I looked at my watch. I had already switched it to Tokyo time—Okinawa time—but my body was still on Eastern Standard. I got my train ticket and moved through the ever-efficient Japanese airport and transit system. Downstairs, I managed to find my way onto the right train, but I wasn't positive and had that uncertain feeling that I might be headed the wrong way. A young Japanese man, my own age, attempted to help me, but he spoke less English than I spoke Japanese—which was quite a feat considering that my Japanese vocabulary consisted solely of counting to twenty (from my days in traditional Japanese martial arts) and the ability to say "left," "right," and "straight." Somehow we managed to make ourselves understood by pointing, nodding, and bowing. He was kind enough to get off the train at my stop, indicate for me to follow, and then manage to say "next hea-yuh" pointing at the ground and then motioning toward the direction where the next trains would come. He hopped back onto his own train just before the doors closed and bowed slightly to me. I smiled and bowed back as the train slid away.

I missed my flight from Haneda to Okinawa by fifteen minutes, but "no plob-rem" the impeccably polite, young lady assured me. I had a ticket in hand for the next flight to Naha, Okinawa, in an hour. LaGuardia this was not.

I hoped Justin would wait for me at Naha. I wouldn't arrive until almost 11:30 p.m. local time. He was already on-island. He had flown in from Camp Pendleton, California, his new duty station after finishing his one-year unaccompanied tour. He had gotten Stonewall's and Arroyo's cases stayed after the stay had issued in Ponder's case.

I thought about Stonewall and Arroyo, still on Okinawa, abandoned by their units for some seven or eight months after the rest of their battalion had returned to the States. I knew they were going to be staying for some more time, too, at the brig at Camp Hansen. I had petitioned CAAF to issue another stay and overturn the Navy-Marine Corps Court's decision. I filed it on 19 December 2000. It was 6 January 2001. I wondered if I had one more rabbit in the hat, but it didn't feel like it. If not, Stonewall, Arroyo, and Ponder were going to be going to jail. It caused a physical reaction in me.

Once in to Naha, I stepped off of the airplane and breezed through baggage claim to see Justin standing with his arms folded across his chest. He looked at his watch and tapped it, while smiling.

"Sorry, man," I spoke as I approached. "Missed my connection in Tokyo He took my garment bag out of my hand, shook with the other, and we patted each other on the back.

"How are ya?" he asked, laughing. "Welcome to hell." I chuckled. Justin had not enjoyed Okinawa.

"I see you've been soaking up the sun in Southern California," I commented.

"Dude," he said as we walked out the front door into the humid Okinawa night. Even in January, it was still warm enough for short sleeves. Okinawa was on the same line of latitude as the Bahamas.

"You slept yet?" I asked.

"No. Does it show that bad?"

"Bags—no, luggage—under your eyes, my friend."

He smiled. We dropped my things into the back of a small white Toyota and he hung my uniform in the back seat.

"I talked to Stonewall and Arroyo already."

"Really? How are they?" It was a dumb question. They knew just as well as we did they were going to jail unless we pulled off another miracle.

"Philosophical," Justin answered. "Resolved." He started the car and pulled up to the booth to pay for the parking.

"Here is your fake money," Justin said politely in English as he handed the Japanese man at the gate a thousand-yen bill.

"Arigato gozaimasu," the man responded, giving Justin his change. I tried not to laugh.

"Arigato," Justin replied and pulled away.

We moved out of the airport into downtown Naha. I watched the familiar neon float by from the shops along Highway 58. The highway was one of two major roads, one on each side of the island, along with the Okinawa Expressway—one of the most expensive toll roads in creation—running almost down the center, through the mountains that cut the long, narrow island into eastern and western halves.

We were silent for a while, the wind and the sounds of the city coming in the half-opened windows. I rubbed my face. I couldn't tell if I was sleepy or if my body was just waking up.

"Ya know," I said. "Hites once said to me that the military justice system works. He said he never had an innocent guy get convicted." Justin nodded his head in response. "I used to believe that." Justin didn't respond. I turned to him so he could keep his eyes on the road. "I don't know if I ever told you that at my law school we had a former Marine teach a comparative law class on the military and civilian criminal justice systems."

"I don't think you did." Justin flipped on his blinker and sped into the right lane, the high-speed lane in Okinawa, while we drove on the opposite side of the road. The driver's side was on the right. It didn't even affect me, as I had only left there three or four months ago.

"Anyway, he was a Marine attorney and a partner at a firm in Portland, Maine. My thesis was that the military justice system is better than the civilian system because you can't separate a system of justice from the society from which it comes. I proposed that because military society was filled with such honorable people, you wind up with a more fair system."

Justin laughed out loud, surprising me. "Rethinking that yet?" He chuckled and it hit me that maybe I was too naïve to be a lawyer. Justin and I were the same age. Despite my seven more years on active duty, I had more illusions about the Marine Corps than he did. At that moment, I began to think that maybe he was better emotionally equipped than I was for this job.

"I'm fucking tired," I said and slumped down in my seat. I looked at my watch. Almost midnight. Ten in the morning on the East Coast.

"We're in court tomorrow at nine," he said.

"I know," I sighed. "I know." I considered whether I should sleep or just tough it out through the night. I needed to prepare for court, but I had neither the mental nor physical wherewithal to do it. I had an urge at that moment like I never had before, to simply quit, say fuck it, I'm done, and take up an entirely different career. To leave the Marine Corps and just … begin a new life. But quitting wasn't an option and my clients' liberty depended on me, so I leaned my head against the window and tried to grab a catnap before we got to the Bachelor Officer's Quarters.

CHAPTER 22

WHY, INDEED

If both individual and organizational greed largely describe the "Why", the final reason for the refusal to concede the low ground of the AVIP also falls under the broad category of "money," but in the negative sense, rather than the positive one. In other words, saving money also plays a big factor in decisions regarding military members because active military members today represent veterans tomorrow, and that means large costs for the Department of Veteran's Affairs (VA)—large costs that have not been budgeted and are never planned for, and yet mark every war with a regularity that is metronomic in its consistency.

It also has marked government treatment of U.S. veterans from the very founding of the Republic. Revolutionary War soldiers in many cases were not paid for their service as the original government under the Articles of Confederation had no power to tax. Soldiers, veterans, of the War for American Independence, were paid after the war's conclusion in debt certificates known as "Pierce Notes." Because no one believed they would ever be paid back, speculators bought them for 20 cents on the dollar from veterans desperate for cash in hand. After the Constitution was established and Alexander Hamilton was made Secretary of the Treasury, provisions were made to pay off the fledgling nation's debts, but Hamilton's plan would have paid the speculators and excluded the veterans.

> [James] Madison, who had not served in combat, was outraged by this. It was the first moment he and Hamilton really broke on an important matter of public policy. He

> proposed to split the repayment equally between the speculators and the veterans. Unfortunately, this was totally impractical—the government lacked the resources to figure out who should be paid what. Moreover, imposing such a massive haircut on public creditors would have had extremely bad effects on the economy.[1]

In the end, most of the veterans simply never got paid. Now, I am not trying to draw the outlines of a 240-year conspiracy to stick it to veterans; rather, I am trying to paint a picture of a governmental "habit," a kind of generational memory gap in which the new generation of bureaucrats has replaced the prior one, but with the same exact incentives to limit costs that neither the DoD, nor the VA, nor their paymasters—the U.S. Congress—ever plan for: the post-war costs of the most recent clash. That's because Congress as an institution always wants to minimize the possible costs to the American public when they're considering spending tax dollars on military adventurism abroad. Like every government project ever, the estimates in advance of the project are always multiples lower than what it actually costs, cost overruns are the norm, and the can gets kicked down the road. It's part of why our federal debt is now, as of 2020, north of $20 trillion dollars. Let me provide more modern examples of this government behavior and explicit policies.

Men in the United States flocked to join the military after the attack on Pearl Harbor. Famous athletes from Ted Williams to actors like Jimmy Stewart risked their lives in the air over Germany and Japan. More ordinary men, like my grandfather, volunteered with nothing less on the line when they left families with children, but many claimed they were in part induced by recruiter promises of "free healthcare for life." Colonel George "Bud" Day, an attorney and Medal of Honor recipient, raised

---

[1] Cost, Jay. "Spare a Thought for Veterans of the American Revolution." *National Review*. 13 November 2017. https://www.nationalreview.com/2017/11/american-revolutionary-war-veterans-deserve-thanks-remembrance, last accessed 14 July 2020.

funds from over 23,000 enlisted and officer members of the Greatest Generation to underwrite a lawsuit against the government over promises of free healthcare "for life." Colonel Day's lawsuit ultimately failed; however, legislators stepped in to give Day and the constituency he represented "about 90%" of what he was seeking from the government via the lawsuit.[2]

The men who are colloquially, but unofficially known, as "Atomic Veterans" may have numbered as high as 400,000. It's difficult to know for sure when the government swears participants to secrecy under threat of court-martial and then records are destroyed in subsequent years in fires. The Center for Investigative Reporting produced a long-form piece documenting the continuing attempts of these veterans to receive treatment for illnesses they believe are the direct result of their participation in exercises like *Operation Hardtack I*, a series of nuclear bomb detonations near Enewetak Atoll in the Pacific Ocean in 1958. Wayne Brooks, along with the rest of the crew aboard the *USS De Haven*, was repeatedly exposed to nuclear detonations.

> The next morning, a countdown blared from the *De Haven*'s PA system. A nuclear test—code name Koa—was being conducted from a barge in the lagoon of Enewetak Atoll. Its blast would release at least 75 times the power of the bomb that killed more than 130,000 people in Hiroshima, Japan, in 1945.
>
> Brooks, a slender Texan, had enlisted in the Navy a year earlier at 17. That morning, he manned his gun station on deck. He had no special goggles or clothing. He and the other sailors wore long-sleeved shirts and tucked their pant legs into their socks. They did as they

---

[2] Philpott, Tom. "Supreme Court rejects military retirees' appeal in health-care lawsuit." *Kitsap Sun*. 11 June 2003. https://products.kitsapsun.com/archive/2003/06-11/172849_supreme_court_rejects_military_.html, last accessed 14 July 2020.

> had been told, turning away from the blast site and putting their hands over their eyes.
>
> The flash was so bright that even 20 miles from the blast, Brooks, now 75, said, "When you put your hands over your eyes, you saw your bones in your hands and in your fingers."
>
> [...]
>
> His story is not unique. In the aftermath of World War II and during the height of the Cold War—between 1946 and 1962—the U.S. detonated more than 200 above-ground and undersea nuclear bombs. Over three months, Brooks would witness 27 of them.[3]

Brooks was repeatedly denied benefits for his illnesses over many years as the VA and DoD claimed that there wasn't enough evidence to support finding a presumption of "service connection" for his particular health problems. Eventually, after decades of studies—and amid increasing public pressure to acknowledge what had been done to service members—the VA would include a list of conditions considered "presumptively" service-connected. For Wayne Brooks and other veterans like him, however, the intervening years would see thousands or even tens of thousands of possible claimants die, significantly lessening the payments that the government would have to make.

Indeed, any detailed historical look at DoD and VA actions in the aftermath of large batches of veterans returning home and filing claims, reveals a shocking pattern:

- Deny any connection to the claims for as long as possible.

[3] LaFleur, Jennifer. The Center for Investigative Reporting. "America's atomic vets: 'We were used as guinea pigs—every one of us.'" *Reveal.* 27 May 2016. https://www.revealnews.org/article/us-veterans-in-secretive-nuclear-tests-still-fighting-for-recognition, last accessed 14 July 2020.

- When pressed by overwhelming public opinion, the government commits to "studying" the issue.
- Years go by during which large chunks of the cohort die before they ever see a penny.
- Study results eventually trickle in, showing correlation between the claimed diseases and government tests conducted on service members.
- The VA reluctantly capitulates, with Congress (loudly) committing to "make it right" for these veterans.
- Then regulations are drafted that narrow the conditions or provide only a small exception to the general tactic of denying benefits.

Lather. Rinse. Repeat.

Agent Orange was a known carcinogen before it was ever used as a defoliant in Vietnam, yet it took decades for the VA to concede that there might be a link between the high rates of various illnesses among those Vietnam veterans who were exposed to it and the toxic chemicals. In many cases, the VA will not budge until a court orders them to. Even after acknowledging the "service connection" for the dioxin in Agent Orange, the VA interpreted the regulations to exclude Navy veterans who served aboard ships in the waters in and around Vietnam.[4] What is most telling about the decision is its date: 29 January 2019. It took more than four decades *after* the Vietnam War had ended for a court to finally compel the VA to provide benefits to Navy veterans who had served in the waters in and around Vietnam because of court interpretations that use legal doctrines that specifically compel judges to view evidence in a light most favorably to the government—and not its citizens.

---

[4] See, e.g., *Procopio v. Wilkie*, Fed. Cir., decided 29 January 2019.

From nuclear exposures to mustard gas tests, from dioxin in Agent Orange to pyridostigmine bromide pills during the Gulf War to the anthrax vaccine, troops exposed to known or unknown hazards are sometimes sworn to secrecy, ignored, marginalized after their service is completed, denied benefits, and then have to fight a system that is rigged against them for decades. If they are lucky just to survive long enough, they might eventually get some treatment via the socialized medicine of the VA. This doesn't even begin to address the quality of the treatment that veterans are subjected to once the government finally lets them in the door.

Lest it seem that I am taking liberties in imputing these motives to VA officials, or stretching the truth, consider this:

> In 1977, a veteran made the first-ever VA claim referencing exposure to Agent Orange. By 1993, only 486 of the 39,419 veterans who filed claims had received compensation for Agent Orange-related disabilities. According to a 2015 ProPublica report, the VA did not keep records of Agent Orange-related claims until 2002, but, from 2002 to 2015, more than 650,000 veterans were granted benefits related to exposure to the herbicide.[5]

Secretary of the Department of Veterans Affairs Robert Wilkie was straightforward in public statements about his reasons for fighting the case, specifically citing the cost of extending benefits to additional veterans beyond the narrow interpretation his agency had adopted for judging claimants.

---

[5] Jones, Christopher. "The VA is finally being forced to pay for navy veterans' exposure to Agent Orange." *Pacific Standard*, 1 February 2019. https://psmag.com/news/court-of-appeals-rules-in-favor-of-blue-water-vietnam-veterans, last accessed 14 July 2020.

> Secretary of the VA Robert Wilkie, and other opponents of the Court of Appeals ruling, contend that there is insufficient evidence connecting Navy veterans who never stepped foot on Vietnamese soil to Agent Orange exposure. In the past, Wilkie has cited the cost of extending care to 50,000 to 70,000 veterans as a reason why the VA denied Blue Water Navy veterans claims of presumptive exposure to Agent Orange.[6]This is all *in addition to* the legal limitations that the government has already placed on service members' right to sue under *Feres* and its progeny. While one changed vote on the high court could overturn *Feres*, it remains the law, but the DoD may not be anxious to test the vitality of the *Stanley* and *Feres* decisions in light of this program's flaws and the possible exposure. Even were the DoD to win in court, Congress could very well undo such a decision in the face of sufficient public outcry, as it has historically, by subsequently expanding the language of the Federal Tort Claims Act or carving out a specific exception to *Feres* for such cases.

Another consideration is the possibility that BioPort itself could still be exposed to liability from family members of service members who were harmed. The Federal Tort Claims Act allows service members or their estates to sue a government contractor, although there is a "government contractor defense" to such suit—yet another judicial creation to limit government contractor exposure.[7] BioPort, however,

---

[6] Id. See also Lambrecht, Bill. "Charged by win in Agent Orange case, veterans groups vow to press on." *Houston Chronicle*, 30 January 2019. https://www.houstonchronicle.com/news/politics/texas/article/Blue-Water-Navy-veterans-from-Vietnam-era-13573428.php, last accessed 14 July 2020.

[7] This government contractor immunity was created by the Supreme Court in a case called *Boyles v. United Technologies*, which involved the crash of a Marine CH-53 helicopter off the coast of Virginia.

with its atrocious history, is in no position to meet the requirements of even that deferential government contractor defense.[8] Neither is the DoD in a position to help, as it appears that the DoD intentionally ignored what it knew for some time: that the anthrax vaccine was not licensed for the use to which the DoD was putting it.

The FDA is not anxious to have to answer in court, either. It would likely not want to have to defend its actions, specifically why it never stepped in to regulate BioPort, why it allowed expired lots released, why it allowed the DoD to operate "on site," why it deferred to DoD interpretations of the scope of a license, and the list goes on. The FDA's own decisions in disciplining previous manufacturers may come back to haunt it. Even under an abuse of discretion standard, its actions are less than pristine.

One final point to be made is that the VA and DoD engage in this pattern of behavior in *all* cases involving veterans' benefits, not just injuries and service connection for disabilities, but even for things like post-9/11 education benefits. In some cases, the VA gives the benefits and then subsequently seeks to claw them back by re-interpreting regulations to exclude veterans and their families who have already received them and then engages in aggressive collection practices, garnishing tax returns, and turning children of veterans into debtors overnight.

> Kelli Hower was six months pregnant with her first child last spring when the phone call came. At first, the Michigan woman thought it was a scammer. But it turned out to be all too real.
>
> The caller was a debt collector, on contract with the U.S. Treasury Department. And he had bad news: Hower owed the federal government $12,000 for college tuition

---

[8] Id.

> payments and living expenses she'd received through her veteran father's benefits under the Post-9/11 GI Bill.
>
> Hower, 30, couldn't believe it. To start, those were benefits she'd used years ago. And her father Bruce Coxworth, 57, of Swartz Creek, Michigan, had earned them. He'd served 22-1/2 years as a military police officer with the Army National Guard, with active-duty assignments that took him far from home.
>
> "They said, 'You owe the federal government $12,000—and we need it now,'" Hower says. "I started crying. I said, 'I never got any letters, so what are you talking about?'"
>
> Hower and her father are among more than a dozen families who contacted the *Chicago Sun-Times* after a story Nov. 10 on military families hit with hefty college bills they were promised would be covered by the government under the Post-9/11 GI Bill.[9]

In the end, however, the song always seems to remain the same for veterans and their families: broken promises, broken bodies, and bureaucratic indifference.

---

[9] Zimmerman, Stephanie. "More GI Bill horror stories: Vets say government reneged on promise to pay for kids' college." *Chicago Sun Times.* 22 November 2019. https://chicago.suntimes.com/2019/11/22/20975706/post-911-gi-bill-military-snafu-mistakes-college-tuition-military-veterans-student-debt, last accessed 14 July 2020. See also Zimmerman, Stephanie. "GI Bill college help came for one vet's family but others still dealing with military's broken promises." *Chicago Sun Times.* 20 December 2019. https://chicago.suntimes.com/2019/12/20/21030379/post-9-11-gi-bill-college-student-debt-veterans-affairs-va-navy-army-durbin-kinzinger-panetta-kildee, last accessed 14 July 2020.

CHAPTER 23
CONVICTION

I left the courtroom before the judge announced his sentence. I couldn't watch. It wasn't technically my client, but I still couldn't watch.

When my turn came, I tried everything. I objected every time the prosecutor gave me a reason to. I grilled the government witnesses until the judge made me stop. I was on the phone to John Richardson back in the States. When the judge stopped my cross-examination of a witness because of something he read in a personal e-mail, I was all over him, too.

"Sir, I don't think you can consider personal e-mails in this court in limiting my cross-examination of a witness." I was fuming. I had just asked the witness if he knew that the anthrax program was essentially shut down because of failures of the manufacturer.

The judge had interrupted me: "I can't allow you to ask a misleading question of the witness if I have information that tells me different."

"Sir, are you saying that the program has not been shut down?" My voice was not very respectful.

"Captain Saran, someone forwarded me an e-mail which was an article in which a DoD official asserted that the program would be starting back up in October of this year."

"Sir, you absolutely cannot consider that extra-judicial information, and as a side note, the DoD says every three months the program is going to start back up and then they have to come back and take their foot out of their mouth because the manufacturer fails another inspection!"

I sat back down and shuffled through some papers. Justin was reading my mind and handed me the most recent letter from the Assistant Secretary of Defense for Health Affairs that directed another slowdown in the program. "Thanks," I said.

As I leaned over, Lance Corporal Stonewall whispered in my ear, "Who is sending him e-mails about this case or the program?" Sharp kid.

"Sir, at this time we would like to have this document marked as the next appellate exhibit."

"Please do," he said, leaning back in his chair. "I presume you're going to tell us what it is?"

I handed a copy to the prosecutor. Chris knew that the conviction was guaranteed; he barely looked at it. He wanted to get these cases done.

"Sir, this is the most recent official memorandum, directing the Service Chiefs to limit who gets the anthrax vaccine. This is dated November 2000, just two months ago. So whatever e-mail you may have received, whatever the DoD's PR department may be cooking up, only troops in Southwest Asia for more than 30 days are now required to take the vaccine. And, sir, could we ask the military judge who he received these e-mails from?"

I had stepped off into it now. I knew the judge pretty well. He got tight-lipped when he was angry and he would look down a lot. I could tell he wanted to throttle me.

"I received a personal e-mail, as I often do, from my father. He knows that I am handling these cases and forwarded me the e-mail, knowing that I might be interested in it." He was about to get even madder.

"Sir, your father is or was a senior Marine Corps officer?"

"A colonel in the Reserves."

"Might we have a recess, sir?"

"Court's in recess."

Before Kolomjec could say "all rise," the judge was out of his chair and out the door.

Back in my old boss's office, Lieutenant Colonel Carol Joyce was calling the Chief Defense Counsel for the Marine Corps on the phone. I had worked for Lieutenant Colonel Joyce three times now through a strange series of coincidences. My first summer at law school I worked at Camp Lejeune when she was a Major and the Chief Trial Counsel, head prosecutor, for the Base. I worked for her the next summer and then when I came to Okinawa, she was the Regional Defense Counsel for the entire Pacific Region, covering Hawaii, mainland Japan, and Okinawa. By strange coincidence, her husband, Lieutenant Colonel Frank Joyce, was a CH-46 pilot, and had been the Executive Officer of the squadron I had deployed with to the Mediterranean Sea. He showed up not long after I left the squadron to go back to my parent squadron in 1995. It was indeed a small Marine Corps.

After conversing with the CDC, I went back into court, challenged the judge, and was shot down coldly.

"Captain Saran," Major Stone replied icily, "I do not appreciate such a spurious challenge of the military judge! Now, let's move on."

I had never actually heard him raise his voice in court. We stared at each other. I smiled, but the way my wife said annoys her and makes her want to slap me. It occurred to me that this might not help my client on sentencing, so I looked down and shuffled some meaningless papers. I could feel my face flush. I bit down on the inside of my cheek until it broke the skin slightly.

I lawyered on.

When court ended that day, I knew that either we got a stay by the next morning or Ponder and Stonewall would be going to jail. Private First Class Arroyo was sentenced to 105 days in the brig, reduction to the lowest enlisted paygrade, and forfeitures of $600 pay per month for three months. He requested a Bad Conduct Discharge which, if awarded by the judge, meant his case would get automatic direct appellate review. The judge did not give him one. That meant there would be no review by an appellate court, not even a verbatim transcript of the proceedings. Only a summarized record would be prepared. No anthrax refuser had received more than 45 days from a judge or jury prior to that case. I had pled Marines guilty to some pretty good assaults and gotten less than what he gave Arroyo. I wondered if I had helped to get Arroyo whacked by my actions. I didn't sleep that night and it had nothing to do with jet lag.

Lieutenant Colonel Joyce and her husband took the defense shop out to dinner the next night. We ate at a nice restaurant and I talked with "Mister" Colonel Joyce, as I mentally referred to him, about flying. Frank Joyce, as the XO of the squadron I had been with, had also served as a member of the Aircraft Mishap Board that investigated the crash of Clark "Swab" Cox and "Cletus" Boggan, two of my former squadronmates. We began to discuss what he knew of Clark and Cletus's crash over dinner.

Cletus had been a "new guy" when Clark and I returned from our six-month deployment with a transport squadron aboard the *USS Kearsarge*. I didn't know him that well, but well- enough to have mourned his death. Clark, on the other hand, I had known well. We had flown together in the Cobra training squadron, checked into the same fleet squadron a few weeks apart, shot our first TOW missiles together, been deployed to Twenty-Nine Palms together, conducted an air-to-air Sidewinder missile shoot together, deployed to HMM-263 as the two junior guys together, lived on the same ship, got all of our instructor qualifications together, and lived four houses away from each other in base housing … And on a perfect day flying on the boat, blue skies over the Mediterranean Sea, just he and I trying to see how many "bounces"—landings on the ship—that we could do in an hour, Clark produced my favorite phrase about flying, after I had flown one of my best approaches to a perfect landing:

"Oh, buddy, you flew that like Steve McQueen."

Clark crashed into the ocean and died off the North Carolina coast the day I left Camp Lejeune to go back to law school after my first summer there as a prosecutor. Had I stayed flying, that would have been my deployment cycle.

"But it might have been you, instead," Colonel Joyce finished my thoughts for me.

I drained my Kirin and ordered another beer. Justin was into his third or fourth. After dinner, back in our rooms, we continued drinking and had more alcohol than two lawyers who were going to lose the next day in court should. I stayed up praying for a fax to come in until I dozed off, half-drunk, at 0430. I knew the magic hat didn't have another rabbit in it.

"Accused and counsel, please rise." I touched Stonewall briefly on the arm and rose slowly to stand at attention. Justin and I looked quickly at each other. "Lance Corporal Stonewall, this court-martial sentences you as follows: to forfeit five hundred dollars per month for three months, to be confined for a period of ninety days, to be reduced to the rank of E-1." Some would say a victory; no punitive discharge and therefore no "bad paper." I knew it meant no appellate review. No court was going to get to second-guess the judge's opinion. Our appellate writ had been denied in large part because of the high standard of review required to overturn a judge's decision on motions in the middle of trial. On direct appellate review, the standard was much more favorable, although the Navy-Marine Corps Court's opinion left me little doubt how they would rule on the anthrax program. They had found that the vaccine was not investigational because the Navy said it wasn't in a Navy instruction. I was not sure when the Navy gained the authority to license drugs, but it didn't matter.

Back in my old office, the two "chasers," as we called the guards, waited outside the door to take Stonewall to the brig in cuffs. He now had a federal conviction.

"Well, sir. I just want to say thank you. You and Captain Constantine did more than defend me, you took this on as a personal cause, you championed me, and Arroyo, and Petty Officer Ponder. We all appreciate that, sir. No one could have done a better job than you both did, sir."

"Thank you, Jason."

Justin answered for both of us. I couldn't find my voice.

I'm not cut out for this, I kept thinking.

"Petty Officer Third Class Ponder, this court-martial sentences you as follows: to be confined for a period of sixty days; to be reduced to the rank of E-2." Ponder's wife and son had probably saved him from worse. His wife's iron will in lobbying members of Congress and keeping media attention on Ponder's case and his command probably got him back from Okinawa. He was to fly back with his Platoon Commander the next day and be confined at Pensacola, Florida, a few hours' drive from his wife and son in Mississippi. Stonewall and Arroyo, unknown, went to the brig at Camp Hansen, Okinawa.

Justin and I tried to drink ourselves silly, but our hearts weren't in it. We didn't sleep that night. The next morning, our defense clerk picked us up. Slightly hung over and running late, we made him take us to Burger King for coffee and some grease.

Naha to Narita.

We sat in silence next to each other on the plane. I dozed for a while. At Narita, we pooled our yen to pay a tax for leaving the country. Justin considered it the ultimate insult. "Great," he grumbled, "I've got to pay to *leave* this friggin' place." It was enough to make me laugh. There was a certain *Monty Pythonesque* humor to the final indignity.

On Saturday, 13 January 2001, Justin headed for the West Coast, where he was serving as the Deputy Staff Judge Advocate for the Third Marine Aircraft Wing. It had been 10 months since we had both picked up our anthrax refusal cases. When Justin's tram pulled away from the terminal, he waved; I touched my hand to my forehead in a brief salute. In an hour, I had a flight to catch back to the East Coast, back to my job, of all things, as a prosecutor at Marine Corps Base, Quantico, Virginia. I could not stop thinking about Jason Stonewall sitting in the Camp Hansen Brig.

I had never believed Franklin's adage: "Better that one hundred guilty men go free than that one innocent man spend a day in jail." Now I had some inkling of what he was talking about. I was incredibly offended by the convictions and incarcerations of Stonewall, Ponder, and Arroyo.

Talking to Jennifer Ponder on the phone was not going to be easy.

CHAPTER 24
AFTER ACTION

As I sit writing this, 25 August 2001, the DoD has recently asserted that if the manufacturer, BioPort, Inc., passes an October inspection, the anthrax program will re-commence. I hope to be out of the Marine Corps by then. These are the unseen casualties of the program. Notwithstanding my personal journey to disillusionment, I remain dedicated to the Marine Corps and the principles the Marine Corps stands for. As a result, I feel compelled to offer a kind of "after-action report" or lessons learned section on the AVIP.

First, compulsory inoculation as a pretreatment for biological warfare has not received the kind of public debate and scrutiny that it should. Before we pass such programs off as "just another shot," there needs to be some discussion about the competing interests involved. Routine immunizations are not at issue and the DoD's attempts to paint the anthrax vaccine as routine are disturbing.

Chemical and biological warfare defense has changed the face of terrorism and warfare. Genetic engineering of agents may make vaccines useless. Individual immune response may vitiate any vaccine's effectiveness. Adverse reaction rates vary from vaccine to vaccine and must be known before mass troop inoculation begins.

Long-term effects are important for veterans who leave active duty. If a vaccine or treatment causes long-term health effects, a veteran has to show "service connection" for the disability in order to rate VA benefits. If the long-term effects are not known, veterans may well be left with severe disabilities, diseases, or other effects and have no way to get help down the road. Interactions between treatments should also be studied, as well as the potential threats, lest the Gulf War situation be repeated and troops are given a defense which may enhance the effects of certain agents while protecting against others.

These kinds of broad considerations, and a host not listed, must be studied and balanced before any vaccine or treatment is given. The use of pretreatments necessitates a comprehensive policymaking process, rather than the helter-skelter approach taken by Secretary Cohen for political considerations. Title X, section 1107, appears to strike this balance and require the President to assume the political responsibility and consequences for such a decision. In short, Congress should enforce this statute strictly and treat violations of it as contempt of Congress and call those who violate it to account or cut off funding for such programs.

Additionally, the President should closely scrutinize any such program. A mass vaccination program, if not done properly, threatens the health, welfare, and rights of 2.4 million service members, something no single terrorist weapon could do. The President must have consultations with both proponents and opponents of any program before a decision is made to ensure that he has all of the accurate information. This is because, unfortunately, it appears that those in senior leadership positions would rather tell those at the highest level of leadership what they want to hear than the truth.

Finally, senior Generals and medical officers have to be prepared to sacrifice their careers for something higher—their oath to the Constitution. There was a time in the military when senior military officers spoke their minds and were willing to accept the consequences for saying their piece. In the case of the anthrax program, no senior military or medical officer was willing to do so. They must, however, because ultimately, such well-intentioned but ill-executed programs threaten something even more essential to the welfare of our Armed Forces: Trust.

This trust has become even more important now that we have gone to an all-volunteer force. Gone are the days of ordering conscripts, some without high-school diplomas, to comply because someone in authority said so. We now live in the information age and new troops, even young, eager ones, have grown up with a healthy dose of cynicism. If leaders in the military are going to be effective, we have to deal with the unvarnished truth, pleasant or not. Spin never works. It always comes across as just what it is—an attempt to manipulate the truth for some purpose, rather than deal with those who serve with the same level of integrity that we demand of them.

Unfortunately, right now, junior troops are the ones standing up for what's right and military courts are refusing to allow them to be heard. Congress should grant relief to anyone who has been disciplined for refusing this vaccine and call on the carpet those political and military leaders who have foisted this program off on unsuspecting and trusting troops. Anything less will leave a stain on the honor of our military. Given its history and its desire to continue with such programs in the future, the DoD can hardly afford to give away what's left of its tattered credibility.

PRESENT DAY

It's … odd to read something you wrote almost 20 years ago. I left the prior chapter in the original perspective and voice from when I wrote it in the immediate aftermath of the courts-martial of David Ponder, Jason Stonewall, and Vitolino Arroyo in order to convey the context of the time in which I wrote it and the age I was then. I'm not going to poke (too much) fun at the earnestness of my early-30s Self, but I can't help but smile when I read it. How serious I was about "fixing"—or at least reporting on—what I believed was an extraordinary and unique event that I just happened to stumble into like Scooby and Shaggy and the whole Gang after the Mystery Machine got a flat near that spooky-looking hotel. In my defense, it really was my first direct contact with the Leviathan and I was naïve.

The story—and the fight—didn't end with the convictions of my clients. I continued to work behind the scenes with Tom Rempfer, Russ Dingle, Lou Michels, and others in our band of merry malcontents, even as I worked in my day job as the chief prosecutor for Marine Corps, Base Quantico, Virginia. Of course, 9/11 threw a wrench into everyone's lives; mine more than some, but certainly less than others like those in the Twin Towers. I was an active-duty Marine Captain when the planes hit that September morning. I was still processing what it all meant when the anthrax letter attacks happened exactly one week later—18 September 2001.

Those two events conspired to make every page of what I had written about the government's anthrax program instantly worthless. My literary agent's enthusiasm for my book excoriating the DoD AVIP evaporated faster than water on Phoenix asphalt in summer. *Like a mirage.* Pundits began seriously discussing vaccinating the entire U.S. population and there

I was doing the literary equivalent (to my agent) of screaming "WOLF!" at the top of my lungs. It was just another part of the rollercoaster ride, one of the bigger "lows" that continued to dominate that part of my professional life for many years, long after I had left my original clients behind. There were a few highs, as well, even the hope of Justice.

In March 2003, Tom, Lou, et al. put together a group of plaintiffs and filed for a temporary restraining order/injunction and a declaratory judgment against the DoD, the Department of Health and Human Services, and the FDA.[1] By then I was in training for deployment to Afghanistan to do my part in the Global War on Terror, but I helped out as I could, mostly moral support and some editing of briefs. For a while it even looked like Justice might be done when the judge in the case issued a temporary injunction and a thoughtful justification as to why. It looked like there was finally a jurist who listened and understood the arguments.

> Pending before this Court is a Motion for a Preliminary Injunction. The central question before this Court is whether AVA is an "investigational" drug or a drug unapproved for its use against inhalation anthrax. Upon consideration of plaintiffs' motion for a preliminary injunction, the opposition, the reply, and oral arguments, as well as the statutory and case law governing the issues, and for the following reasons, it is, by the Court, hereby ORDERED that the Motion for a Preliminary Injunction is GRANTED. In the absence of a presidential waiver, defendants are enjoined from inoculating service members without their consent.[2]

---

[1] *Doe v. Rumsfeld*, 341 F. Sup. 2d 1 (D.D.C. 2004).

[2] Id.

When I got the e-mail and read the ruling just before Christmas 2003, I felt a sense of vindication that's hard to describe. In that moment, I thought a great Wrong had been made Right; that the Law had finally come around to correcting the Injustice done to my clients. I was already formulating the e-mail I would write to help them get their records corrected.

Eight days after the injunction, over the Christmas shutdown that normally predominates Washington, D.C., the FDA suddenly issued a new ruling on the status of the AVA, placing it into Category I—stating that the vaccine was effective irrespective of route of exposure! There was zero data to support such a claim. It started to dawn on me that the "highs" of our fight were merely the tops of the rollercoaster ride—and each one would be quickly followed by a corresponding drop—or worse.

In 2004, the Court admonished the FDA, wiped out the hurried order, and issued a permanent injunction, but I couldn't celebrate. I had my fly date for Afghanistan and my concerns were narrowed to life-preserving essentials. Me being me, however, I sent a copy of the court's order to the judge that had sentenced my clients to jail. Yes, I'm *that* guy. Years after an argument, there I was sending an Article III court's decision to the Article I judge just to let him know: *See? I was right after all, fucker.* It wasn't a nail in his door, but the electronic equivalent.

Just another *chunk-chunk* climb to the peak before the inevitable drop.

While I was spending most of the next two years doing my part in the hunt for bin Laden, the FBI was chasing down leads for the anthrax letter attacks. It ended right where those of us close to the issue knew it would: at Fort Detrick, Maryland, home of the United States' biological warfare program. Federal law outlaws the offensive use of chem-bio weapons, so what is developed there is always claimed to be for defensive purposes only, but as soon as the anthrax letter attacks happened, our crew had already narrowed the suspects down to two: Russia and the United States. Anthrax is, comparatively speaking, a rather large and clumpy molecule and trying to aerosolize it—that is, make it into a sufficiently fine powder for dispersal that will fit through sprayer nozzles—requires significant technical capability, a capability known to be possessed by only two labs on planet Earth: Theirs and Ours.

Of course, that's not how it played out in Washington, D.C. Robert Mueller was the Director of the FBI at the time and those paragons of virtue and investigative acumen focused on Steven Hatfill, a bioweapons expert and civilian who worked at United States Army Medical Research Institute of Infectious Diseases, who had been publicly named by some woman on her website. Politicians, including President Bush, rushed to blame Iraq's weapons program. Indeed, the wiki on the subject does a fairly good job of outlining all of the political and media pressure that blamed a whole slew of convenient targets, none of which were close to being correct, but "coincidentally" served a variety of political narratives, for both Team Blue and Team Red.

Meanwhile, in our case, the DoD and other defendants took an appeal and, while the case was still pending, the FDA dotted every I, crossed every T, and made certain that no federal district court could overturn its decision on the AVA.[3] Under the deferential review standards[4] the Supreme Court has laid upon the judiciary, we never had a chance. It was more crooked than a hundred miles of country road, but the DoD was not going to let some uppity lawyers or malcontent soldiers stop a multi-billion-dollar program that was supposed to be the crown jewel of its biological defense initiatives.

By the spring of 2006, my war in the Graveyard of Empires was over and I came home to start my life again. This included solo legal practice and, given my background, I found myself representing service members and veterans in courts-martial and records correction cases. Back then, a google search of my name would mostly return press around my time

---

[3] See Biological Products; Bacterial Vaccines and Toxoids; Implementation of Efficacy Review; Anthrax Vaccine Adsorbed, 70 Fed. Reg. 19 December 2005, p. 75, 180.

[4] See, especially, *Chevron U.S.A., Inc. v. Natural Resources Defense Council, Inc.*, 468 U.S. 837 (1984).

fighting the anthrax vaccine. I also got involved in Tom Rempfer's attempts to correct his service records in light of what had been done to him over his stance against the AVA.

Then came *Kisala.* I can't even bring myself to read it again, even now.

Okay, fine. I did it. I went back and read it.

Yes, it's just as bad as I remembered.

Andrew Kisala was a soldier at Fort Bragg who refused the anthrax vaccine for all of the reasons I've outlined in this book. I know this because I was involved in almost every anthrax refusal case and I had passed along all of my work—motions, pleadings, documents, witnesses, everything—to every lawyer who had a refusal case. Kisala's lawyers made all of the arguments, and even though a federal district court judge, Judge Emmet Sullivan,[5] had found that the FDA had not been licensed for the purpose it was being used in vaccinating soldiers and therefore that the order to take it was unlawful, CAAF made it all retroactively "good" by upholding Kisala's conviction. To be clear, Kisala was given the order, tried, and convicted all the way back in 2000, when my clients were, yet CAAF relied upon the subsequent FDA "fix" to rule that the order had been valid *all along.*

The bottom of that rollercoaster ride turned out to be an unfinished track.

For years, after doggedly—and incorrectly—pursuing Dr. Stephen Hatfill, the FBI had to publicly exonerate him after he sued them for $4.6 million. Hatfill wound up getting an annuity that totaled $5.8 million. Mueller's FBI eventually zeroed in on Dr. Bruce Ivins at Fort Detrick, a government microbiologist whose name was all over the DoD's anthrax program. The FBI eventually made a public determination that Ivins was the culprit of the anthrax letter attacks after his suicide by overdose of acetaminophen in July 2008. Tom Rempfer had been keeping up on the

---

[5] Yes, the same judge who took General Michael Flynn's guilty plea. It is indeed a small swamp in and around D.C. Along those lines, one of the attorneys I worked with on Tom Rempfer's case was Mark Zaid, the lawyer for the "whistleblower" Eric Ciaramella.

whole thing through some friends at the FBI and in and around D.C. He called me to tell me that the FBI had found references to our cases and work in Ivins's private papers and e-mails. The apparent motive for the attack was what we had feared all along: Ivins was disappointed with how the AVIP had been sidetracked and the attacks were an attempt to "make the case" for the program.

> According to his e-mails and statements to friends, in the months leading up to the anthrax attacks in the fall of 2001, Dr. Ivins was under intense personal and professional pressure. The anthrax vaccine program to which he had devoted his entire career of more than 20 years was failing. The anthrax vaccines were receiving criticism in several scientific circles, because of both potency problems and allegations that the anthrax vaccine contributed to Gulf War Syndrome. Short of some major breakthrough or intervention, he feared that the vaccine research program was going to be discontinued. Following the anthrax attacks, however, his program was suddenly rejuvenated.[6]

And so there was the upshot of all of it. I—we—had fought the good fight and that eventually led to our clients being thrown in jail, the law being turned on its head, the FDA and DoD revealing what they really care about, the troops being mass inoculated and experimented upon (just like the good ol' days!), five people being killed, and a bunch of people getting rich from it. All of this might have been enough to break me, but I'd been inoculated (get it!) against that possibility by a

[6] The Department of Homeland Security's website has a report available for download regarding its conclusion that Hatfill was not the culprit and that Bruce Ivins was. "Amerithrax Investigative Summary," U.S. Dept. of Justice, 19 February 2010, p. 8.

conversation with a military colleague while he was working at the Pentagon:

I was on leave back home from one of my tours in Afghanistan. My buddy was working in the Navy's ship procurement program and counting the days until his retirement. He was particularly cynical about his job and it came up over lunch in the Pentagon cafeteria. I was kvetching about the anthrax vaccine and he offered some perspective.

"What's the problem with work?" I had asked him.

"Bro, let me tell you something, okay? The DoD has spent three billion dollars so far on this new DDG-2020 program. Three billion, with a B, all right?" I nodded my understanding and grunted over my food.

"Well, no one has so much as popped a single fucking rivet. Not one. There is no ship yet. And we're three billion in … and just getting started." I looked up to meet his eyes. I had seen a lot of waste—a *lot* of waste during the Global War on Terror, so I couldn't say I was surprised, but three billion is a big number.

"Dude, with three billion dollars, you, me, and Todd would have already built a ship, held the christening, and after I cracked the champagne bottle, it would have slid down the ramp straight into the water and sank. Then we would have salvaged it, fixed what we fucked up, tried again, and sank another ship. But by the third one—" he held up three fingers for emphasis, "we would have an operational ship. And we'd still have another billion left over."

I laughed over my salad at his hyperbole, but his point was well taken.

"Bro, we've done feasibility studies, environmental impact studies, surveys, Congressional junkets all over the fucking country, and PowerPoint presentations until I'm ready to kill myself … and not a single. Rivet. Popped. Three billion, baby. Three fucking billion dollars."

He went back to eating and shook his head, more to himself than to me. That's when it finally hit me. My experience with the anthrax vaccine program wasn't unique; it wasn't some personal hell cooked up to break me, or my clients, or those who dissent from orthodoxy. We were simply grit to be ground up in the gears of the system. *Grist for the mill.* It wasn't even personal. There were billions and billions and billions of dollars flowing through that system, a system that rewards those who know how to leverage it, like the Clintons and Admiral Crowe, like the FDA folks who wanted to ensure that the system had vaccines, or the Chem-Bio folks who believe it really is *the most serious threat evah!*, and a whole host of other organisms that ride alongside the Leviathan. And if it later turns out that Agent Orange causes cancer, or being poisoned with mustard gas has long-term effects, or the VA doesn't have enough money to cover these costs? Well, that's the price of Freedom, baby.

Where's your patriotism?

ABOUT THE AUTHOR

Dale Saran is a former Marine officer who served from 1991 to 2018 in both the active and reserve forces. He served initially as an attack helicopter pilot, was selected for the Funded Law Education Program, and after graduating from law school and Naval Justice School, was certified as a Judge Advocate in 1999. He served as both a defense counsel and trial counsel before leaving active duty. He returned to active duty to serve in Afghanistan and defend Marines charged with war crimes in Iraq. He was CrossFit, Inc.'s first general counsel for six years and is now in private practice in Arizona, where he lives with his wife, two children, two cats, and a dog. He has four daughters from a previous marriage and is currently hard at work on his second novel.

www.ingramcontent.com/pod-product-compliance
Lightning Source LLC
Chambersburg PA
CBHW022035190326
41520CB00008B/589
* 9 7 8 1 7 3 4 6 2 9 3 0 9 *